Discover Your Purpose

Discover Your Purpose

How to Use the 5 Life Purpose Profiles
to Unlock Your Hidden Potential
and Live the Life You Were
Meant to Live

RHYS THOMAS

JEREMY P. TARCHER/PENGUIN
AN IMPRINT OF PENGUIN RANDOM HOUSE
NEW YORK

JEREMY P. TARCHER/PENGUIN
An imprint of Penguin Random House LLC
375 Hudson Street
New York, New York 10014

Most Tarcher/Penguin books are available at special quantity discounts for bulk
purchase for sales promotions, premiums, fund-raising, and educational needs.
Special books or book excerpts also can be created to fit specific needs.
For details, write: SpecialMarkets@penguinrandomhouse.com.

Library of Congress Cataloging-in-Publication Data

Thomas, Rhys (Alexander Rhys), 1960-
Discover your purpose : how to use the 5 life purpose profiles to unlock your hidden
potential and live the life you were meant to live / Rhys Thomas.
pages cm
ISBN 978-0-399-16924-3 (paperback)
1. Self actualization (Psychology) 2. Self-realization. 3. Personality assessment.
4. Conduct of life. 5. Success. I. Title.
BF637.S4T4964 2015
158—dc23
2015016531

Printed in the United States of America
1   3   5   7   9   10   8   6   4   2

Book design by Ellen Cipriano

To my students,
who have all become my teachers.

Contents

Preface

For the past fifteen years, I've been helping people to find their life purpose, so they can figure out and attain what they really want in their life. As founder of the Rhys Thomas Institute, I've polled thousands of my clients and students, and found that what most people want comes down to three basic desires: financial freedom through a career they love and can be proud of, fulfilling relationships both personally and in business, and abundant energy and well-being for a lifetime of enjoying it all.

Is that something you want in your life? This book is about how you can have what you really want, whether it's all three of those basic goals, or whether just one or two are really important to you. In the following chapters, you will be shown the concrete tools you can use to bring about your personal desires in those areas by learning about your unique life purpose and starting to live the life you know you deserve.

Getting what you *really* want in your life is easier than it might appear. The biggest barrier is not knowing your life purpose or how to discover, nurture, and express your special calling in life. Once you know who you are and what your unique purpose is in life, a door opens, and you step through it fearlessly to pursue your dreams and goals, fueled by an endless source of energy to do it.

Who you are is your life purpose. This truth is a discovery you make as you learn about yourself and others in the Rhys Method® Life Purpose Profile System. Then, when you act in alignment with who you are, you not only give your greatest gift to the world, but you achieve success in your career, are fulfilled by your relationships, and get access to extraordinary well-being and energy.

Knowing your unique life purpose quality—as revealed through each of the five Life Purpose Profiles described in this book—and letting that quality inform your life—can transform you from a technician doing a job to a master with deep knowledge of your craft. Having a true calling in life can separate a Gandhi, a Martin Luther King Jr., or a Mother Teresa from someone who toils to tediously build a cathedral brick by brick, never seeing the magnificent cathedral that results from their efforts.

You discovering your spectacular, defining "core" quality is what the Rhys Method® Life Purpose Profile System and this book are all about. It is that self-knowledge that students in my school acquire, because knowing who you are is the key to healing mastery. To heal others you must heal yourself first, and, in the broadest terms, healing means becoming *whole*.

The three basic steps I teach for anyone to have what they want in life are simple. First, get clear on what your life purpose is—not the one that others think you are supposed to live but the one that is yours by birth, your soul's choice. Second, acquire the courage to step toward your life's calling and not fall into old unconscious patterns that stop you. And third, tap into the energy available to act fearlessly in alignment with that calling every day, until you break your habits of procrastination and start living your life motivated by a deep sense of calling and mission.

How do you do this? You can use the Life Purpose Profiles as tools to attain inner direction, fearless courage, and limitless energy for yourself. The path of the Profiles is also about your ability to understand and relate to others, and to help them get what they want in life. As you cultivate your own unique abilities, you become someone who can motivate and inspire others, not just in your own language but in theirs, too. I am sure that if you are reading these pages, you would love to own the market in your business or be the spouse and parent of the year to your family. With my system, that is entirely possible.

I have worked with thousands of heart-centered and successful people who have already studied many systems and looked under many rocks to find their true calling but still feel that something is missing. Like they did, you may be wondering if there is more to life. I have been sharing the "more" with clients and students through my work and seminars, and in the Rhys Thomas Institute over the last fifteen years. The success and expansion of my school have been fueled directly by the use of the Life Purpose Profile System that you are about to learn in this book. The transformation that has happened for thousands can and will happen for you.

When people discover their deepest sense of purpose, they gain an extraordinary source of power. Success in marriage and business becomes totally attainable. And successful people innately know how to inspire, motivate, and influence other people, giving them more courage and more energy, and helping them to break limiting patterns and beliefs to live an extraordinary life. The Life Purpose Profile Program in this book gives you a highly effective transformational tool that will make you an indispensable resource in whatever field you are in.

In the bigger context of having a purpose and being a contribution, everything you want in a career and finances, in personal and business relationships, in vibrant health and abundant energy is within easy reach—all yours to have in lasting happiness and joy.

Knowing your life purpose is all you truly will ever need in order to stay motivated and be sustained in all your efforts. In this book, it is my honor to give you a program that makes all that possible.

Introduction

Today, the array of self-discovery opportunities we look to is dazzling: meditation, martial arts, yoga, mainstream religions, life coaching, New Age spirituality, Eastern philosophy, and a vast variety of inner and outer disciplines. All of these are paths we hope will lead to self-knowledge and self-realization. While this is all well and good, too often the many paths and books miss the most important ingredient in self-development: the experience of touching your soul and being fully supported to live your life from it.

You may be attracted to a spiritual path or personal growth practice in the hopes of finding your true self, but often the focus is on loftier goals, such as personal enlightenment or spiritual attainment. While those may be worthy goals, they don't easily translate into knowing your life purpose in practical areas, such as your career or relationships.

If you've been struggling with the question of your life purpose, then you need to figure out your *Big Why*—your deepest, truest purpose in life—in everything you do. You also need a structure—something practical yet wise—to hold and support you in being who you are as a unique individual, knowing what you are here to do and then doing it.

We live in a world where no one is holding our hand and affirming our unique true identity, pointing us consistently down the path that is ours and ours alone, the path where we make the choices for our freedom and empowerment at every turn. We travel through life with much less assurance and support, often in a random fashion even with the help we've sought out.

Regardless of which path you are on, it's likely that you don't have the structure and support you need. You may not have the tools you need to live with inner peace, joy, and success on every level.

But there is a path that can help you do exactly that.

The five Life Purpose Profiles you will be introduced to briefly in Chapter 2 and then in greater depth in Part III, provide a workspace, a laboratory in which you study yourself and discover your own truth. You don't need to dissect or analyze who you are; rather, the Profiles connect you to the field of energy you are already embedded in, allowing you to feel your deeper purpose within it.

Having a clear path and structure—a context for living your unique and highly individual life purpose—changes all that. The Rhys Method® Life Purpose Profile System gives you that context and is the only tool you need to bring forth your life purpose and live a life of extraordinary power and success.

PART I

Getting Clear
on Your *Big Why*

CHAPTER 1

The Missing Piece

s this all there is? That little voice in your head just won't let up.

Your life is good. Your job brings in enough money to support you and your family. You may even be climbing the ladder in your career, on your way to becoming a business owner or a CEO.

But that little voice is still there: *This can't be it. . . . Isn't there something more?*

And it's been getting louder.

No matter how much you achieve, no matter how many toys you accumulate, the voice doesn't go away. You try to ignore it, but the empty feeling that accompanies it is hard to ignore. It hooks you every time, and there's a good reason it just won't go away: you haven't discovered your *Big Why* yet.

What you have discovered is your *little why*—how to survive and get your bottom line covered. But even when you do that, there's still a sense that something is missing. I call that missing piece your Big Why—and when you find out what that Big Why is for you, you'll have found the answer to the question the little voice in your head has been asking.

The simple answer is, No, this isn't all there is. There's a lot more. And what that is will lead you to effortless fulfillment of all that you want in life.

The French call it the *raison d'être*, your "reason for being." Buddhists call it *dharma*, your path in life. It goes by other names: your *calling* or *mission* in life; your destiny. But all of these references point to the same thing: you are here for a purpose, and knowing that purpose, that Big Why, is the key to all of your success and happiness in life.

That little voice and the emptiness inside you, that sense of life passing you by when you haven't achieved real happiness yet—they are all calling you to your Big Why. In this book, you are guided back to your original state when as a child you knew the answer to this question: *Who am I and why am I here?* The Life Purpose Profile System contains the maps you need to reconnect with yourself, to bring that self forth into every aspect of your life. Only when you know the way, and are on track with your unique purpose that drives all your choices and actions in life, will success in life be yours, because your life purpose is authentically who you are.

Our Evolving Life Purpose

Our understanding of who we are and what our purpose is in the world has evolved throughout human history. In the beginning, as self-awareness was dawning in humanity, our purpose was defined by personal and tribal survival. It was enough to know yourself as a man, woman, mother, father, tribal member, hunter or gatherer, food preparer, tool maker, and so on. How well you responded to your environment and fit into your tribe or family was likely the deciding factor in your survival. To fulfill this purpose, individuals and tribes would kill other humans when they needed to secure natural resources such as water or food.

Inner peace wasn't on the agenda.

Consciousness evolved, and individual survival and small tribes gave way to society, government, religion, and corporations. A person's purpose then became associated with their contribution to the group; each person applied his or her skills to a job. People were divided by gender roles; men were leaders and workers, and women were nurturers and caretakers.

This is the understanding of "life purpose" most prevalent in our world today: Our life purpose is limited to our jobs and our roles in family and society. Our sense of self-worth depends on the amount of external influence we have and the money and resources we control. Within this system, we have the illusion of freedom, but when material success and recognition are the primary ways we define ourselves, our sense of life purpose and its expression are limited. Society supports a pattern of striving that does not bring us inner peace.

This way of thinking is evolving so that more people are learning to prioritize inner peace, personal freedom, and self-awareness. At this stage, we stop trying to fit into someone else's notion of what makes us valuable. We no longer define ourselves by our lineage, country, religion, government, or any other external system that might want to use us to further its own agenda. Traditional gender roles fall away because men and women are equally capable of achieving deep inner knowing and transcendence.

Today, we are evolving into this new kind of humanity. Jung called this new human the *individuated self*, Maslow called it the *self-actualized self*, Wayne Dyer calls it the *no-limit person*. I call it the *core soul self* to underscore an identity that includes not only your accomplishments and your potential but also the spiritual and energetic dimension of your human experience. I will show you how that dimension comes in five types. Everyone falls into one of those five categories, which helps account for human differences and motivations.

The need to find our unique life purpose is now more important than ever, as we let go of old identities and roles based on gender and occupation, and have an unprecedented amount of leisure time and resources. We are less willing to spend a lifetime witnessing our goals and dreams vanish as circumstances dictate what we can and cannot do. This was the fate of the mythological king Sisyphus, who pushed a boulder up a hill only to have it roll back down on him over and over again for eternity.

There may be times in your life when you feel like Sisyphus, endlessly pushing a rock up a hill. But with self-awareness, that rock is not just any rock; it is your rock that your soul has chosen for you and that refines you, strengthens you, and forms you into the person you were born to be. This is the rock of getting up every day and surrendering to your destiny—it never tires you but always inspires you because it is your deepest purpose in life. You want to know, *must* know, more than ever, what your unique path is during your time here on earth, so that life is not a futile, repetitive waste.

The question *What should I do with my life?* may no longer be the right question. Instead, you might start with the question *Who am I?* Knowing who you are, not what you should do, is the missing ingredient in your life purpose pursuit.

Your Core Soul Self

To understand what I mean by your core soul self, let's look at the term *soul*, which *Webster's Ninth New Collegiate Dictionary* defines as "a person's inner spiritual self." It is your inner spirit, or self, that you will be getting to know in this book.

I use the term *soul* not in any religious context but rather to point to an ineffable quality that is within us all and forms an essential part of our being. Your soul has always been a part of you, even before your birth, and carries the qualities that make you unique as a human being. You can know your soul through your deepest feelings and emotions, often coming to you as a sense of energy that is not entirely physical. This "soul energy" is your life energy, the force that animates everything you do. It reaches through you in every moment, connecting you to the world and letting you contribute your unique flavor to all of life. It transcends the physical world, it is eternal, and it is your truest essence.

Barbara Brennan, the spiritual healer and former NASA physicist whose classic *Hands of Light* put energy medicine on the map, writes of the soul in her recent book, *Light Emerging*: "It has been there within us since before the beginning of time . . . it is beyond time, space and belief. It is the individual aspects of the divine . . . We recognize it easily as that which we have always known ourselves to be since birth. In this place, we are wise, loving, and full of courage."

Your life purpose is not chosen by you but by your soul. Because it is your soul's choice, it is nonnegotiable. It never changes. It is yours and yours alone for life, and only when you tap into the energy of your soul does your life become directed, purposeful, and even magical.

In the last forty years, I've worked as a sports coach, teacher, speaker, healer, and founder of an energy medicine school, interacting with thousands of people to help them reach their highest potential. I have never met a person who did not have an essential life purpose.

To truly know your soul is to free yourself of all illusions that limit your creative force. This freedom comes as you realize that your power to create—your life purpose—is a gift you have been given. You accept that gift when you stop chasing after someone else's ideal life and rediscover the source of your own life—your unique core soul self.

It would seem that since your life purpose is your soul-derived birthright, living it should not be difficult. You were born doing it. You can't help but know it and live from it. But because life inevitably inflicts wounds on us and we form beliefs in response to these wounds, the job becomes more complicated. You must first identify your life purpose, then align with it and allow it to become your source of motivation and energy to courageously act according to it. That is the life you were meant to live—and can live when you have the right tools.

You Are Your Big Why

You are your life purpose, and you always have been. If you are waiting for the right circumstances to show you your purpose in life, you are missing the point.

The reality is that you are already fully on your path; you just don't recognize it. You don't recognize it because you don't know yourself well enough, in all of your many dimensions, to see how you fit into your own life. If you did, nothing would stop you.

Know thyself is great advice, but there is little backup support provided for the task. The media barrages you with infinite options for who you can be and what you can do, as if it's simply a matter of choosing one over the other. So you try on different versions of who you might be and then get stuck worshipping status, money, and beauty. Or you let yourself be molded by the expectations of society or family, following in the footsteps of your parents, so you survive but are dead inside, an outer shell with no inner essence guiding and empowering you.

But the truth is, each of us has a specific purpose, and until we uncover it, no amount of striving for validation or fitting in will ever bring inner peace and true happiness.

One of my mentors, Wayne Dyer, tells a story about Mahatma Gandhi, India's hero who not only led his own country to independence but also influenced political activists all over the world with his methods of nonviolent resistance. We know Gandhi's method as *civil disobedience*, which Martin Luther King Jr. demonstrated when he fought for and gained equality for blacks in this country.

During his campaign for independence, Gandhi was known to travel around India by train. At his frequent stops, he would share his inspired message by walking through the streets and speaking to groups of people. Once when he was pulling away from the train station in Calcutta, a young man clinging to the side of the train pressed a piece of paper and pencil into Gandhi's hand and said, "Write your message down, so I can bring it back to my people." Gandhi handed back the paper with nothing written on it, and with a gentle smile said simply, "I am my message."

Why you are here, and what message you are here to share with the world, is revealed by your circumstances, not created by them. If he had wanted to, Gandhi could have lived a comfortable life as a lawyer, which was his profession before he sought to lead India to independence. Instead, he heeded his inner calling—his Big Why—to devote himself to prayer, fasting, and meditation in solidarity with the impoverished people of India who longed for their independence.

You, too, can discover your Big Why. Your life purpose is always yours, and once you identify it, you can pursue goals and desires from a place of alignment with who you are and what you're here for, not from what others tell you or from what you think you should do.

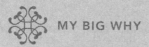

MY BIG WHY

In 1998, I had a midlife crisis that turned my world upside down. For most of my adult life, I'd felt something big was missing. By the time I was thirty-eight, that sense had finally become too painful to ignore. I could no longer go on striving toward what was not making me happy or fulfilled.

You may think thirty-eight is young for a "midlife" crisis, but looking back, I see that mine was the kind of crisis that could happen to anyone at any age. In fact, what happened to me is now happening to people of all ages, young people in their twenties and thirties, as well as baby boomers and empty nesters. Everywhere there is a rising tide of people asking, as I did, *What is missing in my life and how do I get it back?*

Today I am on the other side of what turned out to be a profound transformation in which I found the missing piece in my life. But back then, I felt isolated and cut off, struggling to survive in my own private hell.

If you knew me then, you'd never guess I was so desperate and alone. I'd achieved success at a relatively young age, becoming one of the top tennis teaching and coaching professionals in the country, a spokesperson for the industry nationally. I had a highly coveted position as the director of a prestigious country club, making $150,000 a year while wearing a warm-up suit to work every day. Married for fifteen years, I had two wonderful boys, aged seven and eight, and a beautiful home outside of Boston.

In terms of my personal development, I'd been pursuing inner peace and happiness through self-help gurus like Wayne Dyer and Tony Robbins for over ten years. Along the way, I'd studied psychology, Eastern philosophy, quantum physics, and the latest mind-body applications to health and performance. I'd earned a black belt in Tae Kwon Do and examined my life with a psychotherapist. If you'd asked me how it was all going, I would have told you I was living my dream, that I had it all.

But behind the pretense lay the stark truth of my life. I'd been struggling for years in my marriage over issues that never got resolved. I spent all my spare time working, leaving my two young sons growing up without the father they deserved. In spite of my long hours at work, I never felt secure in my position. I had chronic sinus, lower back, and digestive issues. To evade both the physical and psychological pain, I numbed myself with alcohol and a hefty dose of denial about how bad I was feeling in any given moment. I can look back now and see the toll of living a lie.

As I approached my late thirties, that world of unfulfilled striving was crumbling. For years, I'd been clinging to the illusion that success meant earning a lot of money. This meant I could never do what I really loved, for fear I'd get stuck in a second-rate, poorly paying job if I broke away. I smiled, but I wasn't happy. I'd become completely numb to life. The only "feeling" I had was a sense that something was missing in my life, something that should have been there if I were ever to be truly happy. But I had no idea what it was. I knew it only by its painful absence.

In my desperation, I did something that seemed crazy at the time. I signed up for a three-year program at the Institute of Healing Arts and Sciences, a school in Connecticut that offered courses I hoped would help me to heal, so that my relationships, work, and overall success as a man would all fall into place. In my state of denial, I thought that solving all my problems would be simple. After all, how big could that missing something be? I'd done so much work on myself already—surely there wasn't much new I would need to learn.

But I was wrong. In the program, I learned how to awaken the life force energy in me that I had shut down over the many years of denying my true nature. I could see that who I wanted to be and who I had become were actually two distinctly different people. I had been parading falsely as an "achiever" and businessman with just enough energy to pull it off, while lying to everyone about who I really was. People around me accepted the charade, and because I appeared so successful, no one tried to stop the train wreck my life had become.

During the three-year program, I came to see I'd been the Tin Man from Oz, searching for my heart but with no idea what it looked like, having armored myself against any real feelings. Through my training at the school, I found a deeper truth that was calling me to something greater than what I'd been striving so painfully to attain: my life purpose from my soul's perspective.

As I did the inner work to awaken and embrace my own deeper purpose, I started to notice that, as I had been, many people were hiding their quiet desperation behind a smile, a drink, or distraction. Failed relationships, careers that were more like torture than work, responsibilities rather than passions, *have tos* not *want tos*, and dreams that were put on hold for too long seemed the common lot. The "something missing," I learned, not just for me but for everyone, was joy, passion, enthusiasm, love, connection, and tapping into authentic meaning and purpose in life—all the things material success had never brought me.

Like everyone else, I was taught that the best way to conduct my life was to think first and then take action based on my ideas—to figure it all out to the best of my ability and then do the "right thing." But I had it backward. Figuring it all out had kept me safe but stuck, never fulfilled and happy. The best way to run my life, it turned out, was to listen to my feelings and let them guide me. When I learned to feel my deepest feelings—those not generated by my thinking mind—I found that those feelings called me to my highest purpose in an infinite number of ways.

The more I worked on myself and encountered others who had similar experiences, the more I began to feel a part of a wave of people on course to discover their true purpose in life and inspire others to do the same. I also noticed that there were few avenues for people to take in awakening from their numbness and start living with purpose. There needed to be more support for this critical evolutionary movement, and I was having glimmerings that I was to be part of that growing community of support.

My Big Why—the answer to the question *Why am I here?*—was taking form and expressing itself uniquely in my life. I began to teach what I'd discovered to everyone I could. My feelings were calling me in every moment to act on the best that was in me, and I discovered that those qualities were the core drivers for what I am here to do on the planet—not only in my personal life but as part of my contribution to a greater good. This realization has led me to my Big Why, my unique mission in life, which is to teach all who wish to learn that our own truth is infinitely stronger and more intelligent than anything others tell us to do, or what we *think* we should do.

Today, after many hours spent listening to my subtle inner callings with the help of tools I developed for myself and eventually others, as well as working with thousands of workshop participants and individual clients, I have come to realize that my deepest feelings are actually the "words" my soul uses to talk to me. To know who I am, I had to feel my soul communicating with me, guiding me in every moment to *be me.*

My life today provides a sharp contrast to how I used to be. Knowing who I am and what my purpose is, I live every day with energy and passion, enthusiasm and creativity. I am in better shape physically in my fifties than I was in my twenties and thirties, I found the courage to leave an unhealthy marriage, and I regularly share my "crazy ideas" with my two sons, with whom I have a loving relationship.

I also quit that top job as director for the prestigious country club, and in 2005 I opened the Rhys Thomas Institute, located outside of Boston. I teach my students how to awaken to their truth through a method I learned and then developed further, so each one can stand fully in their life purpose every day, as I've come to do. Knowing and aligning with my life purpose fuels my high level of energy, and I no longer need alcohol or any kind of substance to "get me through" the day. I run on my own inspiration and excitement about life.

You may be suffering as I did. Perhaps you recognize from my story that you, too, have been denying your truth in life, not even aware of what it is. But just as I did, you can learn to release old patterns and defenses that are stopping you from living the life you want. Once you find your Big Why and take action to live it, you will get what you truly want in life.

Is what you want in life a career or job you can be proud of that supports you and your family? Or is it rich and fulfilling relationships, both in your personal life and in your business? Maybe what you want is the energy and well-being, the stamina and good health to enjoy your life. Or maybe it's all three.

But one thing is for sure: It all starts when you find your life purpose.

What's Next . . .

In the next chapter, you will be introduced to the Rhys Method® Life Purpose Profile System, based on an understanding of the five different kinds of soul-driven people in the world. The system is designed to support your newly evolving self—your core soul self, not the persona you might try to project to others. The goal of the system is to empower you to make conscious choices and act courageously, based on inner knowing rather than on external circumstance and social norms.

The pleasure of knowing and being you is the first step to finding your individual life purpose and transforming your life. Then, as you share your truth with others, you will find that you have a larger life purpose that is destined to play an essential part in the transformation of all your relationships, your society, and the world.

CHAPTER 2

The Five Life Purpose Profiles

You are about to take a look at the human race in a way you have never seen it before. This new perspective, with the freedom and power it makes possible, can radically change your life and all of your relationships for the better.

The extraordinary life you've always dreamed of is possible through the Rhys Method® Life Purpose Profile System, which guides you toward understanding and mapping a path to human authenticity and potential. In this chapter you will learn about the system's origin and uses, as well as the promise it holds for you to discover and live your own unique life purpose.

Origins of the Profile System

The Life Purpose Profile System has its roots in the work of Alexander Lowen, a physician and psychotherapist whose groundbreaking research was presented in his 1975 best seller, *Bioenergetics*. Lowen had been a student of Wilhelm Reich, the controversial psychiatrist who proposed that a person's character depended on how emotional trauma had impacted his or her mental and physical health. By working with thousands of psychiatric patients in sanitariums as well as with private clients, Lowen and Reich came to the conclusion that both mind and body needed to be treated in order for a person to heal. Their work stood in opposition to Freudian analysis, the dominant approach of the day, which had patients examine their pasts in order to attain mental and emotional healing.

Lowen went on to develop a theory of five distinct types of character structures in people based on physical, mental, and emotional tendencies. He was looking mainly at energetic excess or deficiency as they showed up in a person's physical body. The qualities of these five groups were so pronounced that Lowen could challenge any psychologist to bring him a patient, and within minutes hand back a detailed history of the patient's behavioral patterns, life challenges, and reasons for any neurotic tendencies observed.

Lowen called his five types *character structures* and saw them as the underlying motivators in a person's life. He spent many years developing a full-body approach to mental and physical health based on his understanding of how energy blockages limited a person's ability to express feelings or needs. His main contribution was to bring attention to *body armoring*, a person's unconscious, defensive responses that result in a decrease in physical function and eventually illness. He believed that until a person becomes conscious of negative patterns and is able to open up energetically to hold more life force, healthy functioning would not be possible. Lowen devised exercises that helped patients to release their body armor, and thus their defensive patterns, in what became a popular treatment modality in the '70s.

While Lowen's approach took a giant step forward in mental health treatment by emphasizing the importance of the physical body, the system I developed takes the next big step, which is to include the "core" aspects of a person's makeup at the level of the soul. My system provides not only an awareness of a person's physical, mental, emotional, and spiritual makeup, but also offers guidance and tools that tap into the vast potential within each person to guide them to their unique purpose in life.

Development of the Rhys Method® Life Purpose Profiles

The Rhys Method® Life Purpose Profile System came about over the course of my training at the Institute of Healing Arts and Sciences, a school dedicated to training energy medicine healers and integrating energy medicine into hospitals. The institute used Lowen's work as the basis for understanding the connection between physical and emotional illness.

As a student and later a teacher at the institute, I had the great privilege to work with master practitioners of an offshoot of bioenergetics called *core energetics*, developed by John C. Peirrakos. I was able to see both the physical manifestations of defense mechanisms and the emotional manifestations of blocked energy typical of Lowen's five structures. Recognizing how and where energy is constricted in the body when people armor themselves against feeling was incredibly eye-opening to me.

Equally stunning was the realization that this healing dynamic was something I had glimpsed in my work with people over my entire professional life. As a tennis coach, I'd worked one-on-one with people and seen how they were able to release and use their energy, and how that related to their body type. This experience was my immediate frame of reference for understanding Lowen's character structures, and as I learned the tendencies of each type, I could visualize students I'd coached who exemplified each type. Also, as a martial artist, I could see Lowen's structures as they appeared in my training, and I was excited about how these body templates opened up a way for me to understand more about healing.

But I soon came up against a limitation in the bioenergetic system. As I studied both bioenergetics and core energetics, I found it difficult to accept their almost exclusive emphasis on defensive patterns people develop in response to early life trauma. Even the names used for the five character types—*schizoid, oral, masochistic, rigid,* and *psychopathic*—reflected a focus on pain and suffering rather than on capability and potential. I pored over Lowen's books but found no description for what it might look like once a person became free of unconscious defenses. If people's defensive armor no longer restricted them, I wondered, what kind of people would they be?

I began to create an expanded version of Lowen's five structures, starting from a place of honoring a person's unique gifts rather than focusing on how they are broken and aiming to fix them. Lowen's work was a therapeutic model in which the character structures used to define a person resulted from specific traumas in life. In my view, any character flaws existed only in the shadow of a greater soul quality within the individual. "Schizoid" could never define the whole of a person. Creating an identity out of one's defense, when that defense was the problem to begin with, seemed counterintuitive and counterproductive to everything I was learning about healing.

This understanding enabled me to reframe Lowen's five structures and develop the five Life Purpose Profiles. My profiles include the defensive postures, but they focus on the soul qualities in defining the person. In defense, a person's decisions in life are automatic and reactive rather than conscious, driven by an underlying fear and uncertainty in life. Free from defense, a person is able to meet and embrace life's uncertainties as opportunities to choose the life he or she wants.

Your core soul self, the *undefended* you, is the source of all your energy, passion, joy, and inner peace. Your defense, on the other hand, is a master wall-builder whose job is to protect you from being vulnerable or hurt. It will never bring you lasting happiness or unity. No peace or joy is possible as long as your energy feeds your fear of losing what you have instead of feeding your ability to reach for what you are capable of.

Walls protect but simultaneously isolate. The breaking down of our psychological and spiritual walls is an essential part of the evolution of the consciousness of humanity toward universal acceptance and oneness. The catalyst for our universality is each person discovering his or her deepest purpose and linking it to the purpose of every other man, woman, and child on the planet. For that to happen, we must understand the deepest aspects of a person, those that exist at the level of our soul.

Introducing the Five Life Purpose Profiles

My Life Purpose Profiles use Lowen's five character types as a frame of reference—both Lowen's types and my Life Purpose Profiles focus on the same body structures and their defenses, which we will delve into more deeply in later chapters. But where my profiles diverge from Lowen's types is in the inclusion of a person's *core soul qualities* that help the person manifest his or her life purpose in the world.

Furthermore, I've observed that there are five distinct expressions of the soul's purpose in human beings. We all fit into one or another of the following primary soul "flavors": *Thinkers, Feelers, Caretakers, Achievers,* and *Leaders.*

Think of your own family members—especially your siblings or children. Weren't they each unique as babies and children, even though they may have borne a physical resemblance to others in the family? Any parent knows that each child is like no other, that each one comes with his or her own personality.

You may understandably have a resistance to being labeled or judged. After all, people have used many repressive classification systems for generations that ultimately negate the integrity of other human beings. Slavery, the caste system of India, one religion claiming supremacy over others, prejudice or stereotyping, male and female gender roles, and racial profiling of terrorists have all failed humanity and stand as a warning, not as a model for understanding our fellow humans.

The Rhys Method® Life Purpose Profiles are not labels that limit and contain and negate. Rather, they are an acknowledgment of the unique greatness that is in each of us. Once we see our gifts, we can make the choices we must make to do our part in transforming our lives and those of others on this planet.

I offer you an opportunity to see yourself through a lens that is dynamic and empowering. My goal is to educate and ultimately liberate. My profile system is never imposed but simply offered as a structure to bring about personal fulfillment, higher consciousness, and unification with others in a more peaceful world. As each individual comes into alignment with his or her life purpose, the planet becomes balanced and whole.

John Gray, the author of several popular self-help books, proposed a similar idea when he wrote that men are from Mars and women from Venus. He showed how understanding gender difference can help men and women communicate better, and live in harmony and peace.

The profile system is based on an understanding that no one was born a blank slate, ready to be defined by the conditions and circumstances around them. Yes, we are influenced by our environments, but only after we bring our own unique "planet" to the party. Then, our unique core soul self responds to the events and circumstances in our life from a deeper set of principles. We are each a unique combination of our environment and our nature, grounded first in our original core soul self.

Each of us has one primary Life Purpose Profile that then blends with a secondary profile to give us our unique expression. The remaining three profiles also come into play, if only to a minor degree, making each person's overall profile a composite of all five.

Each human being will express his or her unique quality based on the infinite number of factors that create a whole person, but one's specific life purpose—as thinkers, feelers, caretakers, achievers, and leaders—never changes. The result is that no two people are exactly the same, even though everyone falls into the five major life purpose callings. How you express your life purpose—the job or career you choose or the role you play—is something you create according to your unique choices in life.

Below, I've listed the core soul qualities of each of the five Life Purpose Profiles:

1. *Creative Idealist* (Thinker/Creator/Visionary)—the most creative thinkers, connected to the higher mental and spiritual realms
2. *Emotional Intelligence Specialist* (Feeler/Lover)—the most empathic, loving, and sensitive people who live from the heart
3. *Team Player* (Nurturer/Caretaker)—the most supportive, serving people who hold families, nations, and whole societies together

4. *Knowledgeable Achiever* (Doer/Achiever)—the most master-ful, organized, and successful people who complete difficult tasks and remind everyone else of the big picture

5. *Charismatic Leader–Charmer* (Leader/Hero)—the most will-ing to take risks to motivate and lead others out of injustice, fighting for causes worth fighting for, in addition to inspir-ing others to be and do more in their lives

The charts on the next page show both male and female represen-tations for each profile, illustrating how a person's physical body is an expression of his or her energetic makeup. (Keep in mind that these are idealized representations and that a person's secondary profile and their other three profile qualities, to a lesser degree, will also be a factor in their appearance.)

For example, as a Creative Idealist, your energy moves up, into, and out of your head, giving you a tall, thin body. As an Emotional Intelligence Specialist, due to your sensitive nature, your body will be flexible and soft at your belly, concave around your heart. As a Team Player, your energy is reflected in your solid, supportive body and open, friendly face. As a Charismatic Leader–Charmer, you will concentrate your energy up in your neck and shoulders for communication and battle, giving you broad shoulders and a narrow waist. As a Knowledge-able Achiever, your energy serves your performance, and so you have well-balanced muscles and a strong body.

Your life purpose and the way you express yourself to the world is directly affected by the type of body you are born into, a point made adamantly by Lowen in his character structures. I believe that there is nothing random about the body and life in general—our physical char-acteristics were designed to express our soul's deepest purpose.

Profile Characteristics

Creative Idealist	Emotional Intelligence Specialist	Team Player	Knowledgeable Achiever	Charismatic Leader–Charmer

Distant, fearful eyes; head tilted; body core tight; disjointed limbs; left-to-right or top-to-bottom imbalance	Sweet, gentle, soft features and muscles; large eyes with a longing in them; S curve in lower back	Sense of density, compact body, tired eyes	Every hair in place, pelvis tucked under, tight muscles, "perfectly balanced" body, strong chin	Head forward, archetypal beauty, intense energy in eyes, extended solar plexus, seductive energy

Profile Characteristics

Creative Idealist	Emotional Intelligence Specialist	Team Player	Knowledgeable Achiever	Charismatic Leader–Charmer

"Mad scientist," tall vertical energy, no eye contact, introspective, fidgety, wandering	Soft, unformed body; fat held in lower belly; gentle, loving, sad, and sweet; nonthreatening	Square body, open face and heart, friendly, attentive to others, giving	Very neat, washboard stomach; can appear rigid, alert, thoughtful, and detached	Aggressive, large shoulders, wedge shape, bully belly in solar plexus; will stare you down; can go from 0 to 100 in seconds; dangerous

Universal and Spiritual Profiling

The five Life Purpose Profiles describe the five major human qualities that exist in every culture on earth. Genetically, humanity may be one species, but within that species each of the seven billion people on this planet expresses a unique set of human traits not found in any other, as well as a predisposition universally to express one of five essential human qualities.

There are many ways human beings are grouped or profiled, including socially, politically, and religiously, but without understanding the five profiles with their unique energy and spirituality, few will have the support to find their true life purpose. The five types are *inter*-dependent, making unique contributions to humanity.

Astrology, numerology, Myers-Briggs, and other workplace personality tests are all systems that attempt to define us but are not holistic enough. The Life Purpose Profiles are based not only on physical, mental, and behavioral qualities but acknowledge the nature of each person's soul—the energetic component, including capacities such as intuition, power, brilliance, clairsentience, and empathy. The profiles point to a person's essential goodness and potential for oneness with others, supporting their commonality with all humanity.

These are aspects of human beings that few scientific disciplines touch on. Scientists are our modern-day priests, but they are limited by the view that only what is tangible and observable is real, and the soul's energy doesn't fall into that category. Yet this is changing. Quantum physics, still not fully embraced, reveals a very different picture than the materialist universe that most accept. The Heisenberg principle tells us that we are inextricably connected to all we see, that pure objectivity is impossible because our very presence influences events and people we observe.

The Life Purpose Profiles include all that and more, giving unprecedented access to a new paradigm of self-knowledge. Just knowing your profile gives you a quantum leg up on how to live. You will find that when seeing life through the lens of your profile in my program, you are catapulted into a new realm where you can choose and create your life rather than live in response to events and circumstances.

Knowing by Feeling

During my training as a healer, I developed my ability to see another person's core soul quality as his or her highest potential. As a tennis coach for almost twenty years, this ability had always been with me, but it was now showing up in an exciting new way.

In my second year of training as a healer, I discovered a powerful tool that could help others tune into themselves to explore their own deep abilities. I was introduced to the practice of using a set of crystal bowls as transformative agents. The sound that comes from vibrating a crystal bowl resonates perfectly with the human energy field. This is because the human body is almost 100 percent crystalline in structure; water is a liquid crystal and our bones are made up of vast crystalline networks. When a crystal bowl is intoned, the sound amplifies and awakens the human energetic field, opening a channel through which we can receive a felt sense of our true self, our soul.

Over the next five years, I acquired an extensive set of these healing crystal bowls, ranging in size from as small as six inches in diameter to as large as twenty-four inches, the largest ones being capable of reverberations that shake fixtures loose from the wall. I used them in my private practice with clients, and also packed them in the back of my pickup truck and drove throughout the New England states, offering what I called Crystal Bowl Meditation workshops at different centers.

At first my motivation was to simply share what I thought was a powerful healing modality. In the workshops, as I intoned the different-size bowls for a variety of sounds, people would spontaneously release their stress and tension, sometimes healing a deeper issue or illness that was connected to that stress. My technique was simple: I played the bowls and then asked people to describe what they experienced. They related experiences of deep, essential states of being, such as inner peace and knowing, as well as love, compassion, and courage. I recognized these states as one or more of the core soul qualities in the five profiles that I was beginning to develop.

When I realized that the bowls were connecting people to their deepest soul self, I felt like I'd discovered a decoder for knowledge previously kept under lock and key. I started including descriptions of the profiles in my workshops, showing participants how the experiences they were having with the bowls were calling them to their life purpose. People were at first shocked that I could discover so much about them with so little information. Soon, however, they wanted to learn for themselves how to gain this awareness and follow the inner calling that awareness pointed to.

The crystal bowls were a gateway, offering people an opportunity to let their soul speak through them. What my students and clients described after a session led me to see that they were receiving their highest soul quality as it resonated with the vibration of the bowl. At times, the vibrations showed people how these qualities were being blocked, causing pain or discomfort in a particular part of the body. After thousands of readings, I discovered that each person's experience was unique, and yet the message was always consistent with the person's Life Purpose Profile. Both the pain of blockages and the elation of wholeness that the bowls evoked led to epiphanies and the release of energy, transforming each person's sense of self.

The crystal bowls taught me a profoundly important truth: to know who you are, you must *feel* who you are. This is a truth I will be revisiting again and again in this book. Thinking only gets in the way of finding your true life purpose. Rather, you must *feel* who you are and what your true calling is, and the bowls are powerful tools for doing that, teaching you to trust what your body already "knows."

Lasting Transformation

The crystal bowl healing sessions I did with so many showed me how self-realization can cause a person's ego, along with his or her defensive patterns, to be released for a period of time. But I also saw that releasing this part of a person's identity was not a guarantee of real and lasting transformation. Real transformation required more: first, an internal awakening to a higher truth; and second, the context in which to understand and hold that awakening for sustained and continued growth.

Many transformational, spiritual, and personal growth teachings can guide people in the awakening/epiphany phase. They do this through powerful techniques such as meditation, emotional release, psychotherapy, personal process work, goal setting, and more. But when you release a part of your identity, even though you are glad to be rid of what caused you pain, you are left directionless, like a boat without a rudder adrift in an open sea. Without some structure for understanding and integrating your new experience of yourself, you will most likely go back to the familiar way you've been navigating through your life.

In order to make permanent change, your new sense of self must have a greater context in which to flourish, one that goes beyond simply a personal desire for change and a rejection of some pattern in your life. You need a foundational understanding of what that change looks and feels like, and where it is leading you.

The Life Purpose Profile System offers that foundation by giving you an accurate description of who you are at the deepest, truest level of yourself, in addition to identifying your path in life. People who work with this system begin the process of change not just to fix what is broken in them or to alleviate pain, but to embody the extraordinary quality within themselves that they know is their truth. With the five Life Purpose Profiles, you don't rely on hope but rather on a deeply held soul memory to do the work of real transformation. Your specific profile, you will find, acts as a bridge to support you as you let go of your false sense of self and come into perfect alignment with your true self.

When you identify and own your specific Life Purpose Profile, you can look back at your life and see every decision you've ever made in a new light. You have always been on your path, and the profile system shows you what that path is. Looking through the lens of your profile, your negative life patterns are revealed as shadow aspects of your true self. Those shadow aspects lead to deeper self-awareness and should not be cause for self-rejection. Within this framework, you are able to make better choices. This is real transformation—not a reaction to past choices, but a move toward a deeper, inner truth—the only path to lasting change I have ever seen.

The Promise of the Rhys Method®
Life Purpose Profile System

The Rhys Method® Life Purpose Profile System is a profound, life-changing experience that guides you to align with your life purpose, release your defensive patterns that block your life force energy, and embrace the extraordinary individual that you are. Owning your unique profile, you can begin to move beyond simply surviving to having direct self-knowledge at the level of your soul. It is then that you can start living the life you really want.

PROMISES OF THE RHYS METHOD® LIFE PURPOSE PROFILE SYSTEM

By doing transformational work within the context of your profile, you can:

- Gain awareness of your essential life purpose and experience the inner peace that goes with that awareness.
- See more clearly the unique power within others and, as a result, interact with them more effectively.
- Connect to your essential life force for passion and energy to live a full life.
- Enlist the universal laws of attraction to draw to you what you need in fulfilling and manifesting your life purpose.
- See how everything in your life supports you in developing and living your life purpose instead of draining your focus and energy.
- Become a master communicator, transcending all demographics, life experiences, races, and levels of intelligence to know the heart and soul of anyone you relate to.
- Learn to forgive family members so you can move on in your life. By simply understanding your parents' profiles and the profiles in your failed relationships, you see how those relationships needed to turn out the way they did.
- Own your power and let go of blame and victimization once and for all, stepping up in your own self-esteem and in esteeming others.

With the supportive context of your profile, you learn to command the Law of Attraction, magnetizing to you all that matches your truest essence. This is your greatest power to create, and it comes from who you are in your core. You cannot keep anything in your life for long—things or people—that is not some part of your life purpose, so the

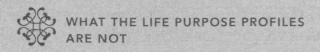

WHAT THE LIFE PURPOSE PROFILES ARE NOT

By seeing what the profiles are *not*, you get a better understanding of what they are. They are *not*:

- *A description of your personality.* Your profile goes far beyond your personality to acknowledge what is and always has been the greatest and truest aspects of your nature.
- *A goal for you to strive toward and achieve.* You can only get there by letting go of your false, defensive self. Being who you truly are does not involve striving.
- *A recipe for happiness.* Happiness is a by-product of knowing your true self, aligning with your life purpose, and making congruent choices in your life. It emerges when you are not on the defensive; happiness cannot be sought or planned. Sometimes you need to experience anger or grieving if that is what is being called from deep within you.
- *An excuse to be dysfunctional in certain areas of your life because those areas are not your profile's strengths.* You are an energetic composite of all five profiles, and while primary and secondary take dominance, all others can be strengthened to bring forth your best self.
- *A measurement of your self-worth or value over others.* The profiles make very clear that all five of the human life purpose traits are essential for a peaceful and unified humanity. Making them a caste system where one or two traits are better negates their true power. When we understand the truth that the meek shall inherit the earth, we understand that power is an internal state, not a badge of honor or a cause for division and isolation.

- *A way to blame your spouse, girl/boyfriend, or children.* Once you're familiar with the profile qualities and can see them in the people in your life, don't be tempted to play "gotcha" when others don't exhibit the highest qualities of their profile.

more you live your life purpose, the more you attract and keep what supports your success and happiness.

Aligning with your profile enables you to receive the guidance of your soul to connect with others, so you never feel separate or isolated. The guidance you receive also shows you who your true soul mate may be and how you can find and support love in your life. You gain a profound new perspective on all the significant people in your life—past and present—and the importance of expressing your core qualities in all of your relationships. This builds a stronger marriage and more loving and lasting relationships with your children as they grow.

Another gift of knowing your profile is that it enhances your ability to interact with people in your work. For example, as a coach or therapist, you develop an uncanny ability to read your clients when you first meet them, creating instant rapport and surprising them with your insights. Then, you can tailor your healing treatment specifically to fit their unique needs. In any workplace situation, you will find yourself judging less, supporting more, and enjoying greater camaraderie with co-workers that you never thought possible. You naturally help others get what they want in life by supporting them in their truest expression. This, in turn, helps you get all that you want in your career and life in general.

The Bigger Picture

The Rhys Method® Life Purpose Profile System offers a doorway to transformation in the consciousness of individuals and societies. It begins with understanding who you are. Once you truly know yourself, you can learn to hold and express that self, first with those closest to you, and then in your career, social relationships, and greater mission out in the world.

Finding and honoring your core soul self, who you truly are, is your life purpose. Once you know your life purpose, whatever career you take on becomes the vehicle for you to be a transformative agent whom others follow. Martin Luther King Jr. was a great example of someone who found himself and simply stood for who he was in the world. He did not stand *against* his white oppressors; rather, he stood *for* the freedom and empowerment of blacks, and the unity of all mankind. He never said to his followers, *Be like me.* Instead he said, *Honor that which is true within yourself.* And as he fought his own demons to do the same, he lit a spark in individuals that culminated in a massive movement that changed a culture.

We are not all here to change the course of an entire race of people or start a new religion or nation. Some of us are here to simply be the best we can be and do unto others as we would have them do unto us. But when each of us becomes aware of our gifts and readily shares them, the gross imbalance in power and resources that keeps our world locked in war and injustice will fade into the pages of history.

The profiles provide a path that takes you directly to the place where you can know your truest self. Once there, you become the one who speaks those words that awaken others, and the entire world transforms.

We all play our part. You can find out what yours is.

What's Next . . .

In the next chapter, you can answer a questionnaire to help you identify your own primary and secondary Life Purpose Profile. Knowing your profile is your ticket into the program offered in Part III, where you begin the transformative process of becoming and standing fast as who you truly are in the world.

CHAPTER 3

Discover Your Profile

In this chapter, you will have opportunity to discover your primary and secondary Life Purpose Profiles.

You will begin by taking the Profile Questionnaire, which is composed of one hundred statements designed to reveal your core soul qualities. Once you have identified your profile based on your questionnaire score, you can do a guided meditation called Your Secret Place that connects you to your profile on an emotional level.

The exploration you do in this chapter prepares you to enter the Life Purpose Profile Program that is offered in Part III of this book. However, you'll want to first read Part II and find out how your defenses have prevented you from living your life purpose. With your new awareness, you will have the courage to recognize and dismantle your defenses and get back your extraordinary power to live the life you were meant to live.

The Profile Questionnaire

The purpose of this questionnaire is to help you take the first step in discovering which profiles are operating most strongly in your life.

Read each statement. If the statement is generally true for you over most of your life, or represents a common feeling or pattern from your past, then check the box. The profile isn't a box you are trying to fit into but rather a window that lets you look at the whole of your life, so answer in accordance with your overall life experience, not just the present moment.

The statements are organized in groups of five, and you may find that only one of the five fits you. However, if you find that several statements within a group resonate with you, go ahead and check multiple boxes. If none resonate, choose the one that comes the closest to what is true for you.

QUESTIONNAIRE

☑ 1. When I get stressed, my mind races, and I jump from idea to idea and from thing to thing.

☑ 2. I am sensitive to lighting, loud noises, and textures of clothing fabrics (including clothing tags or seams). I guess I can just say that I am sensitive.

☐ 3. I feel embarrassed when people ask me more than once what I would like to do. I don't really know or care what we do, so I say, "Whatever you want."

☐ 4. I am very protective of my children and a lot of my decisions are based on protecting them and advocating for them.

☑ 5. I have been in a relationship with someone who had half my motivation and work ethic, and I tried everything to help get them back on track, but they were hopeless.

☐ 1. I love to meditate and find it easy to totally let go of the world and fly.

☑ 2. I am moved deeply by beautiful art, music, and nature.

☐ 3. I really don't like to step up and speak in front of groups, but I love talking to people!

☐ 4. I tend to know when someone is dangerous and protect others from them.

☐ 5. Sometimes I feel like I'm the only one among my family, friends, and co-workers who can see the bigger picture.

☐ 1. I often "leave my body," as strange as that may sound!

☐ 2. I avoid violent movies or television because it is difficult to let go of the images and strong emotions they evoke.

☐ 3. I never want to stand out or make any situation about me or my needs. I much prefer to help others succeed.

☐ 4. I absolutely KNOW I have an amazing ability to manifest spectacular things in my life, but I often sabotage myself in an equally big way.

☑ 5. I edit better than most editors.

☐ 1. Others would describe me as gentle, smart, artistic, poetic, intuitive, and a spiritual seeker.

☐ 2. My friends love me because I am so deeply caring, loving, and understanding. I can totally hear them and I am compassionate toward their feelings.

☐ 3. I love getting to know new people, neighbors, and co-workers and like to make people feel welcome and part of a team or family.

☐ 4. I have always been theatrical in my emotions from early childhood, from joy to rage to depression. When I feel it, everyone knows it.

☑ 5. Once I take the time to assess a situation and share what I find, I am not interested in the opinions of others who have not looked as deeply into it as I have.

☐ 1. In some strange way I have never really felt like I belong on planet earth.

☐ 2. I often have a hard time letting go of draining relationships because I don't like to abandon anyone. I would hate it if someone abandoned me in a time of need.

☐ 3. I don't like my body. I have always been a bit square and have a hard time with my weight.

☐ 4. I have had painful past experiences where someone I trusted stabbed me in the back/betrayed me (and I still hate him/her!).

☑ 5. I value clarity and decisive actions as my highest values.

☐ 1. I am extremely creative and love free flow of consciousness.

☐ 2. I have a gentle healing touch.

☐ 3. I can get stubborn but could never hurt anyone.

☑ 4. By thinking big and seeing myself as a winner, the power of the Law of Attraction works for me.

☐ 5. I get very frustrated with people who are supposed to be knowledgeable and in charge but who are unprepared or disorganized in their approach.

☐ 1. My thoughts are often wide and expansive. I can contemplate the entire universe and how it works, and then not know what to eat for dinner.

☐ 2. I get drained and exhausted and will cry when I feel this way.

☐ 3. Instead of asking for what I want, I ask others what they want because that's more important.

☐ 4. In the past when I didn't stand up and fight back when wronged, I really judged myself for wimping out—that is unforgivable to me.

☑ 5. I enjoy learning and mastery. I am willing to spend money on more training, certifications, and degrees so that I can be more expert at what I do and have a higher level of mastery.

☐ 1. Sometimes I wonder if my ideas are genius or if I'm actually crazy.

☐ 2. Others would describe me as sensitive, sweet, loving, and caring.

☑ 3. I am trustworthy and committed, often betraying myself before I would betray a friend.

☐ 4. People find me very charismatic, and I have never had trouble getting people to like me or follow me in projects I am passionate about.

☑ 5. I am not a needy person. I take care of my own needs. I don't want what I can't have. What I can have is plenty.

☐ 1. I like to create a mind-made world of art, books, computers, and ideas that are out of the reach of most people. Maybe I have a bit of the hermit in me.

☐ 2. My parents used to tell me, "You're too sensitive," and I often wish I weren't so sensitive (it feels like a curse, not a gift).

☐ 3. I will take all the time necessary to prepare food or take care of the health needs of others but often neglect my own needs since I have little time to take care of myself.

☐ 4. I often volunteer to run a big project or family event, not because I want to but because I want it to be run my way. I don't trust that others will do it right.

☑ 5. When I am feeling good, I see the big picture regardless of past events that didn't go well. I encourage others to see the big picture as well. Life is too short to be stuck in the past!

☐ 1. I can tune people totally out and be lost in my own thoughts even while they are talking to me.

☐ 2. I have a great capacity for feelings and sensual pleasures, from food to sunshine to rain to snow to silk to whispers—I love them all.

☐ 3. I have a great memory for people (names and faces) and details they shared with me.

☐ 4. Under stress, the warrior in me comes out, allowing me to rise to the occasion.

☑ 5. I never let myself be lazy and just do nothing.

☐ 1. I see all of the interconnected patterns in life through a deep understanding of science and mathematics.

☑ 2. Sometimes I just want a compassionate and understanding ear, not a solution and a to-do list.

☐ 3. It is difficult for me to say no when I am asked for help. I just can't leave someone in need, ever! I wish I could sometimes.

☐ 4. My résumé has a string of jobs that weren't quite what I was looking for, even though I was great at them.

☐ 5. When I am really tired I often go for a workout—it gets my energy back up again and I don't need any extra rest.

☐ 1. I am a bit of a conspiracy theorist (and intelligent people agree with me!).

☐ 2. I seem to have a deep well of love that comes from the core of my being. I can't believe I ever felt like there was never enough love in the world.

☐ 3. I have lots of people connections and networks, and people often rely on me as a resource for my great networks.

☑ 4. When I was younger, I could be great at anything (sports, school, performing) if I really wanted, without actually working as hard (or being as disciplined) as others.

☐ 5. I am seen as an expert or authority in my field based on my accomplished record.

☐ 1. I have hyper energy and don't need much sleep.

☐ 2. I see everyone's heart, and it makes my heart sad when someone is hurt and alone.

☐ 3. I get uncomfortable when others try to pay me back for the nice things I do for them or thank me too much or publicly.

☐ 4. In my career I often somewhat jokingly say, "I am just in it for the money."

☑ 5. When I think about how I have been wronged in the past, I become angry and say to myself, "I should have known better. I should have done it differently."

☐ 1. I can get easily distracted and go off on a tangent for hours.

☐ 2. My body is soft and flexible and I prefer yoga and walking to competitive sports or running.

☐ 3. I often feel that my good nature and helpful demeanor are taken advantage of by my family and people throughout my life.

☐ 4. I *love* winning but hate practicing and preparing for competition.

☑ 5. I never really let myself enjoy my accomplishments for two reasons: I could have done more/I could have done it better. And there is always so much more to do than waste time celebrating.

☐ 1. I never do things the same way twice (that would be boring).

☐ 2. Others would describe me as fragile and needy at times, and I hate it. Being gentle doesn't mean I'm weak.

☐ 3. I am extremely careful never to make anyone feel rejected or judged.

☑ 4. I find it difficult to trust people I don't know and many of the ones I do know.

☐ 5. Once I make a mistake, I will never do it again! I always learn from my past and rarely repeat an error.

☐ 1. I have a secret fear that if I really show my brilliance and put myself and my ideas out there, I will be attacked by small-minded people in power.

☐ 2. As an adult I have been told that I am empathic, compassionate, and loving.

☐ 3. It's really hard to "put myself first" because I know it would feel like I was being really selfish (and I vowed never to be selfish).

☑ 4. Whenever I really want something, I have many tools to get it. I can use charm, argument, or some kind of leverage, or I can hold out longer than anyone you have ever seen to get what I want. I am a tough negotiator.

☑ 5. I have extremely high moral standards and pride myself on being the bigger person, taking the high road in all situations.

☐ 1. I value enlightenment as one of my highest values and have studied many spiritual disciplines.

☐ 2. When I was a child, I could read subtle clues about how my parents or teachers were feeling beyond what their words and actions said.

☐ 3. Other people just don't seem to care as much as I do about doing nice things for people in the world, so I will do what others are unwilling to do. Only later do I feel sad about the whole thing.

☑ 4. If someone I love is being hurt or wronged, I feel extremely protective and go on the attack for the benefit of the person.

☐ 5. When I manage staff, I give very specific guidance for them to follow.

☐ 1. I find myself changing topics multiple times during a conversation as new ideas come into my head.

☐ 2. I don't like large groups. Ten minutes in a big group and I get drained.

☐ 3. I am uncomfortable if people try to "pay me back" for helping them out because that's not why I did it!

☑ 4. My body easily responds to conditioning and weight training. I can bulk up or slim down quickly when I am motivated to do it. But I don't always have the motivation.

☐ 5. I don't easily give authority to anyone unless they show me they are intelligent and have mastery in what they do. Then I watch and learn from them.

☐ 1. My body is wiry and I much prefer endurance exercises such as running, biking, and climbing that I can do for hours every day. I never tire of it. It's my healthy addiction.

☐ 2. I don't want a solution to my problem, just someone who listens and cares. Not everything can be fixed quickly. My feelings are like that—I need time to process them.

☑ 3. I find myself asking other people's advice in tough decisions in my life because I am not totally sure what I want. I like to hear the opinions of those I respect.

☐ 4. I don't really have any long-term goals. I like to make big things happen now and let the future figure itself out.

☐ 5. Under intense stress I just work harder and raise the bar of my personal expectations, even if it burns the candle at both ends. I know how to succeed and do not stop until I do.

☐ 1. My reaction to people in authority over me is either fear or avoidance. I rebel anonymously.

☐ 2. I made a vow never to hold back on my emotions or compassion because my parents were so cold, aloof, and critical. I never want my children to feel that or have to hold back their feelings.

☐ 3. I love learning about people's lives, opinions, and families. I am a good listener.

☐ 4. I try many different directions in life, different jobs and relationships, but nothing seems to bring the lasting satisfaction I am looking for, even though they seem to for a while.

☑ 5. I get frustrated with people who are not on time and situations that drag slower than they should.

Tallying Up

Now that you've checked the boxes for statements that resonate as true for you, count up how many checks you made for each number and then fill in the chart to get your score:

Questionnaire number:	1	2	3	4	5
Number of boxes you checked:	1	3	2	6	12

Scoring Your Questionnaire

To determine which Life Purpose Profile is your primary one, refer to your highest score and then match its box number to your profile below. Your secondary profile is your second-highest score, and the remaining three scores correlate to your remaining three profiles, ranked according to how many checks you made.

Box 1—Creative Idealist

Box 2—Emotional Intelligence Specialist

Box 3—Team Player

Box 4—Charismatic Leader–Charmer

Box 5—Knowledgeable Achiever

Once you've identified your two top-scoring profiles, go back through the questionnaire statements and read all those that belong to your two profiles, including the ones you did not select. (The statements on the questionnaire are listed in the same order as the scoring box and profile names.) Every statement that you read from your primary profile should resonate with you at some level, and many of the secondary ones will also.

You may have scored very evenly among two, three, or four profiles, making it difficult to determine which are your primary and secondary profiles. If this is the case, you will want to consider exploring further in the Charismatic Leader–Charmer profile. Charismatic Leader–Charmers are capable of living through any of the profiles, since they have natural actor/actress abilities and the different profiles are all avenues for that theatrical expression. To live their life purpose, just as for any other profile, Charismatic Leader–Charmers must come into their true nature, which is hidden behind the other profile qualities they may demonstrate.

Helpful Hints for Understanding Your Score

In some cases, the profile you scored highest in is not your primary but rather your secondary one. This is because you have been living through your secondary profile in your choices, leading to certain actions and behaviors in your life. For example, a primary Charismatic Leader–Charmer with secondary Emotional Intelligence Specialist who does not own his or her power may score higher as an Emotional Intelligence Specialist. If it isn't clear which profiles are your primary and secondary, take another step in the discovery process with the meditation described in the next section, which will help you make a clearer determination of your true profile.

An important point to keep in mind is that the questionnaire is only as accurate as your recognition of the truth—distinct from your conditioned behavior or thought patterns. Often in life, you are expected to play roles or behave in ways that are contrary to your true life purpose.

For example, gender expectations are among the strongest forces shaping you and can cause you to adopt the qualities of a secondary or minor profile. If you are a woman who grew up in a household where the girls were encouraged to be nurturing and supportive, you may have checked statements indicating Team Player rather than another profile. If you are a man who has always been expected to succeed in your career and provide for your family, you may have checked statements indicating Knowledgeable Achiever over statements pointing to your true profile. Regardless, your primary profile's core qualities and defenses will always color any secondary profile you adopted, creating a blend that is heavily weighted on the side of your true primary profile.

As mentioned in the scoring section, if your scores are evenly distributed across the board with high numbers in each, then you should explore being a Charismatic Leader–Charmer. The Charismatic Leader–Charmer is good at adapting according to different situations and filling multiple roles. You may exhibit the qualities of one profile while at work, another with your children, and another with your parents and siblings. Strangely, the one you rarely play is the Charismatic Leader–Charmer.

Keep in mind that every person is a composite of all five Life Purpose Profiles. Some profiles remain in the background and others are highly specialized, expressed only at certain times or with certain people. Knowing which profiles are most dominant for you is the purpose of this exercise. Then when you read the profile chapters, you can focus on those that may be the biggest players in your life. However, if your scores indicate a profile that does not seem to fit after you read more extensively about it, you have two options: Retake the questionnaire and make sure that what you checked is accurate, or have someone who knows you well take the test for you and see if that person comes up with the same results. If you are still struggling with results, there is a more comprehensive assessment at www.discoveryourpurposebook .com/members.

Your Secret Place Meditation

Even if you are satisfied that your scores on the questionnaire accurately identify your profile, I still recommend you do a guided meditation that I have outlined below, Your Secret Place. (A recorded version is available for you to listen to at discoveryourpurposebook.com/members484. Following this guided meditation before you explore your profile in Part III will help you to fine-tune your selection by *feeling*, not just *thinking*, which profile is yours.

To live your life purpose, you must be able to distinguish between how you feel when you display your profile's qualities from how you feel about other qualities that are not aligned with your profile. You reso-nate most deeply with the *feeler, thinker, caretaker, leader,* or *achiever* because your molecules and bio-systems were designed for you to live and feel your best in the energetic field that is characteristic of one of those states. Once you reconnect with this dynamic quality of who you are, your core qualities are naturally expressed, first in yourself and then in the world. Your unique energy is your extraordinary power and fulfills your life purpose.

The Your Secret Place meditation not only reveals your profile but also shows you the difference between being in your core soul self and being in a defensive state. At some point in your life, you chose to live your life in a defensive state, which is smaller and less extraordinary than who you really are. An elaborate facade of masks and behaviors was your response to the inevitable wounds that happen in life. But this is not the real you, rather a version of you that is fearful, perhaps isolated, and not empowered to live the rich, full life you know is possible. (In Part II, you will be reading all about your profile's defensive state: its origin and forms, and how it has been keeping you from living your life purpose.)

Once you realize the difference between your core qualities and your defensive behaviors, you can begin to let go of old, unproductive patterns. You will know how to discern between the essential self and the defensive self, which is the path to living a life of purpose and enlightenment. Only then will you have the courage and ability to access your unique power and be who you truly are.

Preparation

Going to your secret place in this meditation will help you remember your extraordinary gifts, the ones you were born with and have forgotten. Take a deep breath and get ready to awaken to your extraordinary qualities. They will point you in the direction of your life purpose.

Find a quiet place to do this inner investigation—either a favorite space in your house or out in nature. I suggest you choose a place where you can be alone for a half hour to embark on this discovery. You are free to sit or lie down; just make sure that wherever you go and however you position yourself, you are comfortable.

You may also want to play some soft and relaxing music. I suggest my *Life Purpose Crystal Bowls* mp3, which can be downloaded at www.discoveryourpurposebook.com/members. The crystal bowl toning sounds will help you clear away any excess mind chatter and distractions.

Keep a pen and a journal near you. This allows you to record your discoveries during the meditation or upon finishing it, while they are still fresh in your mind. You can bring a favorite blanket, book, stone, or object that you associate with inner peace. If you have a childhood photo of yourself, between the ages of three and ten, you may want to have that with you as well.

Now settle in, press PLAY to hear the music or crystal bowl intoning, and surround yourself with your favorite things. You may want to hold your childhood photo in your hand or pressed to your heart. Most important: *Just relax.*

Steps for Your Secret Place Meditation

Twelve steps for Your Secret Place meditation are provided below. A shortened list of these same steps follows for you to use once you are familiar with the process.

STEP #1. SEE YOURSELF AS A CHILD. Choose an age between four and ten years old. Allow yourself to feel what it was like to be this age. See your face. What did you look like? What were you wearing? What did your voice sound like?

STEP #2. IMAGINE STANDING IN FRONT OF YOUR CHILD-HOOD HOME. No one is home right now, and the neighborhood is quiet. Notice how you feel standing there. Notice how your body feels as you look upon your childhood home. What emotions come up?

STEP #3. ENTER YOUR CHILDHOOD HOME. As you walk through the front door, notice how you feel being inside the house. Wander through the kitchen, the dining room, and the living room. Then enter the bedrooms in the house, recalling to whom each belonged. How do you feel when you enter these different rooms in your childhood home?

STEP #4. ENTER YOUR ROOM. Once you have passed through all the rooms in the house, enter your own room and feel what it's like to be there. See yourself surrounded by your favorite toys, dolls, stuffed animals, and pictures on the wall. Notice how it feels to be in your childhood room.

STEP #5. IN YOUR IMAGINATION, GO TO YOUR FAVORITE PLACE YOU WENT TO AS A CHILD. This should be a place where you felt good and loved to spend time. It could be a hiding place, a crawlspace, an attic, or a place outside in nature, in the woods, a big rock, a stream or lake, a play house in the backyard, or a favorite tree you would climb. Maybe your secret place was far from your family's home at a grandparent's house, at summer camp, or a place you rode your bike to. It could have also been some place you found in your teenage years. No one else knows about this place, because it's *your* secret place. Maybe you had multiple secret places. If so, go to each one and choose the one that feels the best.

STEP #6. FEEL WHAT IT'S LIKE TO BE IN YOUR SECRET PLACE AND SEE WHAT YOU ARE DOING. Use all five of your senses—sight, hearing, taste, touch, and smell—to bring yourself back to that special place. Take a few minutes to let this sensory experience soak in. What does the place look like? Are you playing, reading, thinking, organizing, or fantasizing? Do you always bring a brother or sister with you? Do you have an imaginary friend that you don't tell anyone about? Are you imagining that you are a royal figure or a special person (like a superhero)? Do you have any special skills or powers? Are you invisible? Can you fly?

Now notice how you are feeling in your body, mind, and spirit: Are you hot, cold, tense, relaxed, vibrant, heavy, active, or powerful? Also notice where those feelings are concentrated in your body. What are you thinking about? Are your thoughts racing or still? Are you happy, free, open, or calm? Do you feel fully in the flow of life and do the smallest things like a bug crawling on a leaf bring you joy?

Simply notice what comes up for you without trying to change or judge anything that you feel. Enjoy this experience completely. Let yourself soak in it so that you can remember this feeling, because in this state, you are having a direct experience of your life purpose. Write down any details about what you are feeling or experiencing to help you remember.

When you are ready, say good-bye to your secret place. Know that it's always a part of you and that you can visit it again whenever you wish.

STEP #7. RETURN TO YOUR CHILDHOOD HOME. This time, all your family members are in the home. As you walk in the door, everyone sticks their heads out from wherever they are in order to look at you. Notice the difference between how you felt and acted in your secret place and how you feel and act in your childhood home. What happens to your energy? Is it different from what you felt in your secret place? Does your body shrink or expand, get tense or loose, hot or cold? Do you feel a pressure like you are being squeezed or compressed into a tight space? Do certain parts of your body feel more compressed than others? Do the patterns of your thoughts change? What emotions come up? Do you feel connected to your spirit? Now walk through the house and interact with your mother, your father, and any brothers and sisters (if you have them) or extended family members who lived with you, as you would have done as a child. Compare your feelings here to the feelings you had in your secret place. Take a moment to write any differences down.

Notice how you held yourself in your home, how you got attention, how you avoided getting in trouble, what being good looked like, and how you may have vowed to be more like one of your parents than the other. Become aware of how you showed some parts of yourself but not all. Notice how that pattern of behavior became who you are, and your secret place faded out of the picture at some point in your childhood.

STEP #8. RETURN TO YOUR SECRET PLACE. Once again, go back to your secret place and feel yourself fully there. It may take a few minutes to relax into that place again after having been in your childhood home. Once you are relaxed and playing again, enjoy the place of peace and happiness, a time when you were fully yourself.

STEP #9. SLOWLY COME BACK TO THE PRESENT TIME. Take a deep breath, wiggle your fingers and toes, open your eyes. Notice how your energy changes as you come back, once again in the place you live now as an adult. Does it feel similar in any way to when you left your secret place and went to your childhood home? Write down any feelings you have about being back and how those feelings are similar to how you felt entering your childhood home after being in your secret place.

STEP #10. TAKE A MOMENT FOR SELF-REFLECTION. In your secret place, you experienced your core soul quality and the way you express your primary Life Purpose Profile when you are fully undefended. In your childhood home, you experienced the primary defense that you have likely used in your life to hide your whole self. Even if your parents were the best parents in the world, they still created a home and energetic living environment that was theirs and not yours. You had to fit into that rather than change it to fit your own life purpose needs. As you learn about your primary and secondary profiles, you may find that you expressed your primary profile in your secret place and your secondary profile in your childhood home. For example, you might be a Charismatic Leader–Charmer in your secret place, seeing yourself as

making a huge difference in the world, but in your [...]
Team Player since that was what was expected of y[...]

STEP #11. FAST-FORWARD TO YOUR TEENAGE
TWENTIES. How did living in your household shape the person y[...]
were becoming as a teenager? What kind of people are your friends?
What role do you take in your relationships and when you start dating?
Which groups are you a member of? Just feel what it's like to be a teenager and express yourself as you were then. Did you still have a secret
place? At what age did you stop having time to go to your special place
or start seeing it as childish? How did those choices to be the person you
are "supposed to be" influence your choice of jobs in your twenties? If
you got married, feel the role that you took on in your marriage. Was
your energy more like the feelings you had in your secret place or more
like the way you were in your childhood home with your family?

STEP #12. FAST-FORWARD TO TODAY. In your life today, reflect on
how much time you spend in that state of awe and bliss that you felt in
your secret place.

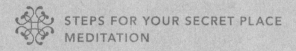

STEPS FOR YOUR SECRET PLACE MEDITATION

1. See yourself as a child between the ages 4 and 10.

2. Imagine that you are standing in front of your childhood home.

3. Enter and walk around the rooms. What does the home look like? How does it feel?

4. Enter your own room. What does it look like? How does it feel?

5. Recall a special place you used to go, and see yourself there.

6. Feel what it's like to be in your special/secret place.

7. Return to your childhood home and notice how different it feels.

8. Return to your secret place to reexperience your feelings there.

9. Slowly come back to the present time.

10. Take a moment for self-reflection.

11. Fast-forward to your teenage years and twenties. How much of your life stayed connected to the person you were in your secret place?

12. Fast-forward to your life today. How much of your life is spent in that state of awe and bliss you experienced in your secret place?

After the Meditation

Whatever it was you were doing and feeling in your secret place during the meditation is what you could be experiencing now, every day, all day long. Living life filled with the energetic state of your secret place ensures you are never tired, but always engaged, passionate, creative, and happy. How you felt when in your secret place is also the direct gateway to knowing and aligning with your Life Purpose Profile.

Meditate on your secret place for a few minutes every morning for thirty days to help fully anchor yourself in the feeling. See how long you can sustain the secret place feeling, that extraordinary power within you, in your daily life. It may take practice to live from the energy of your secret place, but the goal, which you *will* eventually reach, is to feel your secret place energy all day, every day. By practicing in this way, you can generate power to live your life purpose.

The feelings you had when you left your secret place and returned to your childhood home point to defensive behaviors that had you become someone other than who you truly are. Those feelings can be matched to the shadow or defensive side inherent in every profile. Your profile's defense is the unique way you protect yourself when you are feeling attacked or stressed.

Below are the names of the defensive patterns for each profile. (In Part III of this book, I will describe each of the profile defenses in detail.)

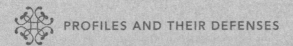

PROFILES AND THEIR DEFENSES

Creative Idealist—Thinker
Emotional Intelligence Specialist—Poor Me
Team Player—People Pleaser
Knowledgeable Achiever—Rule Keeper
Charismatic Leader–Charmer—Enforcer-Seducer

Activity: Reflecting on Your Experience

Many people who come to my classes want the direct experience of being guided by their soul. My answer is the experience you have of your secret place. Residing in your secret place gives you a grounded foundation to venture out into the world and not lose yourself in the process. The struggle arises only when you lose touch with that secret place by being someone you are not.

Following are descriptions of how the different profiles experience their secret places and their childhood homes. As you read the descriptions, recall your experience from the meditation (or review your written notes) and ask yourself this question: *Which profile best represents me in my secret place and which defense best represents me in my childhood home?* (You may have chosen a defense that is different from the one associated with your primary profile—possibly one associated with a secondary profile.)

Creative Idealist with Thinker Defense

IN YOUR SECRET PLACE. Creative Idealists often choose a secret place that is located up high, such as the top of a tree or hill. If this is your profile, you almost always go to your secret place alone. It's rare that you will want to bring other people who might interrupt your time to daydream. You can be doing anything, from visualizing sailing across the sky on a comet to writing a screenplay about your family as sea monsters. There is always a sense of fantasy informing your play.

IN YOUR CHILDHOOD HOME (THINKER). You may have trouble remembering your childhood because you weren't viscerally in your body. In defense, you become anxious, fearful, and nonconfrontational. You would never fight with the people in your family, so you had to remove yourself from the family energetically. In response to conflict, you chose the "flight" over the "fight" response, leading to much mental scattering and disorganization or to overthinking a situation without taking any action ("paralysis by analysis").

Emotional Intelligence Specialist with Poor Me Defense

IN YOUR SECRET PLACE. You have the richest-feeling experiences, often in your room surrounded by stuffed animals or out in nature with a pet—anywhere as long as it allows you to feel a soft and deep connection to things around you. The connection can be with people but more often is with nature, drinking in the beauty of flowers or the little snails that leave silky trails on the stones. You do not need to go far; the feeling alone of a grassy area lets you connect to your soul.

IN YOUR CHILDHOOD HOME (POOR ME). You feel a sense of collapse and defeat—a response to feeling picked on, abused, betrayed, or abandoned. Your energy is heavy, thick, feeling there is nothing you can do, no way to fight back—you are a victim. You may be hypersensitive and needy, and cannot separate your feelings from the feelings of others, often blaming them for the way you feel.

Team Player with People Pleaser Defense

IN YOUR SECRET PLACE. You most often have lots of people with you in your secret place. You may bring friends to a fort, tree house, or park and feel happy when spending time with them. If not friends or siblings, you bring stuffed animals, toys, pets, or imaginary friends to comfort you. Maybe your secret place was in the kitchen with your grandmother cooking, or fishing with your dad, or snuggling on the couch and watching TV with your family. If alone in your secret place, you will be making a gift for someone you love or simply thinking about random acts of kindness to do for others.

IN YOUR CHILDHOOD HOME (PEOPLE PLEASER). In defense, you make yourself useful, stay out of trouble, and do what you are told. You rarely offer help to others, doing so only because you feel obligated. You feel stuck, resentful, and may become passive-aggressive in your attempts to avoid and please at the same time. You may even feel you didn't have a secret place because you did not have any personal time in your childhood.

Knowledgeable Achiever with Rule Keeper Defense

IN YOUR SECRET PLACE. Your secret place might be located in a playhouse, a fort, an office, or somewhere you can organize people and solve problems. You can be doing anything in your secret place because you are extremely skilled in almost all activities that you pursue. You may imagine yourself lining up your stuffed animals in a specific order, telling people (or imaginary friends) what to do, directing plays or dances, playing house or making mud pies in nature, creating a business (such as a lemonade stand), winning an Olympic gold medal, or building a skyscraper.

IN YOUR CHILDHOOD HOME (RULE KEEPER). You feel well accepted by your parents, who dole out praise to you for being a good boy or girl and following the rules, but there is rarely any emotion or affection expressed. You are never needy or demanding and tend to be highly competent and disciplined: walking early, reading early, potty training early, and selecting your own clothes to wear early. Now, you are highly driven but rarely experience a sense of satisfaction upon achieving your goals, having the biggest inner critic and inner perfectionist of all the profiles.

Charismatic Leader–Charmer with Enforcer-Seducer Defense

IN YOUR SECRET PLACE. You usually have amazing and fantastical experiences in your secret place, visualizing yourself as a superhero, warrior, or royalty. You like to go to a place up high to see the world below you, imagining that you are flying and swooping down to save the planet. No matter what you are doing in your secret place, you feel a sense of power, passion, and enthusiasm. When you bring friends or stuffed animals to your secret place, you tell them what to do in such an inspirational and motivational way, you create excitement and ignite them.

IN YOUR CHILDHOOD HOME (ENFORCER-SEDUCER). You are fearful or unsafe in your childhood home and don't trust the people who live there. You may get into fights with your parents upon returning home in the meditation, taking on battles regardless of the consequences. You throw temper tantrums, act cute and seductive (Mommy's little boy, Daddy's little girl), or do whatever it takes to get your way. You are a negotiator, sometimes lying to your parents or faking that you were hurt or sick in order to gain control. In your childhood home, you may feel broken or betrayed, and act like a victim to justify fighting back. Or you may try to protect others whom you perceive as victims, like a younger sibling.

 RHYS'S SECRET PLACE

At age five, I started to play in the woods behind my house. I loved sitting on the small rocky knoll when it was sunny and warm outside. I called it my secret hideout, but it was really the place that allowed me to access a secret feeling within me. While there, I often felt super-charged, as if I could fly or create anything I dreamed up. I collected fallen oak and maple leaves to make a soft bed where I'd lie and look up to see clouds form. I also used the sticks and leaves around me to create fantasy worlds filled with people who had superhero gifts and magical objects. The visceral experience was one of total freedom and exhilaration. Every cell in my body was singing with the joy of being alive, playing in the world in my own special way.

Upon returning home and interacting with my parents and older brother, my energy would shift from feeling the exhilaration and joy of my secret place to a more contracted state of wanting their approval. I hid my secret place feeling from them, pretending that those feelings didn't exist out of fear my family would disapprove or reject something very precious to me. I also noticed none of the big people in my life were experiencing what I felt like in my secret place. They all seemed to want me to be different from who I was, and when I was, I got their attention and approval.

Eventually, I came to spend more time in the contracted state that others accepted than in being expansive and free, and I lost contact with my secret place. I still went to the rocky knoll out in the back of my house, but I went with friends instead of alone, and it was never the same.

Looking back at how I disconnected from my secret place now having rediscovered it, I'm aware that who I am as a Creative Idealist was clearly expressed in those special, private childhood moments. As I anchor those secret place feelings through a daily meditation, I am able to stay connected to the guidance of my feelings, choosing and making decisions naturally. My creativity—thoughts and ideas—are my deepest source of joy. In that state I experience the brilliant playfulness that is a core quality of my profile as I share my crazy ideas with those I'm close to, and out into the world. These indications, which are part of my Creative Idealist profile, tell me I am living my life purpose in every action and in each moment. And none of it involves striving or stress of any kind. I am simply at home and at peace.

It is important to see that what you did in your secret place is what you are here on the planet to do on a larger scale and with other people. For me, my little game of creating superheroes is exactly what I do now in my school and what I am teaching in this book. I want to call forward and "create" a superhero in you. I love nothing more than to awaken the real power in the people I touch. Whether it be the gentle loving gift of the Emotional Intelligence Specialist who changes the world by loving each person like they loved the crickets and ladybugs in their secret place, or the vivacious passion of a Charismatic Leader–Charmer who finds that their true mission in the world looks a lot like the fantasy of the rock they were playing on becoming the ship they then captained to new lands.

What's Next . . .

The journey of living your life purpose begins with knowing yourself at the deepest level—your soul. Knowing who you authentically are, not who you think you are, is your path to fully embracing your Big Why.

Next, in Part II, you will explore the inner forces that created what you *believe* is you but is not truly; rather, it is your false self. The path to dismantling that false self is one of *awareness*, *choice*, and *aligned action*, bringing you into congruence with all you are. When you enter the Life Purpose Profile Program in Part III, your understanding of your inner dynamics will help you engage the process that ultimately results in access to your extraordinary power.

PART II

Having the Courage to See Your Defense

CHAPTER 4

Beliefs, Wounds, and Vows

Did you ever have the experience as a child of wanting to share, do, or express something important to you, but one of your siblings poked fun at you or a parent judged it as bad or stupid? All that energy that wanted to share a deep inner truth and enthusiasm for life got negated, so it hurt deeply in your heart. You may have wanted to do something as simple as sing a song or show everyone a picture you drew, but it was a deep part of you that you wanted to share, and you got shot down. At that point, you consciously or unconsciously decided that you would never put yourself out there like that again. Then, later in your teenage years and adult life, you found yourself paralyzed or tongue-tied at moments but didn't really know why. You are an adult, you have something important to say, something close to your heart and mind, but, all of a sudden, access to expressing it seems cut off.

Even more mysterious, your passion and confidence have totally evaporated, leaving you doubting that what you had to say was even important in the first place. Each time this happens you move further away from having the power to express yourself and act, until, at some point, you give up, play small, and no longer even try.

This puzzling predicament is not unusual—we all experience not being able to speak or act on our deepest truth in certain situations— usually the ones that really matter! In this chapter, I will show you how your beliefs—especially those super-beliefs I refer to as your *vows*— became hardwired long ago as mental constructs that prevent you from expressing your unique life purpose. It is only when you uncover the truth behind your vows that you can call back the energy you repressed so long ago. Only then can you gain the freedom to make conscious choices and act courageously in alignment with who you are and fulfill your life purpose.

The energy you need to live your life purpose is not based on how fit you are or how energetic you feel. Having stamina is helpful, but plenty of people who are in great shape have no clue about their lives or deeper life purpose. The energy you need to live your life purpose comes from a much deeper channel in which you fearlessly challenge limiting beliefs and life patterns based on self-rejection and stand up once again for your highest truth.

Belief and Identity

All of your experiences in life are filtered through your beliefs. It's not so much events that shape your experience as it is how you interpret, analyze, and evaluate those events.

The most powerful of all your beliefs are those that define who you are. As an infant, you felt the world and experienced yourself as a flow of energy rather than as a person. But almost from the moment of your birth, adults tried to hook your attention away from your flowing, formless world and get you into their world of rules and structures and labeling to make the world solid, controllable, and predictable. At a young age you had to give up the feeling of who you are and begin to define yourself so you could be like everyone else. If you stayed in the no-form world too long, your parents and doctors would treat you like you were ill or mentally slow.

By necessity you needed to put your analytic mind in hyperdrive to match your parents' notions about what is real and what is not. You came to see yourself as solid, predictable, and separate from everything and everyone else in your surrounding world, just like Mom and Dad. You learned the family language that turned the flowing unified universe and the flowing unified soul self into static, solid, and separate entities.

By the time you became an adult you were isolated, wandering through a world of objects, each one defined not by what it is but by how it is different and separate from you, or by how the world has labeled or judged it. In these strange mental gymnastics, your experience of what is outside of you tells you more about what you are than your internal guidance and knowing. Your worldview has defined you by *what you are not* rather than who you are.

The more you created beliefs based on evidence and mental experiences in your life, the more you defined your world as solid, separate, and therefore "real." You told yourself a story, based on the thinking function of your brain, to bring solidity and certainty along with the illusion of permanence to your life. In that way, you avoided the fear that goes with living in an uncertain world, in an impermanent body. You labeled the world in a way that let you know it and your part in it were safe and secure, just like everyone else did.

But I want to challenge this very fundamental belief about who you are. If you take a few deep breaths and feel who you are—do not *think* who you are—you will experience yourself as someone more *non-solid* than solid. Your body appears to have a solid, separate form, but according to modern science, even that physical part of you is continually changing, making you a part of a universe that has never been the same twice. At the quantum level, looking at the energies that make up your very molecules, there are no particles that are the same as they were even one minute ago!

In that light, it seems the only thing about you that is solid and separate is your rigid beliefs and your thinking mind's memory of who you are. To be experienced accurately, your true self must be felt as fresh and new in each moment, like an infant in the ecstasy of playfully being alive. Such felt awareness brings you to what is not solid but formless and flowing, touching on your true identity, which is made up of your *core soul* qualities as expressed through your unique profile. It is those core soul qualities that give you a purpose for the form you take in any moment, whether you are *creating, feeling, caretaking, leading,* or *achieving.*

In summary, who you believe you are defines the world that you experience. Your beliefs establish a solid and dependable self, but they limit who you are in life and the choices you make. This is why it is so important to know who you are at the deepest level of what you're here in life to be and do.

If you don't know who you are, believing instead that you are someone you are not, you create a fake life and purpose that invariably feels lost or unsure, as well as a world you don't fit into. Deep down inside, you know that you are being who you are supposed to be rather than who you really are, so that triggers great fear that forces you always to struggle to survive, to "make it." If you know who you are as a soul, you see that everything happening to you has purpose and meaning, and you live in peace and harmony with yourself and the world, never feeling forced to change a single thing.

The Rhys Method® Life Purpose Profile System makes it possible for you to see what has always been your authentic soul self. Through the study of the five Life Purpose Profiles, you are able to create a dynamic self-awareness and soul identity that are far more powerful than anything you've ever thought or believed to be the truth. You will know yourself in a profoundly new way.

Vows: The King of Beliefs

Some beliefs about who you are go deeper than others, especially those formed out of fear and defense when you felt that your identity was threatened. I call such powerful super-beliefs *vows*. Vows are beliefs that went so deep that they became hardwired and nonnegotiable, preventing you from living your life purpose.

The term *vow* typically refers to a sacred promise—one to be taken seriously as in a marriage vow or a spiritual/religious commitment. A vow is something you adhere to, even worship as something greater than yourself and your ordinary needs. The kind of vows I'm referring to are indeed sacred promises, but not the kind that are made from your free choice or for your greater benefit. Rather, vows are those promises you made to yourself long ago in order to be safe. In other words, your vows, similar to beliefs, keep you trapped, but the prison of the vow is deeply unconscious and therefore beyond your ability to escape. Even worse, you cannot examine your vows, only see them by the impact they have in your life.

At their most basic level, vows guarantee that you react automatically to flee from danger, which would be a good thing if you were being charged by a grizzly bear. In that instance, the vow is: *I will always seek safety when threatened violently!* But other kinds of vows, while they are meant to protect, actually cause you to reject some aspect of yourself because that aspect was not recognized, or worse, it was rejected by another.

These deeper, more complex kinds of vows determine your personal identity and mentally created life purpose. They are harder to trace in their origins but occur just as automatically as your reactions to immediate danger. Fleeing a charging bear involves your entire autonomic nervous system, not just your rational and conscious mind, and it is the same with a vow you made at a young age to protect yourself from rejection or abandonment. As an infant, you could not tell the difference between a dangerous animal and an angry parent who hurt you and then ignored your needs—both threatened your survival. Vows, regardless of their content, get lodged in your unconscious mind, and you don't get a chance to consider their value. They run your life.

Not all vows are so dramatic, but they can still be as lethal in their impact on your life. A vow can be as simple as telling yourself that you will always be polite and nice. As a belief, you consciously decide that never being angry at people is a better choice than being rude or aggressive. But if you vowed always to be polite, you find yourself being nice automatically and holding back your anger, not responding authentically even if you are clearly being abused by another. These are the kinds of vows that steal your power, making it impossible to act in a healthy way.

Certain news events demonstrate the power of vows over any rational conscious choice. Religious zealots who become terrorists or kill doctors at abortion clinics are willing to sacrifice themselves and kill others in the name of their vow. These are extreme examples, but every vow you make, regardless of the outcome, generates the same level of unconscious conviction that these zealots and terrorists exhibit.

The vow to be nice and polite is laid down in your body-mind with the same amount of force and energy as the vow to die a martyr, causing endless harm. Vows are *always* and *never* statements. You may have vowed, *I will never be as abusive as my father was and hurt other people.* Or the opposite: *I will always love and care for my family, like my grandmother did when she took us in.* These kinds of "nice" vows make you a slave to an ideal and prevent you from showing compassion to yourself when you need it. Such an idealistic vow leaves you feeling like you are never good enough as a parent, never measuring up. At the same time, you stand in righteous condemnation of parents who are strict or assertive with their children.

Simple vows about being good or not being bad start out innocently, but soon they snowball, growing in size and impact to determine your every decision throughout your entire life. Your vows may not lead you to kill other people, but they kill *you*—your true self— paralyzing you when you need to express yourself or act from a sense of your true mission. They force you to judge others who exhibit the traits you've rejected in yourself. You move farther and farther away from your true self and the energy you need to live your life purpose. Your actions may not make the evening news, but they can wreak havoc in your life and in the lives of those you know, causing just as much violence as the terrorists and bombers we read about.

Vowing Against Your Truth

Even though vows look like you are choosing to be good, they are actually your unconscious choices not to be *you*. Because vows are always against your true self, there are no good vows.

For example, if you vowed to be like your grandmother who was always warm, giving, and selfless, then you deny your own needs and take care of others first in moments when you really need to take care of yourself. Furthermore, your vow to be one way or another doesn't necessarily relate to the actual situation in which you made the vow. Your grandmother who appeared selfless may have taken lots of time for herself, but you never noticed that. Instead, you fixated on her "always" being giving and selfless, creating an impossible ideal that made your selfishness sting. In essence, you created a perfect snapshot of how life should be, which stands in opposition to who you really are.

Setting an ideal that you can never live up to, even on your best day, demands that you use all of your energy to be that ideal while ultimately failing. Yet you have to appear "good" all the time, driven by your vow and hiding from the fact that you are a phony at some level. Living someone else's life, or half of your life, is never going to make you happy, no matter how wonderful that life may seem. You need to find your own unique life purpose hiding behind your vows to be whole and fulfilled. Nothing else will suffice.

Vows become the "nonnegotiables" in life, reigning over all your beliefs as unquestionable truths. Every time you say, *This is just the way the world is!* you are referencing a deeply held vow and lie. Beliefs, on the other hand, are cognitive and can be challenged when circumstances clearly do not support them. A vow doesn't get cognized or even *re*-cognized, sneaking past any rational process of your thinking mind before becoming real in your feelings, thoughts, and actions. A vow is fashioned as the truth of *who you are and what the world is*, and unless you become conscious of the vows you've made and release that energy, they negate you.

Core Wounds and Vows

In childhood, your unique core soul qualities—what makes you who you are—were rarely seen, heard, or understood by your parents or guardians. From such ignorance or even outright rejection of your deepest self-expression, you became wounded at your very core. In your wounded state, you vowed against the core qualities that they denied, making a promise to yourself that only the opposite qualities would thrive.

It is this basic inability of a parent to see, hear, or understand the true nature of their children that forms the core wound for every human being. We all suffer not from specific traumas, as psychologists would have us believe, but rather from something far deeper and more common: the realization that who we are in our very souls is not welcomed by those who care the most for us and unconsciously want us to be more like them than ourselves. You may have escaped specific traumas in your childhood, but none of us escaped this universally human experience.

In his book *The Four Agreements*, Don Miguel Ruiz calls this process "human domestication," referring to how a child's true self is bred out and eliminated through repeated rejection of undesirable traits and affirmation of accepted traits. Those traits that elicit love and approval are vowed *for* ("I'll always be quiet and polite when an authority is correcting me") and those that don't are vowed *against* ("I'll never talk back to an authority"). Even early in the game, a good portion of your core self is left behind. The truth is that you need to speak when judged and that if you don't challenge authority you live the life of a lemming.

Every time a child chooses the approval and love of their parent over his or her own truth and integrity, a vow is made. To a child, it's a life-or-death choice—his or her very survival seems to be at stake because the attention and love of adults is what the child cherishes most. These kinds of early vows are often made in the first two to three years of life, at a time when life is a full-body, energetic experience rather than a mental or cognitive one. For a young child, painful events are absorbed into their very sense of self.

In response to early wounding experiences, each of us reacts in a way that is specific to our unique profile in life. When wounded, the Creative Idealist will retreat, run away, or dissociate; the Charismatic Leader–Charmer will stay and manipulate or fight; the Knowledgeable Achiever will manage himself internally to figure out how to be successful and good; the Team Player will comply and put up with it; and the Emotional Intelligence Specialist will get overwhelmed and cry. These responses are hardwired into your nervous system, leading you to make vows that specifically hide your core soul qualities, creating beliefs about yourself and the world.

Once you vow, consciously or unconsciously, to see some part of yourself as bad or good, you set up the *always* or *never* knee-jerk responses that drastically limit the pleasure you can experience in life. Vows always carry heavy doses of shame and guilt about that part of yourself needing to be rejected. Then add the fear that goes with hiding and you have the perfect storm that creates a vow.

Later in life, when you stand up and choose to put yourself first, you feel the guilt and shame that you felt as a child. So you will need to get used to working through guilt and shame if you are going to challenge your vows and take back the energy you lost because of them.

Vow patterns begin a domino effect of self-misunderstanding and trigger thousands of false beliefs about who you are and what your purpose is in life. All future choices, beliefs, and vows must honor your original vow in order to be acceptable. Vows are the antithesis of freedom, always going against anything that is part of your true core self. Vows seem to be your free choice, but that freedom of choice is an illusion. Your choices in jobs, relationships, and who you allow yourself to be seen as are all set in stone, and you cannot go against them without feeling like a bad person, full of guilt, shame, self-hatred, and isolation.

The Polarizing Effect of Vows

Vows always lead to inner conflict because when you live from a vow, every event becomes polarized as either *good* or *bad*. Vows don't let you see your wholeness but instead force you to live in judgment of yourself, preventing you from experiencing the full range of your human qualities. This polarizing effect is the source of so much of the pain and suffering you experience in life.

Any personal crises you experience, whether a midlife crisis or a mental or physical health crisis, come straight from the buildup of hardwired vows you've been living by and see no way to change. In energy medicine, we have discovered that almost every form of illness or relationship problem can be mapped back to a rejection of the true self. You've tried running away or impulsively rearranging people and circumstances in your life but still you are trapped. That is because regaining your freedom is not a matter of escaping or making big changes to your outer circumstances. In fact, your freedom has absolutely nothing to do with what is going on around you—the people, the circumstances, the events you may point to and blame—but rather everything to do with what is going on inside you: your thoughts, feelings, and beliefs, all sourcing from invisible vows.

As you read about each Rhys Method® Life Purpose Profile in Part III, you will see that a person's vows are directly related to the core soul quality of the particular Life Purpose Profile. Those qualities include both the positive and negative sides of your individual traits, which explain how you can vow *for* or *against* (in *always* and *never* statements) and still reject your true self. The sensitive Emotional Intelligence Specialist child may vow never to feel, the giving Team Player child may vow never to be humiliated again by being too nice, the super-performing Knowledgeable Achiever child may vow never to be fully satisfied with achievements in life, the Strong Leader child may vow to fight authority rather than become one, and the Creative Idealist child may vow to keep her ideas to herself.

The rejection of your core soul qualities creates far-reaching, devastating internal conflicts, so that your strongest vows and supporting beliefs block you from living your purpose and being your true self, both internally and externally.

Every powerful structure has its weak point, and a vow's weakness is revealed when you begin to choose those qualities that are inherent to your soul, not your defended self. Just as Superman, the Man of Steel, lost his strength and helplessly flopped to the floor in the presence of Kryptonite, your vows lose their strength when in the presence of your authentic, core soul profile self.

Your core soul self, as identified in your unique profile, existed before your vows were made, and thus has roots far deeper than any beliefs, no matter how hardwired they may seem. The feelings you have when the crystal bowls are intoned or when you are in your childhood "secret place" are your vows' Kryptonite. Vows say *no* to life and pull you back through self-rejection, while your soul says *yes* to life and is felt as a deep calling and self-acceptance.

Simply seeing yourself and others clearly, not through the lens of your fear-based beliefs and vows, allows you to know your true place in the world and be empowered to do what you are here to do. From that grounded place, you begin to rebuild your life, attracting to you people and events that support your life purpose rather than your fears, beliefs, and vows. A new kind of snowball effect starts working for you rather than against you, and an entirely new way of life opens up.

The good news is this: if you are defined by what you have rejected in yourself, then what you have rejected is exactly what must be restored so you can know and be fully who you are. This is the secret gift of vows: in hiding who you are, they are your most valuable clues to your true identity and your life purpose. Uncovering them is the important work you will do in the Life Purpose Profile Program in Part III.

ABOUT YOUR VOWS: A SUMMARY

1. **You never get rid of your vows.** Vows are deep-rooted beliefs hooked into your nervous system to become autonomic, impulsive reactions. You can see them only after they have triggered a feeling or behavior. To recall the energy that vows deny, you must feel that pattern of self-denial emerging and make the choice to honor your core soul profile quality.

2. **There are no good vows.** Regardless of how "good" some vows may sound, they all limit you and make you someone you are not. Who you are, as expressed through your vows, comes from a negative life choice, triggered by childhood traumas and fears rather than from your real life purpose.

3. **Vows keep you stuck in the past.** You know that you are letting an ancient vow run your life when your behavior is childish and you feel like a victim. When a vow is triggered, you experience current events from the lens of a child or infant who is terrified of being rejected or unloved.

4. **Vows divide and polarize your world.** Your vows divide the world into the "good people" who do the "right thing," and the "bad people" who do the "wrong thing." The line is drawn not according to any objective standard but according to your subjective internal judgment. That line cuts through you and slices off the energy you need to live your life purpose, channeled through deep self-acceptance and knowing.

5. **Vows suck your energy.** Vows make your life hard work rather than enjoyable and purpose-filled. Once released, you can re-channel your energy and begin to double and triple the energy available to you at any time.

6. **Vows are never your life purpose.** Over a lifetime, your vows become the principles you think you must stand for and act on

to give you a sense of purpose. But in vowing to be a *good*, caring, and strong person, you are choosing not to be a real person but rather a perfect person, which is never your life purpose. Trying to be what you are not leaves you unable to live an inspired life pursuing the career, relationships, and sense of well-being that are your birthrights.

7. **Vows, when broken, always bring up guilt and shame.** Accepting that you will feel guilt and shame when breaking an ancient vow is the beginning of true personal growth. Feeling the guilt and shame and acting anyway is the path back to wholeness.

8. **Vows fade when you start to live in your core soul qualities.** Only by replacing your vows with your true identity do you become free to call back the energy that gives you the courage to live an extraordinary life. When you choose your core soul qualities over your vows, you start to build a life that is authentic, pleasurable, and fully able to weather life's storms.

What's Next . . .

In Chapter 5, you will see how vows polarize your higher- and lower-self traits to create your profile's defensive patterns. Dismantling those defenses, by seeing your specific vows and releasing them, is the work you will do in the Life Purpose Profile Program in Part III.

CHAPTER 5

Shadow, Higher/Lower Self, and Defensive Mask

To truly benefit from the Life Purpose Profile Program offered in Part III of this book, you need to understand your self-sabotaging patterns, which will appear through the defensive aspects of the profiles. These defensive patterns aren't necessarily bad since we all need to use them sometimes. Your vows to be someone you are not are the actual mechanisms that create what psychology calls your shadow, or rejected aspects of the self, and the resulting defensive mask presents itself to the world as if it were you.

In this chapter, you will explore your higher self and lower self, which, when divided, leave you caught between an animalistic need to survive, control, and isolate, and a spiritual need to sacrifice personal needs for the needs of humanity. People must come into balance between the two if their true life purpose is to be achieved. When your shadow is not integrated, your life force goes into a *defensive mask* of piety or depravity or normalcy, depriving you of the energy and wholeness you need to live your life purpose.

Living your life purpose requires an integration of the divided needs of your lower and higher self. Only when these seemingly opposing needs are balanced and integrated can your life force energy flow freely throughout your system to support your true life purpose. To embrace the lower and higher self simultaneously takes a higher level of consciousness that sees the importance in both.

Lower Self, Higher Self

You have learned how Alexander Lowen's study of bioenergetics profoundly influenced me in developing the Life Purpose Profiles. Now you will learn how the teachings of another master thinker who unlocked the deeper mystery of our human condition further influenced my approach.

Eva Pierrakos developed a body of knowledge known today as The Pathwork. The Pathwork is a collection of teachings that emphasize the importance of recognizing, accepting, and ultimately transforming the dark and unconscious "animal" side of our human nature, referred to by Pierrakos as the *lower self*. The goal of human life, she believed, is to transcend our animal lower self and take our true place with the saints and mystics in what she called the *higher self*.

Lowen and Pierrakos were two of the greatest visionaries in the field of human energy work, and together their approaches provided a structure for me to use with thousands of my clients and students. I was able to expand on their theories to discover a deeper truth, which is that each person has both a *lower-self purpose* and a *higher-self purpose*. The two have become divided and vie for our life's energy in every moment, creating a deep confusion as to who and what we really are. As a result, we create a *false self* and pretend we are not confused.

Furthermore, my work and life experience showed me that it is the balance of both higher and lower, not the transcendence of the lower self, that is ultimately liberating. While Pierrakos taught that the lower self must be transcended for its imperfections, she did not acknowledge the equal imperfection of the higher self in its tendency to idealize and dissociate from reality, or to parade as a spiritual false self. I came to see how living only in the higher self can be just as isolating and destructive as living only in the lower self. In my view, both must come into balance through acceptance if we are to have the energy needed to live our life purpose as a unified *core soul self*. I have discovered that one cannot exist without the other. They are simply the opposite sides of the same fabric.

This understanding gave rise to a new view of human duality that is the foundation for the transformational program in Part III of this book. In the program, each of the Life Purpose Profiles contains specific lower- and higher-self traits that are in need of integration and balance. It is in acknowledging the two forces equally that you bring forth your *core soul profile self*, reflecting your inner congruence. When higher- and lower-self traits remain unbalanced, your soul self cannot be accessed and lies dormant, and a false self runs your life.

In the Shadow

The primary way you lose touch with your life force and therefore your life purpose is by making vows that reject the needs and desires of your lower and higher self. In psychology, such rejection creates what is known as the *shadow*, a concept introduced by Carl Jung and made popular recently by author and transformational leader Debbie Ford.

Translating their concept to mine, I see both a dark and a light shadow. Your dark shadow is the lower self, those selfish and ugly parts you wish you were not, and your light shadow is your higher self, the higher transcendent parts you don't embrace for fear of acting superior to others or seeming delusional. The important point is that your shadow is made up of both your higher self and lower self, and that the rejection of either self leads to you not living as your core soul self.

Rejecting a few destructive lower-self qualities or not fully embracing the visions and genius of your higher self may not seem like a big deal, but it is. When you reject these essential elements of yourself, the life force energy that seeks to emerge through the awakening of your soul self is blocked from flowing freely through your system. By its nature, it must go somewhere, and so it goes out of your system through an energetic process called *projection*.

When you reject the raw, pleasurable energy of the lower self through a vow—*I will never be selfish and mean like my brother was*—and also reject the higher self—*I'm no genius, my ideas are dumb*—all that energy is projected into what becomes a mask of the false self, the *defensive mask*. This then becomes your default identity—who you think you are, not who you truly are.

Let's look more closely now at those two life energy currents, your lower and higher self, that struggle against each other in a drama of duality.

Your Lower Self

Your lower self represents your instinctual and survival-based drives, the part of you that inherently knows what you want and how to get it, whether socially appropriate or not. It is the source of your raw life force, physical power, and vitality—the sentient part of you that reflexively moves away from pain and is drawn toward pleasure.

The lower self is run primarily by the reptilian brain—the limbic brain and brain stem—that is in charge of your autonomic nervous system and basic body functions, such as sex, eating, and aggression. Its entire focus is the care and survival of your body and individual needs, much like an animal surviving and evolving in an unfriendly world.

The lower self's goal is to use its raw strength to survive and/or control its environment, and if that doesn't work, it uses its cleverness.

The lower self manages your life force energy, passion for living, and the level of health and pleasure you can have in life. It knows at all times what you like and what you don't like. For it, there are no *shoulds* or *ought tos*. It is impulsive and never postpones gratification; being in denial or being patient is a function of the higher self. The lower self tells you that without looking out for number one, you will have nothing for anyone else. It is like a two-year-old who loves to laugh, cry, scream, and get what it wants when it wants it.

The goal of your lower self is simple: fulfill your desire for pleasure, survive each day, and collect or hoard whatever survival resources you can. The lower self lies, cheats, seduces, complains, rages, belittles; worships power, money, and sexuality; withholds attention and love to gain compliance; does anything to gain the upper hand and feel superior to others; and hates to lose! Such self-centered and narcissistic qualities were responsible for humankind's survival long ago. In today's society, however, the lower self has to hide itself, as we have become less survival- and brawn-based, and more achievement- and communication-based. But the lower self has not gone away in our modern times—it's only been relegated to the shadow where it must be more stealthy and subtle.

An essential need of your lower self is to be right; being wrong or losing in battle long ago meant starvation or death. Today, being wrong or failing to win in acquiring some basic need is no longer a matter of life and death, but losing still feels like death to the lower self, creating a huge need to hide your instinctual feelings from others. Because of this, your lower self is often judged harshly by both yourself and others, leading you to disown its purpose and project it out onto others, harshly judging those who have the same lower-self traits you reject in yourself.

Your dynamic lower self is the center of all innate and spontaneous sensations, both good and evil, and feels no guilt, shame, or fear when expressing any of these raw emotions in the moment. It is the center of your deepest laughter and pleasure in life, living only in the moment and expressed when you giggle, dance, and play with your children.

When you are making love and feeling physical ecstasy, you are in the lower self. When you are totally irreverent, goofy, alive with passion and joy, spontaneous, genuine, and full of life, this is also the lower self. When you go to war and are fearlessly willing to die for your cause, you are fully in the lower self. It is the lower self that knows the grace of God in your very bones and cells. Once you know yourself fully in your lower self, you are then able to honor life in all forms through direct interaction with it.

To the lower self, any energy flowing freely through the body is good. Screaming at someone and snuggling with someone on the couch are equally acceptable behaviors in the lower self. The lower self is the raw life force, easily shifting from action to rest based on the current environment. Guilt and shame are mental creations, and the lower self does not stand in judgment of any actions. It deals with life in the moment and has only one rule: if life brings pleasure and gets you what you want, stay with it. If it doesn't, walk away with no regrets and try something else. Life has no pretense, it just is.

Your Higher Self

Your higher self is capable of transcending your personal ego to see how your individual actions affect all people and the future of humankind. It knows that the highest purpose of your actions is not to exploit or defeat others but to unify and find harmony with them, to become even more than you could be as an individual. The higher self is the essence of spiritual responsibility. Your choice to live from the guidance of your higher self, rather than the fears of your defense, strengthens your ability to walk your spiritual path.

In your higher self, you have impeccable integrity and know inherently what is right and wrong, while your lower self might look the other way for personal gain. The higher self is connected to your innate and spontaneous soul that expresses love, compassion, and appreciation in each interaction. It is the aspect of you that is expanding outward, connecting and unifying you with all of mankind. The higher self sees that hate and criticism fragment and isolate people, creating war between nations. It rises above such limited thinking and actions, not through denial or dissociation but in seeing the perfect order of all of life and how suffering and joy are both part of it. The higher self is a conscious witness to how you fit into the world and the spiritual connection that exists between your life choices and all of mankind.

When your higher self is activated, it guides you to choose your highest potential in love, compassion, peace, and intelligence. It creates community and knows the importance of seeing and supporting humanity as a whole. It knows that humanity, though made up of individuals, cannot be divided by social boundaries or political borders. Its essential quality is to see each person's highest purpose in his or her gifts to all of humanity.

All religions since the beginning of time have stemmed from those who have awakened their higher self. Through the higher self, all people are trying to find meaning in their existence. We all, at some level, long to know that we are part of a whole and that our actions do make a difference. Your higher self lives in a state of oneness with the highest potential within you, as well as the highest potential within all of humankind. It acts as your conscience, knowing innately that you will only be happy when you treat others as you would like them to treat you.

The higher self, just as the lower self, does not need rules; the present moment and the flow of the universe in the present moment offer a unique opportunity to the individual to express both the highest spiritual and individual purpose. A person who has vowed to live by biblical scripture, or is addicted to a pleasure such as amassing money, has vowed to release his or her true power of choice. The power to truly be able to make life choices in each moment is a terrifying power that most people prefer not to have. Christ had no bible, and Martin Luther King Jr. had no game plan for emancipation; they had to enlist all of who they were and create a way of being in a human body. That is each of our birthrights. That kind of power comes from the integration of the lower and higher self, and when that cannot be accomplished, the false self is created.

False Self and Defensive Mask

The false self is a state of consciousness created by vowing against and rejecting your true nature and deeply polarizing your higher- and lower-self traits. When you reject parts of yourself, the energy that would normally stay in your body is rejected and gets projected out to others as a mask or shield. This projected self is the embodiment of all of your vows of always or never. It is what psychologists call your *ego ideal*. It stands in front of the real you and protects the vulnerable parts of you that you vowed to hide. It is the idealized version of your higher and lower self, held in place by the sheer power of your will; your vows tell you that anything else is wrong. Your false self takes an enormous amount of energy to maintain, since you constantly have to prove it is real to the world. Your true self never has to prove anything—it is effortless and feeds you rather than drains you.

False self behaviors are so painful and glaring that you can't miss them in your own life. To make lasting change, your false self must be challenged and dealt with through increasing awareness, enabling your core soul profile self to once again become your primary experience in life. The path to letting your core soul self emerge is to identify your Life

Purpose Profile and begin doing the work of transformation within its powerful context.

To understand how your vows create the false self and defensive mask, I invite you to follow a simple guided visualization. (To see a graphic representation of the guided visualization, go to page 88.)

Guided Visualization

Imagine a laser beam of sheer pleasure moving up from the earth and through your legs into your body, filling you with raw, powerful life force. This is the life force of your lower self. Ride this beam of sheer pleasure as it fills you with a deep, primal sense of trust to fully inhabit your body and all of its infinite senses and abilities to experience life through thought, word, and action. As you feel this pure pleasure, let it fill you to your fullest with no regrets.

Visualize another laser beam coming down from above your crown as pure starlight, entering your body through the crown of your head. This is the energy current of your higher self. It fills you with pure brilliance and consciousness, awakening you to unique personal qualities as well as your part in the whole of humanity.

As the higher-self beam descends and meets your lower self beam at your heart, see the combined beams expand outwardly in all directions, connecting you with the hearts of every other human being. As these two currents flow unimpeded into and through you, you stand fully in your power with the courage to follow your dreams and live an extraordinary life.

Now visualize the same process again, only this time you will see how your vows divert the two pleasure currents of life out of the body and into the defensive mask, which is projected out in front of the true self. This leaves you exhausted by life, knowing that joy and pleasure exist but are elusive to you.

The Divided Higher/Lower Self and Projected Mask

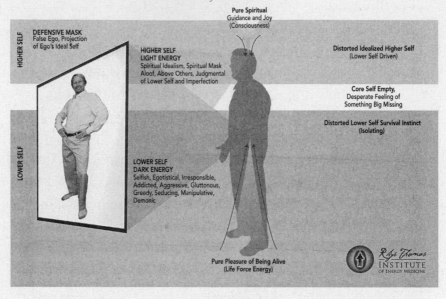

HIGHER SELF

DEFENSIVE MASK
False Ego, Projection
of Ego's Ideal Self

**HIGHER SELF
LIGHT ENERGY**
Spiritual Idealism, Spiritual Mask
Aloof, Above Others, Judgmental
of Lower Self and Imperfection

Pure Spiritual
Guidance and Joy
(Consciousness)

Distorted Idealized Higher Self
(Lower Self Driven)

Core Self Empty,
Desperate Feeling of
Something Big Missing

Distorted Lower Self Survival Instinct
(Isolating)

LOWER SELF

**LOWER SELF
DARK ENERGY**
Selfish, Egotistical, Irresponsible,
Addicted, Aggressive, Gluttonous,
Greedy, Seducing, Manipulative,
Demonic

Pure Pleasure of Being Alive
(Life Force Energy)

Roy Thomas
INSTITUTE
OF ENERGY MEDICINE

The Core Self

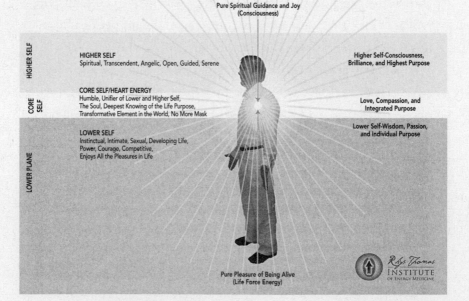

HIGHER SELF

HIGHER SELF
Spiritual, Transcendent, Angelic, Open, Guided, Serene

Pure Spiritual Guidance and Joy
(Consciousness)

**Higher Self-Consciousness,
Brilliance, and Highest Purpose**

CORE SELF

CORE SELF/HEART ENERGY
Humble, Unifier of Lower and Higher Self,
The Soul, Deepest Knowing of the Life Purpose,
Transformative Element in the World, No More Mask

**Love, Compassion, and
Integrated Purpose**

LOWER SELF
Instinctual, Intimate, Sexual, Developing Life,
Power, Courage, Competitive,
Enjoys All the Pleasures in Life

LOWER PLANE

**Lower Self-Wisdom, Passion,
and Individual Purpose**

Pure Pleasure of Being Alive
(Life Force Energy)

Roy Thomas
INSTITUTE
OF ENERGY MEDICINE

Picture two huge deflector mirrors intersecting the laser beams before they meet and merge in your heart. These deflectors represent your vows in life *always* or *never* to be who you really are in aspects of your higher and lower self. The mirrors deflect both of the incoming beams and project a single image outward onto a giant video screen located three feet in front of your body. The distorted image on the screen is your defensive mask that others look at in order to see you—and that you look through to see them, and ultimately, to see yourself.

Your projected defensive mask presents an ideal but false image of who you are. Even worse, when so much of your energy is tied up in the process, you are cut off from the energy you need to live your life purpose. Living through your false or defended mask is emotionally draining. When your energy is projected this way, a feeling of emptiness arises from the void that is created, keeping your vow more alive than the real choices you might be facing in any moment. When you are in defense, you feel that life is unfair or passing you by because you have no power to change things, and you are not actually living your real life.

Left undisturbed by your vows and defenses, the energetic currents of the higher and lower self run unimpeded throughout your entire mind-body system and are the same energy currents that create the brilliant stars and galaxies you see in the night sky. When they come into balance, they awaken a core soul quality that is not higher or lower, but the synthesis of both. That integration of the two represents the foundation of your life purpose, which is then activated fully in every breath and action you take in your life.

In the Life Purpose Profile Program, you must be able to accept both your lower- and higher-self traits that are so often rejected to bring forth your core soul profile qualities. In your primary and secondary Life Purpose Profile, you will gain an awareness of your specific lower-self and higher-self traits, and what it looks like when the two meet to emerge as the expression of your highest evolution: your core soul self.

No Easy Choice

If you want to find and live your life purpose, you cannot take the easy way out and choose to live from one self over the other, negating the less convenient one. If you do, you will remain divided and immature.

If you look at your life or the lives of people you know, you can see this tendency to live from either the higher or lower self, and how it results in a mask of defense rather than true integrity.

Choosing the lower self as your idealized self and rejecting your higher self, you live a life of striving—you work for the money, the prestige, or just to survive. You spend your money to self-gratify through drinking, smoking, sports, vacations, and luxury cars, and you might donate to a good cause for the tax deduction. You are religious but not spiritual, and you see other religions and the people who worship through them as inferior. You vote for government leaders who believe in military solutions to international problems, strengthen borders between countries and people, and give your business an edge over the same business in other countries. You often have a limited set of emotions—happy, sad, aloof, and angry—that seem to fit most life situations and make life choices simple.

If, on the other hand, you live with the higher self as an ideal and reject the lower self, you tend to be self-sacrificing and place your needs after the needs of others. You may donate your time and money to worthy causes and work as an educator, caretaker, intellectual, or psychologist, or in a service business. You are a spiritual seeker rather than a religious follower. You see the essential need for unity, community, and people supporting people but stand in judgment of those who do not. You fight for the underdog, often earning very little, but see the essential truth that the world is deeply interconnected. If you let one part die, the rest of it is soon to follow.

You may demonize the lower-self people, for example, by feeling that you are above the pettiness of most people. You vote for politicians who are ecologically minded and driven by altruistic ideals. You have a strong need to nurture others and extend compassion, as well as the need to be seen and understood as a good and righteous person.

Surprisingly, for those who live in their lower self, all of their higher-self qualities still exist; and for those living in their higher self, all of their lower-self qualities still exist. Until the two worlds of the lower self and the higher self come into balance with each other, no one will ever be safe and feel at home in the world.

What's Next . . .

In the next chapter, you will learn how the *core soul self* has the capacity to balance and meld the lower self and the higher self in order to create a divine and purposeful life. But first, we will take a closer look at life behind the mask as a defended false self, including the virtual reality and the negative pleasures that substitute for living a real life of positive pleasure and purpose. It is through a deeply felt awareness of your false self and its world that the road to heaven is paved.

CHAPTER 6

Virtual Reality, Negative Pleasures, and Accepting Duality

When your lower self and higher self are opposed to each other, your life becomes hell. You live in confusion and fear because if you placate one aspect of yourself, you deny the other. As you vow never to be selfish or stupid, always a good and caring person, you deny your lower-self instincts to take care of yourself. This includes allowing yourself to make mistakes, which are a valuable part of the learning process.

Life becomes exhausting in this state of inner conflict. With no clear sense of purpose to guide your life, you experience frustration, anger, self-criticism, self-abuse, and anxiety, as well as shame and guilt that you have no purpose in life. All of these experiences are signs that you are resisting some lower and higher aspects of yourself, and when you resist the whole of who you are, you can't live your real life.

Instead, you live in the self-created hell where you divert more of your life energy toward defense rather than toward your life purpose. That defense has many forms, but can be seen most easily in what I've described as your *defensive mask*. Now you will learn about how that defensive mask creates an entire world you think is real—your *virtual reality*—and an experience of life that settles for less than you deserve.

Your Virtual Reality

Your projected defensive mask becomes a filter through which you see the world as you think it is, not as it actually is. I call this view a *virtual reality*, one that exists only in your mind as your impression of life becomes increasingly distorted. For example, if your boss comes into work after having an argument with her spouse and doesn't say good morning to you, you may spend the day thinking you did something wrong, or you may meet someone whom you immediately dislike because that person looks just like the kid who used to bully you in grade school.

In both of these scenarios, your defensive mask created a reality that exists only in your head. It's as if you were wearing a pair of virtual reality goggles and headphones, reacting solely to the mental images you see and unable to distinguish them from the real world. You are totally lost in the projected virtual reality playing out in your head. Your defensive mask keeps you trapped in a virtual reality that never shuts off and always creates fear and pain. The pain comes from being isolated and out of touch with reality and your real place in the world.

Trapped in your virtual reality, you have a continual feeling of not being good enough, and what you accomplish doesn't give you lasting fulfillment. The spontaneous life force coming through your lower and higher selves is diminished. You can no longer trust yourself or your feelings, so you create a mask of your ideal self that both protects you from being seen as clueless and imperfect and simultaneously reinforces your own rejection of who you really are.

With your virtual reality goggles on, you see only what is in your head, not what is really around you. You create a life that, like a video game, constantly repeats the same destructive patterns. Part of you knows that life is passing you by, but the scene going on in your virtual reality is so convincing that you never challenge it.

Your virtual reality runs on the same energy current you use to create your life in each moment, but your virtual reality is created from negative memories and fears, not from the infinite universe that is literally at your fingertips. It creates a false self, one living in a false world that exists outside the flow of life and that can never live a purposeful, pleasurable life.

We all create the reality we experience in our heads and live out that creation in our lives. When you are in balance, you use your conscious intention and will to transmute your life force energy to crystallize thoughts and feelings into actions around your life purpose. This creates a natural flow with life and an experience of heaven on earth. When your vows and unconscious virtual reality are in charge of that same creative force, what is crystallized into reality does not match your life purpose in any way.

The ability to dissociate from your life purpose and live in a false hell is universal for all human beings—and unavoidable. It is something we must all go through before we can make the conscious choice required to live from our soul self. We must experience the pain of hell before we can see that heaven has been at our fingertips the entire time.

Fear and Defense

Fear rules your virtual reality like a guard dog whose job is to protect you from the devastation of being rejected. But the guard dog soon becomes the master, and you begin to see all people as possible sources of rejection or attack. You live in fear that they might discover you are not perfect, lovable, nice, or smart.

Your fear creates an illusory need to be protected, and so you justify the way you treat yourself and others as a means of defense. Your mask may exhibit your highest qualities of love and compassion for others, but these qualities are expressed out of fear that you will not be seen as good if you don't express them, which makes you feel unfulfilled and exhausted. These actions, driven by fear, have no real impact in the world. The bottom line is that maintaining a defensive mask and virtual reality takes energy away from your ability to live passionately and enjoy the world you actually live in.

Even more important, forgetting or not knowing who you truly are can lead to illness of mind, body, and spirit. Most physical illnesses can be directly correlated to some aspect of the self that has been rejected. In your defensive mask, you are so fixated on being what you are not that you overlook the bodily sensation of pain and don't let that pain be a guide back to your wholeness and health.

In addition to impacting you physically, your virtual reality is a fixated mental state that deeply affects you emotionally and psychologically. When you live in a fearful and defended virtual reality, you tend to oscillate between hysterics, dissociation, and the choice of a narrow set of emotions to express all of your life. Mood-enhancing drugs such as Prozac can take the edge off your virtual reality anxiety, but when you numb your system, you eventually create more dissociation and confusion, and then need a higher dose of the drug. Knowing your life purpose and allowing it to flow unimpeded through your body and soul vaporizes emotional and psychological issues as though they never existed.

For most of your life, your virtual reality has distorted and hidden your lower self and higher self, and has blocked your core soul self from your awareness. It has done this through sheer fear driven by constantly rehashing negative past events and traumas. It is only when you allow the spontaneous sensation of your core soul self to rise up in each moment, without resistance in either the lower or the higher self, that you can come into your wholeness.

Integrating Your Shadow

The power to attract to you all that you need to fulfill your life purpose comes from integrating the higher- and lower-self qualities you've rejected (your shadow). Left in the shadow, those qualities vie separately for their own agendas, while your vows drain you of the energy you need to live your life purpose.

All false self-defenses drain your energy. Choose any exhausting experience you have in life—in your job, your family, your relationships—and you will find a rejected lower self along with its seemingly conflicting higher self lurking in the shadows. But when you embrace both extremes and experience them working in perfect balance, you can take back the energy diverted into your defenses and let it flow fully into your core soul self. Only then do you naturally and easily attract to you all that supports your life purpose.

Look over the two lists of descriptive words on the next page. The list on the left is composed of lower-self qualities you would not want to be characterized as. The list to the right is made up of higher-self traits you'd consider complimentary.

Now look closer to see how the two lists perfectly complement each other. They are not opposites but rather matched pairs that together bring balance, expressing two sides of the same coin.

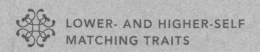

LOWER- AND HIGHER-SELF MATCHING TRAITS

Liar	Brave teller of inconvenient truths
Demonic	Angel of transformation
Narcissistic	Balanced in self-love
Overbearing	Strongly committed
Murderous	Fearless in fighting for the highest good
Pathetic	Gentle and kind
Stubborn	Unbendable in support for others
Spineless	Flexible
Neurotic	Infinitely creative
Lost	Intuitively guided

In Part III, you will learn about the pairs of traits that are specific to your unique life purpose and highest potential. By rejecting one of a pair, either the higher- or lower-self trait, you reject the other, leaving you disempowered and at the mercy of your vows, defensive mask, and virtual reality. Accepting either one gives you the possibility of accepting the other, since they only come in pairs. In that acceptance, your choices in life have power because you make them from being fully conscious of the alternative. When a liar stops lying and speaks the truth, he has power, and we all pay attention.

In the same vein, only someone who is indignant about wrongs done to them can choose to fight for the rights of all people as their highest priority. Treating others as you would have them treat you arises out of that lower-self sense of self-righteousness and victimization. Martin Luther King Jr. became a fighter for the rights of others, but he had to first experience their abuse himself and do battle with it before he could stand for another's right never to be abused again.

The connection between the alpha and omega of your most powerful lower and higher self is the source of the power you need to live your life purpose. As you come to know both traits existing at the same time within yourself, and you choose for your highest good, that is when you start living your life purpose. That is when you start living from your core soul self, and when your energy and impact in the world multiply exponentially.

But you must first deal with the *negative pleasures* you get from hiding your worst and your best behind a defensive mask self.

Positive and Negative Pleasures

When you feel a sensation of pleasure flowing freely in your body, it is a calling that moves you toward, not away from, your life purpose. In fact, all of life, when not resisted, is a positive energy current, a pleasure current, that naturally draws you toward the fulfillment of your life purpose.

Dealing with any life situation, good or bad, without fear or resistance (letting life flow through you), will lead to the ultimate positive pleasure of being engaged fully with life. This openness to what life offers you allows you to be conscious of being the creator of your life both for personal gain and as a contributing part of humanity. The greatest gift the creator has bestowed upon you that sets you apart from all other animals is the ability to choose to consciously create your life in each moment. The less you resist life and are open and vulnerable to the full experience of it, the more you will feel called to your life purpose now. You will break the habit of mentally planning for future happiness that will never really work out; rather, you can be happy now. When you do this, you will be able to hold more pleasure and energy within you daily, which then becomes the energy and passion that you are able to inspire others with, living in the primary pleasure of living with integrity. Primary pleasures—such as love, passion, being afraid but taking action anyway, sharing your life with family and friends—are the only things that ever will make you truly happy. Secondary pleasures—such as alcohol, sex, drugs, blaming others, winning, amassing wealth, being better than others—are empty promises, or negative pleasures, that never fulfill, since they are distractions from life, not a path to it.

All power can be used for both good and evil. The infinite power of *choice* to consciously create your life, your work, and your relationships for good has a flip side that is dark. The power you have to decide and *choose* to flow and say yes to life and get great pleasure from every second of your life can also be enlisted by your vows to choose to say no to life. You can either take the people and materials you are given each moment and make a masterpiece that unifies and flows with life and inspires anyone who gazes at your masterpiece, or you can use your power of choice to reject life as it is and fail to embrace what has happened to you in the past, who you are as an individual, and what is happening to you now.

While you may not reject everything that has happened or is happening to you, you have rejected or at least not fully accepted much of it. For example, the way you wanted your father to treat you, or the way you wish you were making more money than you are. These are simple acts of rejecting your life and the pleasure you could be having. Along with that pleasure goes the energy you need to live your true life purpose.

Now you would think that honoring your vows and rejecting your core self would be the most painful, empty, and soulless thing you could do to yourself, but even when life is put into the mask self that has no real purpose in the universe, it still is an act of creation that elicits a level of pleasure. Since you vowed not to have the primary pleasure of being who you truly are, all that is left in most situations are those negative forms of pleasure.

The defensive mask was created so you would *never* have to be hurt by negative events again, and so you would *always* be good or smart, or at least not seen a dumb. Even though you are lying to the world about who you are, what you want, and what you stand for, the ability to avoid the slings and arrows of outrageous fortune gives you a secret pleasure and a sense of control in a chaotic world. But that makes you less human and more isolated and confused as to who you really are. You become an expert in what you are not and in judging other people, but you no longer see your path.

The simplest truth you must live by is to feel, not think, your life. In doing so, you follow these two rules: (a) Do what you know you should do and are called to do from deep inside, no matter how hard it is for you, and (b) Don't do what you know in your heart you shouldn't do but are doing.

This simple dictum is the path to enlightenment and pure pleasure in life.

Positive pleasure can only exist in the present moment. Vows keep you stuck in a past filled with hurts and have you hoping for change rather than enjoying the present. For example, if you are taking long walks every day with the goal of losing weight, the positive pleasure of walking and breathing and being in nature is lost as you focus on your future weight loss. You are only driven by your vow never to be seen as fat like your father who struggled with his weight his whole life. Judging your overweight body as "bad" and then forcing it to exercise only leads to negative pleasure, punishing yourself for being who you are.

If you are overweight, you can feel the drain that weight has on your life force when the positive pleasure current stays in your body. This awareness will result in your naturally not eating as much and exercising more to allow that energy to flow more freely in your life. But if your vows push it into the mask, all you are left with is the negative pleasure of self-contempt and dieting. Of course, the solution the mask creates for the problem just exacerbates the problem. No matter how much weight you lose, it will never be enough for the idealistic vow. Positive pleasure, on the other hand, is self-fulfilling, not self-rejecting, and it is not something to attain in the future; rather, it is about learning to accept and love who and where you are right now.

In other words, as you consciously choose not to have your life run by your vows, your awareness increases, and your vows become more visible and thus avoidable. You start to reconnect with the primary pleasure current in your body, feeling its presence before it becomes diverted into your defensive mask. Then you can act to channel that energy into your real life, not your virtual life. The key is choosing to create a life that is congruent with reality.

As you increase your felt awareness of positive pleasures, your body relaxes the strict limits placed on your energy by your vows. You can watch your life and the lives of others transform before you, experiencing the thrill of growth and change. But with your vow limitations still intact, you see only what you expect to see, and life is busy and boring, not vital and exhilarating.

Every spontaneous sensation you feel is like a spring of water bubbling forth from the source of all life. When you can feel your life force energy gushing through you, there is no separation between you and life itself. This is living in your core. The genius of the universe is encoded in the life force that creates all things, and as that life force flows through you, you express your divine purpose of living on earth in human form. Simultaneously, you express the universal consciousness of being called to contribute your unique purpose to the whole of humanity. Every emotion you are capable of can arise in the moment to fulfill your life purpose, making all of life a challenge you embrace with relish. Or your feelings can simply be echoes stimulated by a memory that you can't let go of, making life boring and repetitive.

Only if your life force is allowed to course through you in both positive and negative currents are you able to comprehend how the entire universe is constantly supporting you in living your life purpose. From the moment of your birth to the moment of your death, that spring of life and sheer pleasure of being alive flows through you. Only when you have died do you lose the direct link to the pleasure current of the human body and thus your calling to your unique life purpose.

All of life is pleasure. How you experience the infinite wellspring of life and its potential pleasure is determined by the choices you make, both conscious and unconscious, in managing the energy life gives you. Your choices and the actions they engender direct the currents of energy as they flow through you. If you choose to act consciously and are open to the experience of your energy flowing unblocked in the lower and higher self, you always experience the positive primary pleasures of life. Among these pleasures are balanced relationships, love, forgiveness, growth, passion, enthusiasm, brilliance, strength, purpose, vibrancy, and mastery.

When you make vows that you are not choosing consciously but living in automatic defensive behaviors, that same life energy runs through your virtual reality mask to become distorted as a negative pleasure of creating a false self that is less vulnerable. It then gives life to your fears of the past, memories of trauma, low self-esteem, addictions, demands, delusions, manipulation, lies, grief, anger, hurt, complaining, a lack of forgiveness, assumptions, anxiety about the future, victimhood, rejection of yourself and others, arrogance, entitlement, and so on.

Rewards of Negative Pleasure

Whatever you do to maintain the illusion of not being responsible for your actions is a negative pleasure. This includes controlling, blaming, avoiding, not forgiving, and resenting others, because when you do these things, you get a reward, or payback, which is not having to be responsible yourself. But when you live in your core, you take full responsibility for every choice you have ever made, apologizing to anyone you have judged or hurt. To live in your core soul self means never having an excuse or blaming anyone for who you are or what you do. It demands that you embrace the world as it is, and as it has been, with love and forgiveness.

As seen from the eyes of your defended self, being responsible looks infinitely more difficult than rejecting responsibility and blaming others. Blame requires that you resist who you are and the world as it is because taking responsibility is often painful. The negative pleasure you get from judging or manipulating others, procrastinating, taking revenge, and other harmful behaviors is preferable because it lets you off the hook and allows you to continue in your delusional comfort.

To see your defenses in action and be able to choose more consciously, you need to first see the reward you get from living in your defense. After all, if you didn't get something in return for being miserable, afraid, pushy, indignant, angry, accusatory, or blaming, you might just stop doing it.

The top negative pleasure for all of us is hiding behind a defensive mask and living in our virtual reality. Being responsible for everything that has ever happened to you, everything you have ever done, and everything you will ever do is not easy. Your vows are your childlike choices to be *this* or at least *not that*, negating the best parts of your real self. The deep anger and helplessness you felt at some injustice done to you in childhood seem to give you the right to judge everyone through that experience, and so you make assumptions about others rather than bravely trusting in each moment.

Your defenses—your vows, mask, virtual reality, and negative pleasures—cause you to resist life rather than flow with it. That resistance not only becomes your identity but gives you a purpose in life, since you left your real purpose behind when you let your vows rule your life. Now you say, "I know who I am, because I am not *this* or *that*!" but sadly, this kind of negation leads to your believing that what you've been through and had to sacrifice is so much more than anyone else. In your self-righteousness, you justify saying and doing unconscionable things to others, knowing that you shouldn't. You, who were once a victim, become a victimizer, now projecting blame onto others for your behavior and receiving pleasure in doing so.

You can see that every time a vow diverts more of your energy into your defenses, the result is painful for everyone. But even though it is painful, you feel a sense of pleasure from being the "right one" or the "good one," or you get negative pleasure from being the broken or sick one who is then special and privileged and can get out of doing what you don't want to do. Either way, you enjoy a moment when you get to avoid responsibility for your actions, and, in a strange but understandable way, that is pleasurable.

Each of the five Rhys Method® Life Purpose Profiles has its defensive aspects in which negative pleasures are uniquely expressed. The Thinker defense (part of the Creative Idealist) leaves or dissociates and has the negative pleasure/illusion of being above the human condition, living more in the mind or in the spirit world. The Enforcer-Seducer defense (part of the Charismatic Leader–Charmer) has the negative pleasure of never trusting other people and battling with them or manipulating them to gain control rather than trust. The People Pleaser defense (part of the Team Player) has the negative pleasure of being self-sacrificing, making him or her self-righteous and resentful of the self-centered "takers" in the world. The Poor Me defense (part of the Emotional Intelligence Specialist) has the negative pleasure of using his or her sensitivity as a reason to play victim, justifying endless complaining and manipulation in relationships and never owning power in life. The Rule Keeper (part of the Knowledgeable Achiever) has the negative pleasure of a harsh inner self-discipline that justifies aloofness and being critical of the self and others for their imperfections.

Each characteristic behavior seems so natural that it is often hardly noticeable as a negative pleasure. It remains hidden under the guise of protecting you from ever having to decide who you are. In effect, your negative pleasures give you a "hall pass," allowing you to pretend that you are someone you are not and then blame others for why you are the way you are. Negative pleasures are all those petty behaviors that you can't seem to let go of. If you didn't get pleasure from them, you would drop them. But you don't because the rewards are just too great and the alternative is taking full responsibility for your life.

Take Back Your Power

We all must choose between living in the positive pleasure of our life purpose and being who we truly are, or living in the negative pleasure of our virtual reality and defensive mask, negating the very flow of life. Positive pleasure comes from being part of a universe that is forever expanding, creating new life in each moment. Negative pleasure flips the flow of life and creates feelings that are convenient to your personal needs only. Nothing new is being created, and even your feelings come from your thinking.

When you feel the primary pleasure of life, you feel the creative force of God. In allowing that energy to flow simultaneously through your lower self and higher self, you take back your power to become a contributing force, a healing presence for others and the world.

As you learn about your primary and secondary Life Purpose Profiles in Part III, you will see how your defensive mask and virtual reality are sources of your greatest negative pleasures in life. You will learn that, to take your power back, you must accept, not reject, all of your defenses. Rejection only strengthens your defensive mask and virtual reality, making more and more negative pleasure necessary in your life.

Your core soul quality is your greatest pleasure in life, but to be in it, you must accept all of who you are, including the vows that drain your energy into your defense. Only nonresistance can take power away from the mask because the mask exists only when you are in resistance to your true nature and to life.

Albert Einstein said, "The difference between stupidity and genius is that genius has its limits." I don't believe that there is such a thing as a stupid person, but I do believe that many people are geniuses at being stupid.

Living in a defensive mask is stupid. It creates nothing new and only resists change and the natural flow of life. Each of us can know the "mind of God," as Einstein termed it, or we can keep ourselves in painful unconsciousness by channeling our life's energy out of our bodies and into the false self of a virtual reality.

But being able to take off your defensive mask and cease living in a virtual reality is not simply a matter of knowing it exists and wanting to get rid of it. The only true cure for the delusion and suffering of humankind is, as the ancient Greek sage Socrates taught, to *Know thyself*. Knowing who you are as a soul self is the answer to resolving all of your suffering in life. When you are in your core, the defensive virtual world that spins its illusory story in your mind completely disappears. In fact, it's as if it never existed.

When you increasingly embrace both your lower-self and your higher-self traits, you no longer look for your life purpose—you *become* your life purpose. Your energy is full and powerful, and you take responsibility for everything in your life. Whatever appears, even if you have no idea why, you trust for your highest good and you don't resist.

As a child, you knew the pleasure of a fully integrated self. Somewhere between ages two and six, you lost that by doing what every human being does—rejecting your most precious gifts and self in hopes of being loved. You spend the rest of your life searching to find it again, until you realize that it is within you. It *is* you. But to get there, you must first reawaken to the full expanse of your true nature and see it not in some watered-down version but in all its glory.

When you no longer let the virtual person you have created walk in your shoes, something new begins to emerge, as when you were a small child and you did not think but *knew* who you were by how it felt to be you. All of your actions, feelings, and thoughts emerged from that self you knew and felt, and you had no inner conflict going on. It is that spontaneous oneness with all life that shows that you are living your life purpose.

In Part III, you have an opportunity to investigate the five Life Purpose Profiles in detail. You will see yourself in all of them—especially the blend of your primary and secondary profiles—and find a direct path to your life's calling. Once you identify your specific profile blend, you will have an essential tool for seeing the qualities within you that must come into congruence if you are to find inner peace and give your unique message to the world.

To take back your life force energy from your vows, your defensive mask, and virtual reality, as well as release your negative pleasures, you will need to see that the core soul qualities as described in your profile are your truth. They are always available to you in each moment, but you must kick the mental habit of letting your life choices be commanded by reliving the past or projecting into the future. Your core soul qualities are the spiritual principles that you are born to live by. Challenging the power your defense has over you and embracing all of your rejected lower- and higher-self traits will take courage and commitment.

You cannot truly live in your higher self—in love, compassion, and selflessness—without the equal potential to live in your lower self—hate, cruelty, and selfishness. This will be hard to accept at first. A person who has not vowed against hate and has the choice to hate or love can love and truly drink in the power of it. Having vowed never to hate makes love an empty behavior—not a real choice to be open and vulnerable. One without the other is the result of unconscious vows and only feeds a false self that lives behind a defensive mask, trapped forever in a virtual reality where the power of real choice that can change your life in any moment is lost.

The path to spiritual maturity is one of learning how to hold seeming opposites—your higher and lower self—as equal. To come into your true energy current of power, peace, and pleasure, you must begin to see how the apparently opposite qualities within you are actually perfectly matched pairs. When you embrace them equally within, rejecting or denying neither, you can make truly conscious choices.

To step onto this path and embrace your profile takes the courage of a warrior and the trust of a saint. You have begun your warrior-saint training by becoming aware of your defenses—your vows and how they reject your lower and higher self to create a mask and a virtual reality, kept in place by your negative pleasures.

Accepting Duality

The full emergence of your core soul self requires that you accept the duality of your human nature and come into balance with all aspects of yourself. Such acceptance makes you whole and gives you inner peace; only when you accept all of yourself can you choose and act consciously in the world. In the East, this energetic balance point is represented by the yin/yang symbol, showing how human duality exists in balance as dark and light, lower and higher self, feminine and masculine.

Once you achieve this congruence within yourself, you automatically know your life purpose. When the raw energy of desire to connect or individuate arises within you and meets the descending brilliance of your consciousness in any moment, you truly know yourself as the creator of your life. The result is a synthesis of your ability to live in primal trust of your lower self and embrace the peace, love, and purpose in your higher self. When you are feeling this essential connection, you experience yourself as whole and complete. As you then reach out to connect and share your wholeness with others, you project the harmony and fullness of your inner world to them.

You have had moments when you felt no separation between your thoughts and your feelings, when the life flowing through you reached far beyond anything you could normally comprehend. In those moments, you feel the entire universe as one, connected through you as you effortlessly participate in its creation and flow. The expression you then choose for your life purpose is unique to who you are, coming through your art, dance, play, yoga, martial arts, competition, communication, relationships, business, or a billion other expressions of human activity.

But the expression you choose matters less than how conscious you are of the two poles—your dark and light, your yin and yang—making up who you are. Each of us is a complete world when these two magnetic poles work together, one depending on the other and neither existing independently. Your motivations in each and every moment will always carry the potential to be both selfish and altruistic, a seeming contradiction that an enlightened being lives with in accepting the unpredictability of life.

The lower self, higher self, and core soul self are the holy trinity in human form. Their unification represents your highest life purpose as an individual because no one aspect of yourself, higher or lower, can stand on its own for long. Once unified, you know your unique place between heaven and earth, and all of your actions are your life purpose.

Great leaders throughout history have modeled this truth for us. Mahatma Gandhi, Martin Luther King Jr., and Nelson Mandela had to honor their lower-self drives in order to do battle with injustice and enact change within their societies and cultures. All of them had to strike an inner balance between their lower selves and their higher selves. Gandhi and Mandela and King are great role models; they transcended their personal issues and selfish problems to live each moment with purpose as they connected to their Charismatic Leader–Charmer profiles. They all had private lives, as we all do, riddled with problems and struggles, but when it came to a choice of bending to the will of those who were abusers, they did not bend. Even when they were persecuted and attacked for their beliefs, they stayed true to their callings and visions in each moment, not against the abusers but for freedom.

These three great men drew their power to do what they needed to do equally from their lower-self narcissism and their higher-self altruism. They had to accept that they, and no one else, could do what needed to be done. They had to take on the mantle of king and leader to shine as brightly in the eyes of the many as was necessary to motivate the unconscious masses to shift to a new level.

Your life purpose is not something that has happened in your past, or something you hope will happen in your future, or something you can write into a mission statement. Rather, it is something you can train for. You can discipline yourself and find ways to open yourself to your deepest guidance—physically, emotionally, and spiritually. Then you will need the stamina, guts, and drive to follow your guidance in each moment in order to live your life purpose.

Your core soul profile self lives only in the present moment where passion, love, and enthusiasm dance together with anger, rage, and manipulation to support your highest good in each moment. Your core soul self is your soul and loves all aspects of you unconditionally, even those parts that are painfully paddling against the current. When your soul self is fully present, you accept all of you—both the selfish and the altruistic—and the ride gets so much easier, and oh so much more fun.

What's Next . . .

In Part III, I will be giving you the framework to begin to live your life purpose through the Life Purpose Profile Program. Once you have that framework, the seemingly random events in your life and the choices you have made around them will begin to make sense. Understanding your profile blend will give you a context to see yourself through, both in defense and in your core soul self. You will have insight into yourself and others far beyond any the most seasoned therapist or spiritual guide could ever offer you.

Once you align with your unique profile qualities, you will recognize the type of awareness you channel. Your profile will not fix you in space but rather acknowledge your greatness and free you to create your own space and teach others to do the same. At that point, you can investigate your life purpose and bring it forth into the world. Einstein brought forth his life purpose when he unlocked the secrets of the universe, Edison when he captured electricity and made it available, Christ when he spread universal love, the Buddha when he demonstrated universal compassion, and Martin Luther King Jr. when he showed us all an example of conscious leadership. They were all able to give their gifts to the world only after finding themselves first; then they acted on what they were drawn to do.

Finding yourself within a framework that is tailor-made for bringing forth your life's unique expression must always come first.

PART III

Live Your Truth:
The Life Purpose
Profile Program

Orientation to the Program

Whether you are a Creative Idealist, Emotional Intelligence Specialist, Team Player, Charismatic Leader–Charmer, or Knowledgeable Achiever, your Life Purpose Profile is the filter through which your life purpose is expressed. It is also the structure that makes it possible for you to bring forth your extraordinary life by clarifying who you truly are and recognizing the false mask you have been living through for most of your life.

In Part I, you identified your primary and secondary Life Purpose Profiles by taking a questionnaire. Now, in Part III, you can use your results from that questionnaire to explore the features of your profiles, guided by activities and resources designed to support you in three clear steps. Once you've completed the program for your primary profile, you can do it again for your secondary profile, getting a fuller picture of your unique profile blend.

But first, I want to introduce you to the design of the program and the unique process that is the foundation for all of the activities you will be doing in the program.

Keep in mind that the Rhys Method® Life Purpose Profiles are not behavioral labels as so many profiling systems are; rather, they are a deep acknowledgment of your greatness and help you identify how you tend to sabotage that greatness when you are under stress.

Design of the Program

Each of the five Life Purpose Profile chapters that follow takes you through three steps toward living an extraordinary life. In each chapter, you will also read the inspiring stories of my students and clients who have been through an extended version of this program, giving you a picture of what life is like when you are consciously evolving on your unique life purpose path.

At each step of the profile, you are given helpful resources to support you, including a list of books to read specifically for that profile, links to meditations and other tools for further exploration, and energetic exercises you can do to remain in your core soul self. At the end of each chapter, a Personal Profile Summary chart is provided on which to record what you have discovered for daily reference in living more fully from your life purpose.

Here is an overview of the steps you will take in each of the five profile chapters:

In Step 1, *Align with Your Profile*, you gain a deeper awareness of your profile's general characteristics, including core soul qualities, defensive patterns, relationship issues, tendencies in career and finances, and physical and energetic aspects. An activity helps you to embrace your profile's core soul qualities and identify those defensive patterns you've been stuck in for your entire life. The guided meditation, Your Secret Place, is suggested with a link provided to an audio download and interpretive activities, for furthering your profile alignment. (A printed version is available in Chapter 3 of this book.)

In Step 2, *Recognize Your Defensive Patterns*, you use your profile as a lens to focus on and reveal your specific defenses—the *vows* that create your defensive mask and virtual reality, and the *negative pleasures* you have been experiencing all your life. You are guided to release those ancient vows and replace them with powerful *Freedom Statements* that support your truth. An inquiry into your negative pleasures helps you to increasingly choose positive pleasures that fulfill you and bring you what you want in life.

In Step 3, *Live Your Life Purpose*, you are guided to own both the higher- and lower-self traits that are unique to your profile, no longer divided by your vows but free to live your life purpose and who you truly are. Living courageously from your purpose and who you are involves taking new actions. You explore how the Law of Attraction can now strengthen you to live your unique life purpose and bring to you all that you need for remaining in your core soul self for an extraordinary life.

Extraordinary Power Process: Feel, Choose, Act

At each step in the program, you are given exercises that take you through a process to develop your extraordinary power. *Feel, Choose, Act* is the process through which you can engage your profile and, at the same time, learn to bring the process into your everyday life. Once *feeling, choosing,* and *acting* have become second nature, you will be able to achieve what you really want in your life: success in your career, fulfillment in your relationships, and all the energy and well-being you need to enjoy your life.

Here's how the Extraordinary Power Process works:

FEEL by doing the inner work to feel, not think, who you are. As you identify your profile's unique aspects—the core soul qualities, wounds and vows, disowned lower and higher shadow self, and negative pleasures—you'll notice that you resonate inwardly with some more than with others. These *Aha!* moments of profound recognition create a state of awareness that can change your life if you let it. The hallmark of this kind of inner work is a moment of self-acceptance that is felt, not thought. Running that inner feeling through the lens of your profile gives you a deep sense of presence and purpose, leading to conscious choices that call you even deeper into your life purpose and away from your self-sabotaging defensive patterns.

CHOOSE by making conscious choices based on your felt awareness, not your vows. In feeling your profile's unique qualities and patterns, you can make more conscious choices in response to events in your life. When you see clearly the dramatic changes possible by responding from your deepest calling and the devastating effects of discarding that calling, you are less likely to make choices from your false self. In each moment, you can choose your future. The goal is to pay attention to the guidance of your core soul qualities, developing a "soul muscle" of expressing your truth in the world.

ACT in alignment with your conscious choices to be fully living your life purpose. Once you have decided that joy is better than suffering, you must take action and commit to new behaviors that express more of your truth. As you respond by acting in alignment with your deepest inner knowing, not your automatic vows and defenses, you shift from survival mode to standing fully in your life purpose. Every aligned act, even the small symbolic ones, begins to feed you, filling you with energy and courage. It is through your conscious choice and aligned actions that *who you are* and *what you do* become one and the same, accelerating your ability to accomplish your most desired goals and purpose.

Repeat the process! This process seems so simple, but only when you engage in it routinely, every day, can you take back your extraordinary power and become the creator of your life. With daily practice, *feel, choose,* and *act* become your default mode in life, replacing the knee-jerk programming of your vows that has been in charge up until now. Only then are you truly empowered to live the extraordinary life you were born to live.

The profile program that follows is your ticket into that life you've been wanting to live but haven't had the tools to make real until now. Whether you are a Creative Idealist, Emotional Intelligence Specialist, Team Player, Charismatic Leader–Charmer, or Knowledgeable Achiever, your journey to extraordinary power, wholeness, and purpose begins here.

CHAPTER 7

Profile #1: Creative Idealist/Thinker

THE CREATIVE IDEALIST

with Thinker defense

Welcome to the Creative Idealist profile and its defense, the Thinker. You will find valuable information and activities here to help you access your extraordinary power and embody your life purpose.

If this is your secondary or other profile, or the profile of someone in your life, you can use what you learn here to deepen your understanding of yourself and of others.

 CREATIVE IDEALISTS WE ALL KNOW

Historical: Galileo, Ralph Waldo Emerson, Thomas Edison, Carl Jung, B. F. Skinner, Albert Einstein, Marie Curie, and Antoni Gaudi
Contemporary: Bruce Lipton, Kaley Cuoco, Jim Henson, Goldie Hawn, Eckhart Tolle, Yoko Ono, Stephen Hawking, Isaac Asimov, and Rupert Sheldrake

Step 1: Align with Your Profile

In this first step of the program, you learn all about your profile, including those core soul qualities that support you to live in your life purpose and those defensive patterns that cause you to sabotage your efforts. The Big Why story of my student Zach demonstrates how knowing your life purpose gives you power to live an extraordinary life.

About Your Profile

What follows is a general description of your profile, including how it looks when you are in defense as the Thinker. You will take a closer look at your current life situation, including relationships, your career or job, how you handle money, and the physical and energetic aspects of your profile.

GENERAL DESCRIPTION. As a Creative Idealist, you are highly active mentally. You love thinking, whether about math, the sciences, computers, literature, or art. You actually prefer your thoughts to interactions with people or to taking concrete actions in any of your endeavors.

Inventors, writers, and poets often have Creative Idealist/Thinker as their primary or secondary profile; these are all people who are highly imaginative. For the writers and poets, the challenge is in learning to focus on bringing the product of their creativity to the market by engaging an editor, agent, and publisher. For the inventor, your challenge is in getting a patent and investors for a product.

Creative Idealists are also at the cutting edge of higher learning, often studying, teaching, and doing research in mathematics, science, or the arts. Because you love to study and think so deeply, life is often more of a research project than an interconnected, visceral event. You have great ideas but you are afraid that if you were to bring your dreams into reality, you would be attacked or persecuted by the established authorities of the day. Because of these fears, you self-isolate and feel safer in your inner mental world than in the outer world.

Creative Idealists are entertaining and can speak intelligently on many subjects. In this profile, you always want life to be fresh and new, and so you will be the first to know when a great band is in town or when a new restaurant opens. But you are just as likely to become lost in your ideas and work for weeks on end as you are thrilled by new ideas, art, or places you'd like to visit.

IN THINKER DEFENSE, you become trapped in self-sabotaging patterns of behavior, such as when your overactive mind is scattered, disorganized, fearful, and dissociated. Such a high degree of mental activity can be isolating, and it distances you from other people and from your deeper feelings.

You spend so much time thinking and rethinking your options that you live in a state of paralysis, endlessly analyzing the possible outcomes of major decisions. You may have trouble manifesting your visions in any concrete way, tending to wander when it comes to developing any projects you've thought about. The bumper sticker on your car may read, ALL WHO WANDER ARE NOT LOST.

You tend to have little engagement or presence in the world, believing that thinking is safer than putting your ideas out there among those who may be unreceptive or closed-minded. Convincing others can be frustrating and exhausting because you don't have the people skills required for smooth transactions. You have trouble putting one foot in front of the other to manifest your visions in a material way.

You have a primal fear of violence and avoid aggression or even simple disagreements at all costs. When faced with an aggressive person, you will tend to mentally check out, not standing up for yourself and frozen in fear. You avoid the very person you need to talk with in order to deal with a problem, fearing an altercation. The simplest angry words can trigger your fight-or-flight response, and since fighting is not an option, you run or disappear as quickly as you can.

The Thinker defense typically takes the form of either the *spiritual seeker* or the *scientist/engineer* type. Both are typically lost in their thoughts and generally dissociated from daily life. Regardless of which describes you best, you avoid aggression and intimate relationships as a form of defense, preferring your ideas and fantasies to human contact.

AS A SPIRITUAL SEEKER, you frequent New Age bookstores and attend metaphysical classes and workshops, becoming absorbed in finding solutions to personal or societal problems. You may be the perennial liberal arts student who jumps from major to major, or the starving artist, poet, or writer who struggles to do your art and make ends meet. You are playful and free but terrified whenever you get close to finding what you are seeking. You are more interested in your latest epiphany than in dealing with issues in a concrete way. As a spiritual seeker, you have ideas about everything other than how to earn enough money, and you may become a proponent of various conspiracy theories. You can become a loner, feeling married to spirit and never seeing the value of marrying an actual person.

AS A SCIENTIST/ENGINEER, you love research and theoretical knowledge, often finding employment in the fields of math, the sciences, or computers. You are a tinkerer and enjoy finding out what makes things work. You can explain endlessly what you know about your field, regardless of whether anyone is truly listening to you. You often have a strong Knowledgeable Achiever secondary profile, which helps to ground your mental and fantastical tendencies in more practical actions. You, too, can be a perennial student, but unlike the spiritual seeker, the scientist/engineer type stays focused long enough to amass higher degrees and certificates. Lacking people skills, you are happy to work behind the scenes rather than start up your own company or have a private practice.

PRIMARY MATE AND SOCIAL RELATIONSHIPS. Creative Idealists are often happier relating to their own ideas or profession than to a mate in a relationship. If you have a mate, you may be more married to your work and ideas than to him or her and wonder why your mate complains so frequently that you are "unavailable."

If you meet a person who shares your same creative vision, you may bond with or marry that person, but the unifying element is your shared beliefs, not your physical or romantic interactions. This kind of dynamic is seen in the marriages of research scientists or in the pairing up of artists or teachers, in which there is little passion outside of their creative endeavors.

Creative Idealists are more likely to enter into romantic relationships through their secondary profile, not their primary one. In all the other profiles, people need to experience intimate relationships in order to fully awaken to their deepest life purpose, but for Creative Idealists, that is not the case. They come into their life purpose through their ideas and creativity. Relationships are then a secondary part of their life purpose and must be worked through in order for their brilliant ideas to land in the minds and lives of others.

In social interactions, you tend to jump from idea to idea in conversation, which makes others feel as though you are not fully connected to what you are saying. People may label you a "space case," and not grounded, or you speak over the heads of most people with ideas and theories that can boggle the mind or float right by the average person. Meanwhile, your personal experience is not that you are disconnected from the topic being discussed but that you are thinking deeply about it.

CAREER OR JOB. Living more in your mind than body, you create a world where structure and material gain tend to be off your radar. As a scientist, the Creative Idealist will be interested in pure science, not the science of a corporation that is investing in a particular outcome. As an artist, the Creative Idealist will often be a purist who creates art regardless of any remuneration, although the paintings may sell for millions long after the artist is dead.

Because you are creative in your core and see infinite possibilities, you are not afraid of trying things that others would say are too much on the fringe to make a living in. But you believe and live the idea: *Anything you want to do, there is a market for it somewhere—you just need to find it!*

In defense as the Thinker, you may have difficulty sustaining the focus and energy needed to stay on a job or to find those people who want what you've created. Not wanting to be pinned down, you choose jobs that don't last; or you may stay in a job you don't like for years, so that you get left alone and can work at your own pace. You have side projects that give you energy, such as writing or art or inventing, but since you can't figure out how to turn your projects into a source of income, you are frustrated and have to hide what you are doing from your employer. In contentious work situations, you rarely stand up for yourself, which causes you to leave rather than work through any particular difficulty.

HOW YOU HANDLE MONEY. As a Creative Idealist, you will not negotiate well at work for money, spending what you do have on pie-in-the-sky kinds of investments, and you rarely know how much you have in the bank at any given time. You need a Knowledgeable Achiever business coach and investment consultant to help you manage money matters. You are best off sticking to what you are good at, which is creative ideas that other, less creative people will pay you well for. Trying to go it alone in the world of finance and negotiations will lead to mental exhaustion and a drain on your ability to be creative.

PHYSICAL AND ENERGETIC ASPECTS. Your Creative Idealist body tends to be tall and thin, reflecting how your energy runs quickly up into your head and out. You appear light on your feet and, even if overweight, don't convey a sense of heaviness or of taking up any space, supporting your preference to be invisible. In your core, you have a brilliance and sparkle in your eyes, head, and words, and you are playfully free in your actions. You love to bring novelty and a childlike playfulness to any situation through activity and conversation, and will often find it hard to sit still.

If you are athletic, you will likely excel in solitary sports such as jogging/running, skiing, tennis, hiking, walking, swimming, and skate boarding. In these activities, you can let go while your mind wanders, the activity alone holding you physically in place. You can get very good at these kinds of long-distance, aerobic sports that allow for your thinking to exist simultaneously with your performance.

In defense, your energy can be blocked at the base of your skull and your head tilted during conversation, as if you were deep in thought. This head tilt disconnects your head from your body energetically and keeps you dissociated from your feeling centers. Because of your defense, the

THE CREATIVE IDEALIST
PHYSICAL APPEARANCE

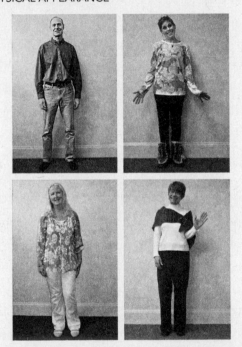

When you are visually assessing a person's profile, notice that Creative Idealists/Thinkers either have a nervous energy or appear slightly vacant, lost in thought even when having their picture taken. Creative Idealists are usually very thin, with a vertically moving energy, and can be very tall; the man shown in the upper left is 6'5". You will often see a head tilt, indicating how the mind and body are disconnected and frequently in different worlds. The Creative Idealists' most salient traits are being funny, silly, and witty. They are sensitive and gentle souls who would rather flee than stand and fight when confronted by any conflict.

muscles of your legs, torso, and neck are often rigid and not highly coordinated.

Your fear of being fully present can create energetic splits in your body. One part of your body may seem full and robust, and the other may seem empty and weak. You may have a strong asymmetry in your face, or a right side/left side imbalance, with your head tilted to one side. You often have visible scoliosis or an obvious twist in your spine, or you may have an upper body that is thin while your lower body and legs are heavy and thick. You can be disjointed or loose in your joints, even double-jointed in multiple joints, or have hyperextended knees or elbows.

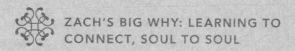

ZACH'S BIG WHY: LEARNING TO CONNECT, SOUL TO SOUL

My student Zach had been curious about spirituality for most of his sixty-six years, even though he would never call himself a New Ager. As a biochemist with a successful career in optical technology, he avoided the touchy-feely crowd, tending to keep his interest abstract and on a mental level. "I didn't even know what patchouli smelled like before I studied energy medicine," he joked. "And the only crystals I'd ever worked with were the ones in a radio set."

Zach was skeptical but curious when his ex-wife recommended he take a course in energy medicine. "I signed up but made sure I understood the refund policy, figuring I'd be out of there after a few meetings." But he wasn't. Instead, Zach completed the full three-year course in healing and self-development, and discovered something about himself and how he related to others that changed his life forever.

Formerly a Quaker, at one time an atheist, and also a student of both Buddhism and mystical Christianity, Zach was surprised that nothing he'd done prepared him for what happened in the program. "It was a totally new experience for me," he reported. "I got a deeper sense of my connection to spiritual energy and to my own soul."

As a scientist, Zach quickly identified with his profile, but he wanted evidence that his connection to his soul was real. He got that evidence when he began to open himself to others. In his second year of the course, Zach had an experience that revealed to him the full power of his profile:

"I was working with a partner who was going through some big changes in her life and she was very anxious, literally trembling as she talked about her lack of confidence and low self-esteem. I listened and felt her pain, then replied, 'You're so beautiful when you are sharing your feelings like this.' I was surprised when she practically turned into a puddle on the floor. Later, she told me she'd felt I'd seen her soul, and how liberating, even life-changing, that was for her."

At first, Zach's newfound ability to connect with others on a soul level frightened him. Creative Idealists have immense power to usher in new paradigms. "I didn't know I could do this, and thought, *I've got to be careful so people don't misunderstand me!*" he said. "But I relaxed about it when I realized it wasn't anything I'd said or done that brought about this woman's profound healing—it was simply allowing myself to feel her pain while I listened to her."

That incident was the first of many in which Zach discovered his ability to impact others profoundly. "I now know without a doubt that it's my purpose in life to connect on a soul level with other people," Zach said. "I had this ability before, but I wasn't conscious of it. Now I pay attention to another person's energy and can choose to open up at times when it might be helpful to them."

Zach has his fair share of Thinker defensive patterns that he is now more aware of as well. "I moved to a new neighborhood recently, three blocks from the ocean, and I'm now on my fifteenth book about the ecology of the area," he said. "I love to learn new things, but my tendency to become so absorbed can be a problem for other areas of my life."

One of those problem areas was his marriage, which had recently dissolved after more than three decades. Zach attributes the divorce at least in part to his having been married more to his work than to his wife. After seeing how this imbalance was a part of his profile's defense, he made some changes. "I wanted to shift the balance between my career and the rest of my life, so I took a salary cut and arranged to have a permanent three-day weekend," he reported. "Now I have more time for what's really important in my life."

Zach summarized how his relationships in general had shifted for him and how he no longer felt so isolated. "I now have friends [classmates] in my life whom I trust completely," he said. "For me, that is huge, and that trust came directly out of my acknowledging the true nature of my soul—along with my defenses."

Zach also came into a new relationship with himself as a result of working with his vows and fully embodying his Creative Idealist profile. "The compassion I discovered that I have for others, I can now give to myself," he shared. "I can honestly say I like myself more—not that I'm glowing with total self-acceptance—but I am making progress!"

Embracing Your Core Soul Qualities

As a Creative Idealist, your core soul qualities connect you deeply to the spiritual and mental realms. You are *highly creative*, and it is through your brilliance, both mentally and spiritually, that you bring new ideas and inspiration to the world—from the latest gizmo or cell phone application to a deep understanding of the soul's reality. In your highest potential, you attain the level of a mystic, a genius, or a saint, or you become a transformative thinker, like an Einstein, Galileo, or Edison.

Spiritually, you have a direct link to dimensions beyond those normally available and can openly channel information from there into the present moment. This makes you a great channel, intuitive, and psychic. You bring forth art, music, scientific discoveries, and new products never before seen, to transform the consciousness of others and awaken within them new possibilities.

Creative Idealists are geniuses in seeing the world and universe symbolically, and when in community, you find creative ways to help the rest of the world understand your vision. Whether in words, mathematical symbols, the visual arts, or science, Creative Idealists have the life purpose of enlightening and awakening others.

YOUR GIFT TO THE WORLD is your ability to stand firm in your truth and not be swayed by the general consensus of current-day thinking. You are connected to the realm of infinite possibility and so can

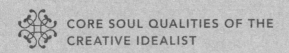
CORE SOUL QUALITIES OF THE CREATIVE IDEALIST

- A creative and dynamic mind in a constant state of expansion—the quality of genius
- A mystic, artist, and creative ("mad") scientist, tapping into the realm of the infinite to bring through wisdom for healing and elevating consciousness
- Transcendent; able to hold both spiritual and material realms
- Playful and irreverent, seeing the world afresh as if with the eyes of a small child

offer others the cure to their mental or spiritual stagnation. In a secondary profile or other blend, you bring your genius and fresh perspective to the other profiles, helping them to transform into their highest level of consciousness.

Extraordinary Power Process: Align with Your Profile Qualities

The Extraordinary Power Process, when repeated frequently in your daily life, supports you to align with your profile and live your unique life purpose. The activities below give you a chance to use the Creative Idealist/Thinker profile to focus that process (described in more detail in *Orientation to the Program* on page 117).

FEEL: DO THE INNER FEELING WORK by identifying with those core soul qualities and defensive patterns that you feel most deeply. Then choose a few to work with that are the strongest. Write in your journal about what it is like to experience those qualities or patterns in your life. Think of a specific situation—for example, at work, in your relationships, in your general health and well-being—and ask yourself the following questions about what it's like to be in your core or in your defense:

- ❖ How do I feel—physically, emotionally, and energetically?
- ❖ What am I saying to myself and to others?
- ❖ What am I attracting to myself?
- ❖ What am I rejecting or avoiding?

As you write your answers, observe the power that is available from your core soul qualities and also the self-sabotage that results from being in your defensive pattern.

CHOOSE: Make conscious choices to create your future, no longer living in the self-sabotaging, knee-jerk reality of your defense. Select one core soul quality you felt the deepest from the reading. Sit quietly and visualize living in that core quality right now. How does it change your relationships, career, health, and finances? Project your life out one, five, and ten years into the future, and explore the same question. Write about your vision in your journal. Then come back to the present moment. Choose how you will do things differently based on living in your core soul qualities.

ACT: Align your actions in your career, relationships, health, or finances. Ask: *What would my Creative Idealist do in this area or situation? How would he or she respond and act right now?* Commit to taking action in this moment, even if it's only making a symbolic gesture of carving out time for connecting with others in a new way or writing down one of your brilliant ideas and deciding who you are going to share it with.

REPEAT THIS PROCESS and continue to *feel*, *choose*, and *act* in this way as you discover more and more about your unique Life Purpose Profile. Soon this simple process will become your default mode, overriding the knee-jerk programming you've been trapped in for most of your life, and you will be free.

Before You Go On . . .

Record aspects of your profile that you can align with on a Personal Profile Summary chart. Turn to page 163 and fill in the first two sections on the chart from your discoveries in Step 1: *My Core Soul Qualities* and *My Defensive Profile Patterns*. (You will have a chance to fill in the remaining sections of the chart in Steps 2 and 3.) Your chart can then serve as a handy reference for the work you are doing to know yourself in this new way.

RESOURCES TO SUPPORT YOUR ALIGNMENT

The following are available at www.discoveryourpurposebook .com/members:

1. **Guided Meditation Audio Download.** *Your Secret Place.* This meditation not only helps you identify your profile but also shows you the difference between being in your core soul self and being in a defensive state.

2. **Crystal Bowls Audio Download.** Daily work with crystal bowls helps you to feel your alignment with your profile, so you are called to your life purpose by energy resonance, not from a force of mental will.

Step 2: Recognize Your Defenses

In Step 2, you use your profile as a lens to examine and then dismantle the defensive mask of your false self that is living in a virtual reality. You identify your core wounds and self-rejecting vows, as well as your negative pleasures, and you begin to replace these defensive patterns with freeing statements and positive pleasures.

The Big Why story of my Creative Idealist student Gladie illustrates how knowing your Life Purpose Profile enables you to live the life you were meant to live, not the life others think you *should* be living.

GLADIE'S BIG WHY: FROM FEAR TO TRUST

Gladie, fifty-six, entered the profile program looking for a new career and, much to her surprise, not only found one but also moved to a new city and healed herself of a chronic autoimmune disease. It all came about as she discovered her true profile and began to dismantle defenses that had kept her driven, fearful, and unable to live a more creative life.

When I first met Gladie, she fit the Creative Idealist/Thinker profile physically and energetically: slim, if not tall, with a nervous, can't-sit-still energy about her. She mentioned she'd had foot and head injuries, a sure sign of the Thinker defense, caused when someone isn't grounded and is in their head much of the time. Furthermore, when she talked, she skipped around from subject to subject in a way that was hard to follow.

She tells what motivated her to come to my school: "I just needed to learn some new healing modalities and expand my bodywork practice." She had been doing trigger point therapy on both people and animals but felt she'd gotten off course by taking on projects that drove her relentlessly.

"I was sure my profile was Knowledgeable Achiever, and I proudly announced it on the first day of school," she said. But soon into the program, she got the first of many surprises. "I realized I'd been living out of my secondary profile with all its defenses and not my primary profile," she reported. "Being a Knowledgeable Achiever worked for me. I was incredibly organized and goal-oriented, and very driven—so much so that I had traveled around the country competing in dog shows with my standard poodle for the past five years. We came in seventh in the nation."

But the stress of having to perform and be perfect at show events eventually became too much for her, and the constant gnawing feeling that she wasn't on her true path just wouldn't go away. She had taken on the competitions to help a family member get trained in grooming and handling dogs for show. But in the profile program, she started to remember what was really important to her—creativity.

At the same time, Gladie was being a caretaker for her aging parents, who lived two houses away in the neighborhood where she'd grown up and lived all her life. "Hiding out as a Knowledgeable Achiever/Rule Keeper, I was overly responsible, a real control freak. I was often frustrated and angry when people didn't do what I knew was best for them." The ties to family and the only place she'd ever lived were strong for Gladie. "I was the connector in my family, but that role kept me from coming to terms with what I really wanted to do in life," she admitted.

In the program, the Your Secret Place meditation helped Gladie to see how she wanted a more creative life. "My creativity had always been there, but I had limited myself, afraid to step away from the norm and fulfill some of my crazy ideas," she said. One of those crazy ideas was to move out of the town she'd lived in all her life. "Once I came into my Creative Idealist, I saw how important it was for me to step out on my own and go somewhere that I'd never been before." With her husband and poodle, Gladie moved to Atlanta, Georgia.

The transition was hard at first, but she flew back frequently for family visits and kept attending classes, exploring her new sense of self more deeply. "People were always telling me I was spacey and unfocused, which I thought meant something was wrong with me," she said. "Then, as I understood my profile more, I realized that's how I'm supposed to be! I'm not supposed to be that other person I've been trying to be!"

Then a new challenge arose. "I got sick in my second year of the program," she said. "I'd actually been sick for a while but ignored the rash on my leg and the headaches, thinking it was just from the stress of moving. Then my joints started swelling and I could hardly walk." Her doctor put her on a full regimen of antibiotics after indications that she had a rare form of gout. But none of this slowed Gladie down, and she returned north to participate in a retreat she'd signed up for previously.

"At the retreat, my knee got much worse, and I wasn't able to take care of myself. In my Thinker, it didn't even occur to me to ask for help because I was so used to doing things for myself." When she couldn't move but had to sit with her leg up, Gladie had the experience of others helping her.

"I couldn't *do, do, do*, all the time, so I started to relax and soon was seeing the humor in it all." Creative Idealists are fun and playful, shifting easily from one thing to another, not predictable. "From out of nowhere, I started making funny remarks and telling jokes—I don't know where it came from."

Gladie went back home and had a surgery she didn't need. More blood work showed she'd been misdiagnosed and actually had late-stage Lyme disease. A friend suggested she start on a raw, low-fat, vegan diet to cure her symptoms. "I was open and jumped right in," she said. "Now, two years later, I have no symptoms. In my new perspective, I've stopped trying to fix myself by taking drugs and having surgery," she said. "My spark of genius came in, allowing me to be more creative in how I approached my health."

Today, Gladie sees private clients in her practice as an Inner Wisdom coach and full-spectrum Energy Medicine Healer. She sums it all up: "The biggest lesson for me was in learning to trust my inner knowing, a direct result of understanding and accepting my Creative Idealist profile." And she has these words of wisdom for the rest of us: "When you embrace who you are, miracles can happen—my miracle was healing myself. Now I help others get in touch with who they truly are, so they can use their own inner wisdom to heal. The greatest gift is to learn to listen to yourself and trust your feelings."

Becoming Aware of Your Vows

Becoming aware of your vows—those hardwired beliefs that filter your every experience through a limited view—is critical for dismantling your defense. The sources of all your vows are events early in life that wounded you emotionally and energetically—your *core wounds*.

For a Creative Idealist, a light spank on the butt when coming out of the womb or the normal bustle, lights, cheering, and machine noises in the hospital room were traumatic and wounding events. If you were taken away from your mother too soon, were premature, experienced a long labor, or had to be in an incubator for a few days or weeks, it was enough to traumatize you and trigger a reaction of deep withdrawal from being present in your life.

As a result of your core wounding experiences, you made vows that involved distrusting the world and avoiding abuse, rejection, or aggression—any form of conflict with others. But a vow to avoid conflict can render you unable to set clear boundaries and therefore leave you feeling that you don't deserve a place in the world. Thinkers often feel like they have landed on an alien planet and don't belong here.

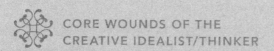

CORE WOUNDS OF THE CREATIVE IDEALIST/THINKER

- Birth trauma during or after delivery
- Early separation from your mother due to birth complications or adoption procedures
- Exposure early in life to noise, harsh elements, or chaotic environments
- Aloofness or coldness by your mother to your needs as a young child
- Hostile parents/caretakers dealing with personal issues that took focus away from your needs for security
- Being left alone and rarely held, denying you a sense of physical connection
- Aggressive or violent parents, or other people, during childhood and throughout your life

Another vow-driven belief of Creative Idealists is that the spirit world is more real than the physical world. The belief that life is an illusion becomes your safety in the face of an aggressive, chaotic world. When nothing occurs as real in the world, a desire to establish yourself in a grounded way will not be a priority in your life.

Or you may become despondent, believing that there is no meaning to your existence. *Since nothing is real, I am not real, you are not real, I am just my thoughts. I vow never to form any attachment or commit to anything or anyone.* These types of dissociated spiritual beliefs, though possibly quite correct at one level, leave you ill-equipped to deal with the physical world and the struggles that go with it.

Once the world is seen from the distance of your mind as something unreal that you don't have to deal with, your virtual reality defense has taken full hold. You lose all ability to feel who you are or why you are here and all power to make things happen in the physical realm. This leads to you living in a low level of constant apprehension and anxiety, and you have no peace or power.

Vows become hardwired through unconscious statements you say to yourself day in and day out. Read and allow yourself to feel the following typical Vow Statements that form the Thinker defense. Do you recognize any as your own?

 TYPICAL VOW STATEMENTS OF THE THINKER

I vow always to live in peace and never be as crazy or angry (as my father/mother).
I vow never to be attached to people or things but to be a bohemian free spirit.
I vow always to live through my art or science, which lets me express my true self.

I vow never to share my thoughts and to stay invisible in groups because no one sees life the way I do.

I vow always to engage only in intellectual arguments, never expressing real conflict.

I vow always to live in my interior world of thoughts and fantasies rather than in the reality of relationships.

I vow always to see myself and all others as spiritual beings, never dealing with physical issues.

I vow always to stay hidden and out of the reach of people and a world that is dangerous, manipulative, and violent.

I vow always to keep what I see to myself, since others will think I'm crazy if I tell them.

I vow always to leave my body whenever threatened with the pain of being hit, yelled at, or negated.

WRITE YOUR OWN: _____

Extraordinary Power Process: Release Your Vows

The activities below give you a chance to become aware of and release vows of the Thinker defense.

FEEL: Choose those Vow Statements from the list that resonate most strongly for you. Mark them and add any of your own to the list. Then select one or more statements to work with in completing the following sentences:

1. A vow I made was always/never to _____

_____.

2. How this vow is influencing my life right now: _____

_____.

3. My self-talk that reinforces this vow: _____
_____.

EXAMPLE:

1. A vow I made was never to show my emotions like my mother did—she was always out of control.
2. How this vow is influencing my life right now: I don't admit to ever being angry in my relationship.
3. My self-talk that reinforces this vow: "I don't care enough to get all worked up over something. Emotional people are dangerous."

CHOOSE: Look at the Vow Statements you marked and, taking one at a time, ask yourself: *What would my life be like if I stopped honoring that vow?* Project out one, five, and ten years from now and ask: *How would not honoring that vow change my life?* Write your answers in your journal.

For example: *If I no longer honored that vow never to show my emotions, I could admit that I'm actually very sensitive and that my feelings get hurt very easily. From there, I could be honest about what I really need in my relationship, not just withdraw when there is an issue.*

ACT: What action could you take to support your choice to no longer honor your vow? Decide to act based on your conscious choice, not a vow. Write in your journal about what happened when you did.

REPEAT THE PROCESS of *feel, choose,* and *act* every time you become aware that an ancient vow has been running your life. Vows are buried deep in your psyche, so it can take years to permanently release them. Be prepared to feel some amount of fear, guilt, and shame as you choose not to honor your vows; a vow is an unconscious promise, and you are breaking that promise when you choose anything other than your vows.

Before You Go On . . .

Record the Vow Statements you resonate with most strongly on your Personal Profile Summary chart on page 163. Fill in the section for *My Vow Statements* with statements from the list or that you wrote in.

Freedom Statements

Replace your Vow Statements with Freedom Statements, which call forth your core soul qualities and support you to increasingly choose more consciously in every moment. Every time you consciously choose a Freedom Statement over a vow, you get back energy and open yourself to an ever-growing life rather than stagnating as a wounded victim.

Use Freedom Statements as a bridge out of defense and onto the path of your truth. The following list offers you a variety of statements, but you can always add your own.

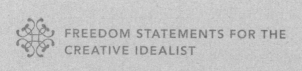

FREEDOM STATEMENTS FOR THE CREATIVE IDEALIST

I am open to letting go of my fears and trusting my gut feelings.
I am open to being a creative genius in all my actions as well as my thoughts.
I am open to being playful and enthusiastic.
I am open to the idea that I have a unique genius, never before seen on this planet.
I am open to the idea that my creative expressions will be accepted by many.
I am open to being totally free to think and share my genius with people.

I am open to being a creative channel to potentially transform a world stuck in the past and in limited patterns.

I love to express joy and enthusiasm in relationships with other people.

I am open to thinking and sharing my ideas in each moment, knowing that what I say may enlighten others who receive my ideas.

I am open to deep, intimate relationships.

WRITE YOUR OWN: _____

Extraordinary Power Process:
Become Free of Your Vows

The activities below give you a chance to replace your vows with Freedom Statements and live from your Creative Idealist soul qualities rather than your Thinker defense.

FEEL: Read the list of Freedom Statements above, speaking each one aloud. Let yourself feel their truth as you sit quietly after speaking them. Notice those you may want to deny and then repeat those statements until you no longer have a negative reaction to them. Notice also which statements register strongly as *Yes, that's me!*

CHOOSE: Speak your Freedom Statements out loud as often as possible to bring conscious choice to your vow-driven, knee-jerk defensive reactions. Tell others your Freedom Statements so that they can see your truth and support you in embodying it.

Sit and inquire within about what your life would be like one, five, and ten years from now if you embody the truth in your Freedom Statements over your vows.

ACT: Explore how you would act differently in key areas of your life if your vows were replaced by Freedom Statements. Choose one action you can take that aligns you with the truth of your Freedom Statement, not your vow, and do it!

REPEAT THE PROCESS of *feel*, *choose*, and *act* often when dealing with your life's challenges. You'll notice how your vow-driven actions begin to fade and you increasingly make choices and act based in the present of who you truly are rather than the past of your false and defended self.

Before You Go On . . .

Record the Freedom Statements that you have chosen to replace your vows on the Personal Profile Summary chart on page 163. Fill in the section for *My Freedom Statements*.

Your Negative Pleasures

Living from your core soul qualities, not your vows, will empower you to embrace your life purpose. But without confronting your *negative pleasures*, real freedom will never be yours. Negative pleasures—those habits and behaviors you know you shouldn't do (or don't do but know you should!) but justify in order to feel good about yourself—must be confronted and left behind if you are going to live your authentic purpose.

In Thinker defense, fantasy is your most common negative pleasure. The payoff is that you get to withdraw and hide from those you feel are scary or hard to deal with, as well as those who want to be close to you. Avoidance keeps you safe in an unsafe world. You see whatever you want to see rather than dealing with reality in any substantive way.

You also find pleasure in creating a million ways to distract yourself from what you know you need to do, leading to little or no results from your efforts. Feelings of superiority lead to more dissociation and fear, and eventually you find yourself very alone. The state of existential aloneness feels good; it even makes you feel unique. You feel good when judging that others have some negative intent because it gives you the right to dissociate from them.

Because the Thinker defense has a great distrust of authority, you entertain yourself with complicated delusions about aliens and conspiracy theories. As a result, you don't have to pay attention to what is going on in the world and contribute to making it a better place. Your negative pleasure comes from being outside the rules of normal life, an illusion of freedom that replaces real freedom.

Excessive computer gaming, Internet surfing, meditation, spiritual practice, writing a never-ending book, thinking up pie-in-the-sky business plans, and recreational drug use (especially marijuana) are a few negative pleasures in the Thinker defense. Many more may lurk under your radar. There are all kinds of activities that keep you forever disconnected from real pleasure in life.

The following list includes typical negative pleasures of the Thinker defense. Feel free to add your own.

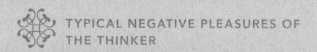 TYPICAL NEGATIVE PLEASURES OF THE THINKER

Being spiritually immune and detached from pain and suffering
   in the world
Having a rich fantasy life that substitutes for reality
Having computer addictions such as Facebook, games, e-mailing,
   and so on, that substitute for relationships and end up keeping
   you isolated

Relying on psychic skills and visions to make your choices

Judging the "idiots" in the world who have "no idea what they are doing!"

Pointing out how bad the state of the world is and feeling justified in taking no action to change things because the situation seems hopeless

Marrying yourself to your studies, research, writing, or poetry rather than a person

Covering a variety of topics in any conversation, talking over people's heads, and outpacing and impressing those who are listening

Entertaining yourself and others with your ideas about how to save the world but blaming politicians and corporations for why you can't do anything

Smoking pot or taking opiates because you believe you do your greatest thinking in that state

WRITE YOUR OWN: _____

Extraordinary Power Process:
Diminish Your Negative Pleasures

The activities below give you a chance to become aware of your negative pleasures. The key to diminishing your negative pleasures is to become conscious of how they are poor substitutes for real pleasures.

FEEL: As you read the list of negative pleasures for the Thinker defense, let yourself feel which ones resonate deeply with you. Mark those and write them in your journal.

CHOOSE: Choose one negative pleasure that you identified and are willing to let go of. Sit with all the pain that this behavior has caused you and others to date. Then visualize your life projected out ten years from now. If you don't change that behavior, what positive pleasure will it cost you?

To help you do this, fill in the following:

1. A negative pleasure that I have in my life is _____
   _____.

2. Having that negative pleasure in my life costs me now and in the future: _____
   _____.

FOR EXAMPLE:

1. A negative pleasure I have in my life is railing against politicians and anyone in power as being amoral and corrupt!
2. Having this negative pleasure costs me the ability to effectively deal with authority and spread the message of change that I truly believe in. In ten years, I could become someone no one wants to be around, alone and angry.

Now write about a *positive pleasure*, one that comes from living in your core soul self. Explain how experiencing that pleasure might look in your life. For example: *If I keep in mind that those in power need conscientious people to guide them to be better leaders, I would feel more grounded in bringing my new ideas forward and sharing them with everyone. In ten years, my ideas would be recognized as a contribution to the well-being of the planet. I can change the world!*

ACT: Once you've chosen a negative pleasure you are ready to let go of, the next time that behavior comes up in your life you can ask yourself:

What positive pleasure am I missing as I indulge this negative one? How would my Creative Idealist respond in this situation? Then take action in accordance with your answer.

REPEAT THIS PROCESS OFTEN. As your negative pleasures become more and more noticeable, see them as behaviors based on fears that you are now ready to grow out of. Don't beat yourself up. Go slow, get support, and let each negative pleasure go, one at a time. You will start to experience more of the positive pleasures that come from accepting your life and the people in it. Soon, the unconscious habits and behaviors you've been substituting for the real thing will no longer seem as attractive.

Every time you let go of a negative pleasure, you can bring back into your life all of the wasted energy that went into that defense. With that energy you can make powerful choices to live your life as a creative presence.

Before You Go On . . .

Record your negative pleasures on your Personal Profile Summary chart on page 163. Fill in the section for *My Favorite Negative Pleasures*.

In Transition . . .

As you transition out of Thinker defense and into your core self, you may find yourself stuck in frustrating old patterns. Your defenses have been in place for a long time. Now newly aware of your defenses, you can make choices and set goals to act differently.

For the Creative Idealist, a good goal is to do some kind of activity with others each day.

ACTIVITY: Choose from the following list:

❖ *Engage in physical and fun activities*, such as playing a game of tennis, going for a swim, or playing soccer, feeling your body from your head to your toes. Transfer your excessive mental creativity into physical creativity through contact, play, or learning with others, so your mind and body must work together.

❖ *Connect with others* at your work: Take classes with others, learn Reiki, get massages, and so on. These activities will stimulate connection with others and trigger and reprogram spontaneous feelings and emotions.

❖ *Commit to any form of relationship*, especially if you tend to be reclusive, be it with a pet (start with fish, not a dog), a person (start with a friend; don't just jump into a marriage!),

RESOURCES TO SUPPORT YOUR TRANSITION

1. **Guided Meditation Audio Download.** *Calling Back Your Spirit* (available at www.discoveryourpurposebook.com/members).

2. **Recommended Reading List**
   - *A New Earth*, by Eckhart Tolle
   - *Wherever You Go, There You Are*, by Jon Kabat-Zinn
   - *The Seat of the Soul*, by Gary Zukav
   - *The Dancing Wu Li Masters*, by Gary Zukav
   - *Zen in the Art of Archery*, by Eugen Herrigel
   - *Care of the Soul*, by Thomas Moore
   - *How to Know God*, by Deepak Chopra

or Mother Earth (start with a window box of flowers) and see them as real, not things to escape from if they don't behave or if they make tough demands on you.

❖ *Make it a point to share some of your crazy ideas* with at least one other person as often as possible.

Step 3: Live Your Life Purpose

Having begun the process of dismantling your defenses in Step 2, you are now ready to integrate your profile's unique higher- and lower-self qualities. As you become less conflicted, and more whole and balanced, you can make choices and take courageous actions in your life, not just react automatically from your ancient vows. You are also able to use the Law of Attraction to attract what best supports your unique life purpose as you create and live an extraordinary life.

Your Shadow: Lower- and Higher-Self Traits

Your shadow is made up of traits that you have rejected through vowing *always* or *never* to be or do something. As you identify rejected higher- and lower-self traits, you can begin to accept and integrate them and achieve a state of inner balance and wholeness. Fully integrating your shadow allows your defensive mask to dissolve and your true core soul self to emerge.

The following chart contains a list of the lower- and higher-self traits *in matched pairs* that you must own and integrate to fully live your life purpose as a Creative Idealist.

LOWER- AND HIGHER-SELF TRAITS FOR CREATIVE IDEALISTS

LOWER-SELF TRAITS	HIGHER-SELF TRAITS
Fearful	Finding solutions in the face of challenges
Neurotically unproductive	Endlessly creative
Fantasy-prone	Seeing the world as metaphor
Rejecting	Accepting the dynamic diversity in life
Phobic	Knowing the power of the mind
Naive	Having the faith of a mystic
Avoiding	Interacting playfully with others
Aloof	Protective of personal time to think
Dissociated	Spiritually unattached
Schizoid	Mentally able to integrate many voices at once
Terrorized	Finding humane solutions for violence
Scattered	Entertaining many ideas at once
Spaced out	Navigating many spiritual levels of consciousness
Loveless	Seeing God's love in all people
Hateful	Seeing the validity of everyone's opinions
Powerless	Moving mountains with just one thought
Lost	Not knowing one's state of mind
Abandoning	Knowing when to let others find their own light
Delusional	Seeing the world through God's eyes
Conspiracy driven	Not fooled by others' ideas

Extraordinary Power Process: Integrate Your Shadow

The activities below give you a chance to integrate your shadow (rejected traits) with your higher-self light.

FEEL: As you read the list of matched-pair lower-/higher-self traits, reach deep into yourself to feel the full range of your raw, lower self at one end and your exalted, higher self at the other. Both are within you to varying degrees. Your raw power and personal needs are found in your lower-self traits, while consciously using that power and fulfilling those needs is in your higher-self traits. When you can own both higher- and lower-self traits and still choose your higher-self traits, then everything you do will be aligned with your life purpose.

Put a check mark next to the lower- and higher-self traits that you feel you exhibit. Also notice traits that elicit a powerful negative reaction, and check them, too. These are traits you have rejected in yourself or in others. (In rejecting lower-self traits, you say to yourself, *I'd never do that—it's too negative, mean, or evil*; while in rejecting higher-self traits, you say, *I could never do that—it's too perfect, saintly, or godlike*.)

CAUTION: No higher-self trait can exist without the lower-self trait alongside it. To be whole and balanced, you must be conscious of both within you. Selecting only those traits that you like will send you back to your vow-created life where only half of you exists.

Using your strongest traits checked, complete these statements for each:

1. A lower-/higher-self trait that I see as strong in me is

   _____.

2. My greatest fear of owning that trait is _____

   _____.

EXAMPLE:

1. A lower-self trait that I see as strong in me is being dissociated, isolated, and "checked out."
2. My greatest fear of owning that trait is that I'd have to face my deep social anxieties.

AND:

1. A higher-self trait that is the partner to my lower-self trait is being spiritually unattached, meaning I am truly a part of all of life, not separate from it in any way.
2. My greatest fear of owning that trait is I would have to feel how deeply I do care about other people and all of life, and no longer hide behind my story of being okay with being separate and isolated.

CHOOSE: Now work with one matched pair of lower- and higher-self traits you identified that you are not owning in their full range. Ask how your life would be different if you owned both higher- and lower-self traits equally, able to accept either freely but choosing the higher-self quality.

Visualize your life up until now and see how damaging it has been to express the lower-self trait unconsciously. Also feel how you have wanted to express the higher-self trait more often but don't, since the lower-self trait cannot be resolved. Now project out this pattern of behavior one, five, and ten years into the future and see what your life looks like with just this one conflict within you.

What would happen if you were able to embrace both, at all times, as part of your life purpose? Notice that if you did not stand in such judgment and fear of being who you actually are one, five, and ten years into the future, you would instead reveal your true power and purpose.

For example: *If I accept that I have always had a tendency to dissociate and often prefer the spirit world to this one, this gives me direct access to my soul and ability to see and sense the souls of the people I come in contact with. Being spiritually unattached, not dissociated, lets me see and honor the highest reason we are all together, and I can serve that.*

ACT: Take actions that align with your new state of inner-balance wholeness. Commit to one action you will take that reflects your new self-acceptance, and then do it. Write in your journal about what happened when you did.

REPEAT THE PROCESS! Once you've worked with one pair of higher- and lower-self traits in this way, repeat the process, covering more traits in both lists. Accepting both higher and lower selves as the whole of who you are is the most powerful spiritual work you can do.

Before You Go On . . .

Turn to page 163 and fill in the section for *Lower- and Higher-Self Traits* on your Personal Profile Summary chart.

Living Courageously

Living your life purpose means speaking and acting fearlessly from your core soul self. To remain in that state, you will need to step out of your comfort zone often and take the road less traveled, leaping courageously over obstacles in your way. What follows are some ways you can live courageously from your Creative Idealist core soul self.

Embrace the innate fear you have of human relationships.

You self-isolate or distract yourself to avoid feeling fear, but only when you embrace your fear can you come into your full power. Accepting that your fear is valid is a start. Creative Idealists who want peace and love have been killed mercilessly since the beginning of time.

Accept your calling to help awaken the unconscious masses.

To embrace the truth of humanity as it is, is to embrace your calling to help awaken the unconscious masses. Einstein is known best for his bulletproof equation, $E = mc^2$, which was a quantum leap in our understanding of physics, but his understanding and embrace of humanity was equally impactful.

Awaken to your feelings.

Your fear of being here on planet earth or your analytical scientific approach to life has blocked your ability to feel your body and the life flowing through you. You tend to feel through thinking and can tell when a great idea is coming. To then relate that great idea to life, you must be able to feel it within you. When both the thought and the feeling are present in you, you become a humanitarian like Einstein and fully enjoy both worlds, mind and body.

Before You Go On . . .

Turn to page 163 and fill in the section for *Actions to Take for Living Courageously* on your Personal Profile Summary chart.

Speak Your Truth

To remain in your Creative Idealist core, you must be willing to speak your truth to others, especially to those with whom you are in an intimate relationship. Practice by reading each of the Essential Word Statements below, visualizing that you are speaking directly to someone you love and feeling your words deeply as you read them.

Make a commitment to speak these essential words—not the automatic words dictated by your vows and defenses—to an important person in your life. Then act to call, write, or speak with that important person to share your truth.

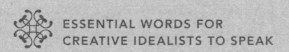

ESSENTIAL WORDS FOR CREATIVE IDEALISTS TO SPEAK

- I love you but know that sometimes I may be afraid of you.
- If any confrontation happens, I may abandon you and myself.
- This is the moment of my greatest need, so please hold space for me. I will be back.
- Each time I leave, and you do not attack me for leaving, my faith in humanity and in our love is renewed.

Before You Go On . . .

Turn to page 163 and fill in the section for *Speaking Your Truth (Essential Words)* on your Personal Profile Summary chart.

The Law of Attraction

According to the Law of Attraction, like attracts like. It follows that you will always attract people and situations that are like you. As your alignment with your life purpose grows, your internal magnet for attracting who and what you want is strengthened. If you are not aligned with your life purpose, no amount of visualizing will help you achieve your desires—in spite of what the popular belief tells you about how constant visualizing will bring you what you want.

With regard to the Law of Attraction, the Creative Idealist/Thinker is the least solid and most invisible of all the profiles. Energetically, you resist anything that can hold you down because the more material wealth you have, the more you need to focus on its maintenance rather than your creative endeavors. For this reason, you are not an effective magnet in making the Law of Attraction work for material acquisitions.

You tend to live more in your mind than your body and create a world where structure and material gain are off your radar. Instead, you find your value through your thoughts and creative expression and don't generally focus on material security, which can become a limiting factor in your creative process. With money comes the expectation for you to perform or produce in a certain way, limiting your availability to create on impulse.

You value ideas and unformed qualities of life that come alive in your mind more than in the material world. Since creative ideas are hardly quantifiable and are in a constant state of change, you are generally not interested in money. As a scientist, you will be interested in the pure science, not the science of a corporation that is investing in one outcome. As an artist, you may be starving now, but your art will sell for millions long after you are dead.

ACTIVITY: EXPLORE THE GAP. The gap is the space between where you are now and where you know you will be when you fully embody your core soul profile qualities and live your life purpose. Looking in areas of life such as health, relationships, finances, and career, inquire about the following:

❖ What am I attracting in my life right now from living in my defenses?

❖ What do I want to attract in my life from living in my core soul self?

Are you attracting what supports your life purpose or what keeps you stuck in your defense? How can you act from your core soul qualities and not your defenses to close that gap and attract what you want? Write your responses in your journal.

Before You Go On . . .

Turn to page 163 and fill in the section for *Law of Attraction* on your Personal Profile Summary chart.

Extraordinary Power Process: Your Personal Profile Summary Chart

Your Personal Profile Summary chart now holds what you have learned about yourself from the Creative Idealist/Thinker profile, either as your primary or your secondary Life Purpose Profile.

Once you have completed your charts for both primary and secondary profiles, use them as a tool to support you in living your life purpose. Follow the Extraordinary Power Process of *feel*, *choose*, and *act* as you refer to each section you've filled in on your chart:

1. Feel: Do the inner feeling work—don't just think.
2. Choose: Make conscious choices—don't automatically react based on your vows.
3. Act: Align your actions with your profile's core soul qualities—not with your defenses—to live your truth.

When you repeat this sequence as often as possible throughout your day, applying it to everything you do, then everything you do reveals the mystery of who you are rather than reinforcing who you think you are. *Feeling, choosing,* and *acting* in accordance with your profile gives you access to your extraordinary power so you can effortlessly manifest your life purpose and live it in every area of your life.

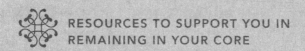

RESOURCES TO SUPPORT YOU IN REMAINING IN YOUR CORE

1. **Guided Meditation Audio Download.** *Your Subpersonalities.* Explore your higher- and lower-self traits through a guided meditation, available at www.discoveryourpurposebook.com /members.

2. **Bioenergetic Exercises for the Creative Idealist,** available on page 164 and also on the same website.

Creative Idealist/Thinker
PERSONAL PROFILE SUMMARY

Profile	☐ This is my PRIMARY PROFILE ☐ This is my SECONDARY PROFILE ☐ This is my THIRD, FOURTH, or FIFTH PROFILE
My Core Soul Qualities (for this profile)	1 _____ 2 _____
My Defensive Profile Patterns	1 _____ 2 _____
My Vow Statements (How I self-sabotage)	1 _____ 2 _____ 3 _____
My Freedom Statements (Solutions to my Vow Statements)	I am open to _____ I am open to _____ I am open to _____
My Favorite Negative Pleasures (How I self-sabotage)	Something I do that I shouldn't do but get pleasure from: Something I get pleasure from not doing that I know I should do: _____
Lower- and Higher-Self Traits (matched pairs)	Lower: Higher: 1 _____ / _____ 2 _____ / _____
Actions to take for living courageously from your profile	1 _____ 2 _____
Speaking Your Truth (ESSENTIAL WORDS you must say to others)	1 _____ 2 _____
Law of Attraction (People, situations, etc. that I am attracting)	In defense, I attract _____ In my core, I attract _____

BIOENERGETIC EXERCISES FOR THE CREATIVE IDEALIST

The following bioenergetic exercises will help you to come into your body more as you align with and manifest your life purpose.

EXERCISE #1: FORWARD FLOP AND BOW. In this two-part exercise, make sure you keep your legs slightly bent and eyes open throughout both parts.

PART 1: FORWARD FLOP. Stand with your feet shoulder-width apart and gently bend forward as far as you can go. Your arms and head should hang loose. Slowly pump your legs to create a vibration in them. Then roll up, one vertebra at a time, until you are standing upright.

PART 2: BOW. Begin to bend backward, supporting your lower back with your hands or fists. Arch backward as much as you can and keep your eyes down on the floor. The goal is to stay in this position until there is involuntary shaking.

Alternate between the Forward Flop and the Bow until you can stand up and still maintain the involuntary shaking while standing or walking. It may take a few months of loosening yourself up in this way to open to a full-body shake.

EXERCISE #2: STOMPING YOUR FEET. In this exercise, stand barefoot on the ground if possible and gently stomp your feet. Then stomp harder. As you build up heat in your legs, say out loud, "This is where I will make a difference in the world," "I love to be here and be creative!"

EXERCISE #3: PLEASURE. In this exercise, pick anything you already do that you really enjoy and slow it down until you feel what you are doing, not just thinking it. Eat ice cream slowly and make appreciative noises as you do. Pick one thing a day that you are going to double the time it takes you to do it, just so you can feel the pleasure in what you are doing.

CHAPTER 8

Profile #2: Emotional Intelligence Specialist/Poor Me

THE EMOTIONAL INTELLIGENCE SPECIALIST

with Poor Me defense

Welcome to the Emotional Intelligence Specialist profile and its defense, Poor Me. You will find valuable information and activities here to help you access your extraordinary power to embody your life purpose.

If this is your secondary or other profile, or the profile of someone in your life, you can use what you learn here to deepen your understanding of yourself and others.

EMOTIONAL INTELLIGENCE SPECIALISTS WE ALL KNOW

Historical: Jesus Christ, Mother Mary
Contemporary: Mother Teresa, Pope Francis, Princess Diana, Meg Ryan, Julia Roberts, Mary Tyler Moore, Tom Hanks

Step 1: Align with Your Profile

In this first step of the program, you learn all about your profile, including those core soul qualities that support you to live in your life purpose and those defenses that cause you to sabotage your efforts. The Big Why story of my student Eric demonstrates how knowing your life purpose gives you power to live an extraordinary life.

About Your Profile

What follows is a general description of your profile, including how it looks when you are in defense as the Poor Me. You will take a closer look at your relationships, your career or job, how you handle money, and your physical and energetic aspects.

GENERAL DESCRIPTION. As an Emotional Intelligence Specialist, you are a highly sensitive and emotional being. While all people experience emotions and feelings, you have a degree of emotional sensitivity that goes beyond what the average person experiences.

You are a gentle soul who can be unconditionally loving, connected through your emotions to the deepest levels of spiritual awareness, compassion, intuition, and love. You find forgiveness easy and natural and have a deep healing quality in your touch and in the way you care for others. You feel humble, gentle, and simultaneously one with any person, animal, flower, or plant you relate to. No other profile can stand in this level of surrendered openness and reverence for other human beings and life.

You live a simple life that draws you toward experiencing the pleasures of all your senses. You love music, but you are more attracted to the lyrics and the deep emotions expressed in them than to the melodies. You love helping others work through their chaos of emotions. You have wonderful, caring energy and demonstrate an easy flow of emotions, with the exception of anger or aggression, which you do not reject in yourself or others but rarely express. In short, you live a life filled with love.

You are generally very present-minded and prefer to live in a small world that is related to your immediate feelings, people, pets, children, house, and family dynamics. Time does not enter into your attention, since what you feel in every cell of your body takes up most of your focus. Time is not needed for those who fully embrace living in the moment. You stay grounded through your deep connection and empathy for others, seeing the work you do and each person you meet as a gift from God. Others sense you as a warm, flowing energy, and you are gentle and receptive with a nourishing quality to you. Your sensitivity gives you the ability to be connected to all of life and everything in the present moment at all times.

IN POOR ME DEFENSE, you are trapped in self-sabotaging patterns of behavior that have you often feeling tired and worn out by life. You process the world through wounded feelings from the past, reliving traumas and abandonment as if they were happening now. You have a hard time getting rid of what appears to be junk but has sentimental value.

You have a tendency to be hypersensitive to people and your surroundings, and you become easily overwhelmed by your strong feelings and mood swings. You fixate on your deepest longings for an open, vulnerable, loving connection. When that need cannot be met in your immediate environment, you feel an emptiness and lack of fulfillment that you project outward and blame others for.

Your defensive patterns are constantly triggered by the perception that your needs cannot be met easily, if at all. Rather than meeting your own needs responsibly, you become clingy and demanding, placing that responsibility on others. Those who are not as needy as you will criticize and reject you, eventually abandoning you because no matter what they do for you, it's never enough. They may admonish you for taking things so personally, leaving you feeling as though your needs and, even worse, your feelings, are rejected. As a result, you break down and withdraw from others, feeling sorry for yourself.

Over time, you get angry at the lack of love coming from others, but since you hate aggression, you are unable to stand up for yourself. You give up, knowing that whatever another gives is never enough to fill the emptiness and satisfy your insatiable longing for love and acceptance.

PRIMARY MATE AND SOCIAL RELATIONSHIPS. Emotional Intelligence Specialists often find Knowledgeable Achievers as their primary mate. You teach your partner how to love and open his or her heart, while your partner teaches you how to set boundaries and realize the gift of your sensitive nature.

In matters of intimacy, you are an extremely delicate being who fearlessly makes every event in your life a sensual pleasure. Above all the other profiles, you are deeply aware that it is the small things, the gentle words, the looks of love, and the giving of sentimental gifts that truly allow intimacy and love to flourish in relationships. Sexuality is experienced by you as a sacred act. With your deep need to merge and become one with another, sex is the ultimate act of love. You will be focused on the love and tender intimacy aspects of sex rather than pleasure.

You make love to the world in everything you do. Smelling a flower, looking at a sunset or sunrise, admiring the green leaves of a tree, and kissing your loved ones all inspire a level of appreciation that none of the other profiles innately feel. You are the greatest teacher of intimacy and love, which you exhibit not by big, grand gestures but by showing others the sheer joy of everyday encounters.

In Poor Me defense, you may be in a relationship with someone who truly loves you but can't understand how overwhelmed you get over the smallest things or why past traumas still affect you deeply. You fear that your partner will not be there for you when you want to talk about these feelings, as is often the case because your partner can't deal with your level of emotion. Your partner does try to help, but you see your partner as patronizing and reject those efforts, which leads to your partner abandoning you in your deepest pain.

In relationships, you talk excessively about your feelings and the injustices you have suffered but rarely express your anger and rage. You spend time processing your feelings rather than taking any action to resolve them. By complaining and failing to take responsibility for your life, you drive your partner away—your worst nightmare. You are just too draining to be around.

Because of your fear of abandonment, you experience anxiety when left alone, even for short periods of time. You blame others for being insensitive to your needs and not knowing how to love or support you.

Once this pattern has played out a number of times, those who tried to love you abandon you in frustration. Every episode of abandonment triggers your feeling of not being enough, and the needy cycle of hoping others will come to your aid begins again.

CAREER OR JOB. You excel in any work that helps others feel safe and understood, especially where you can be one-on-one with people who are in need and receptive to your loving energy. Service businesses and nonprofits that are not too corporate in their atmosphere are ideal workplaces for you.

You may be a schoolteacher or nurse/healer, or a stay-at-home mother or father who offers loving care to his or her children. As a teacher, you might work with special needs students or the elderly, never seeing anyone as less valuable or less deserving of love and attention. You are the heart and soul of any family or business. Whatever form of work you choose, you bring a gentle touch that helps others feel seen, heard, and understood in ways they hadn't been aware of before.

In defense, you rarely feel comfortable at your job and often wish you didn't have to work at all. You chose your job, including that of being a stay-at-home parent, from a defensive stance, thinking that supporting others who are in need would fulfill you when they give back to you. But you find out quickly that all actions have a price, and you always give more than you get, leading to exhaustion. If your work emphasizes paying close attention to details and rules over the feelings of others, you will hate it, and what you do for money will be a source of constant unhappiness.

HOW YOU HANDLE MONEY. You don't generally focus on material security or money because they quantify what you believe should be given from the heart. You have a need for money but no real drive to go out and make it; you don't demand remuneration for the good work you do, even if you are a professional.

Your conflict is in your deep knowledge that the most valuable thing in the universe is love, and love should be given freely if it is real. When you decide to do something, it is for the love of it, not for living wages. This makes you often dependent on family or others to provide that living wage. To ask for what you are worth, as a caring, loving force in any business, creates guilt and shame that you are somehow charging for something you would willingly give away.

The money you make is never enough, further reinforcing the idea that *you* are not enough. Stuck in survival mode and in defense, you often collapse and don't take action, waiting for others to come to your rescue and bail you out. You will generally be content when your spouse, who tends to be a Knowledgeable Achiever, is the breadwinner. Then you can focus on your gift of making life more aesthetically and emotionally pleasing.

PHYSICAL AND ENERGETIC ASPECTS. To others, you may appear soft and gentle with large, deep eyes that drink in life and often tear up even when there is nothing obviously sad. You appear passive and non-threatening, often giving others the impression that you are weak or dependent. You are a conscientious objector to any form of anger, and you hide in the face of aggression or criticism. Under stress, you can appear to be in a state of near physical collapse, with slumped shoulders and concave body posture. Depleted arm and leg energy prevents you from reaching out for the love and nurturance you so desire or standing your own ground and filling yourself with love.

With regard to your health, you may have an overly sensitive digestive system and difficulties with activities that cause overstimulation of your vision, hearing, and smell; you can be overly reactive to pain and illness. Chronic pain conditions, such as fibromyalgia, are often manifestations of your attempts to block your feelings because others have abandoned or yelled at you or otherwise not treated you gently. Instead of letting feelings flow through you, they emerge through seemingly random pain.

THE EMOTIONAL INTELLIGENCE SPECIALIST
PHYSICAL APPEARANCE

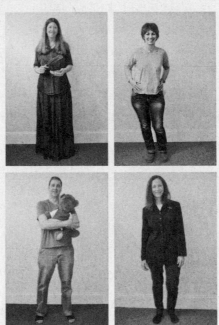

When you are visually assessing a person's profile, notice that Emotional Intelligence Specialists/Poor Me appear gentle, often innocent. Their bodies tend to be soft and flexible, not defined or muscular, and their faces are often childlike in their openness. Eyes are deep and compassionate and often watery, since Emotional Intelligence Specialists are never far from crying with either joy or pain in any moment. Their energy is pooled in the hips and heart area, both energetic centers of emotion. Their most salient traits are their sweetness and ability to love unconditionally. When you are around a person in this profile, you feel the love.

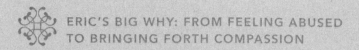

ERIC'S BIG WHY: FROM FEELING ABUSED TO BRINGING FORTH COMPASSION

Emotional Intelligence Specialist Eric is a fifty-four-year-old father of two. Trained as an electrical and mechanical engineer, he had a successful career working in a variety of high-tech fields. His secondary profile is Creative Idealist, which he often found to be a more comfortable mode for his self-expression.

"Having emotions and being male is not accepted in our society, so I avoided anything and everything that looked like my profile for most of my life," he said. For Eric, this self-rejection had its roots deep in his past. "As a child, I was very sensitive, but I wasn't allowed to cry, so whining and temper tantrums were how my bottled-up feelings would come out."

Understanding why he was the way he was made a big difference for Eric. "When I first learned about my profile, I understood why I have certain issues, like getting drained in groups and not liking parties. I go to Walmart and become exhausted. I'm like an energy sponge—I have no boundaries, which makes me very vulnerable."

That vulnerability often takes the form of feeling judged by others. "I'd take a seat at a company meeting, and if all the seats around me didn't fill up, I'd feel awful and alone. I figured people just didn't like me." He learned later that what caused others to avoid him had more to do with his Poor Me defense than anything else. "For an Emotional Intelligence Specialist, it's especially bad when people ignore us because we can feel people's emotions keenly and really want them to like us."

Eric was going through a nasty divorce when he learned about the Life Purpose Profile work. "I'd become so isolated, I had no one to talk with about what was going on in my marriage," he told me. "I was a family person and always worked on my house or played with my kids when I wasn't busy at my job." He had married a Charismatic Leader–Charmer, the profile that was most difficult for him to deal with in a mate because of the profile's aggressive defense. His wife was threatening to take away Eric's fourteen-year-old son, along with the home Eric bought for the family with his inheritance.

Eric had ignored what he'd experienced as his wife's abusive behavior over the years and allowed her to continue to mistreat him, a typical pattern for the Poor Me defense. He described his experience in the marriage: "I wasn't able to set any boundaries and had low self-esteem. I couldn't defend myself. I would escape when things got bad, spend my time remodeling the house instead of confronting her and dealing with her anger."

Things got better as he began to learn more about the profile system. "Understanding my wife's profile as a Charismatic Leader–Charmer helped me to see how she operates in the world—a way that is very alien to me," he said. "Before, I was at a loss and just felt abused by her, instead of trusting my instincts and knowing how to relate to her better."

Eric had other benefits, too, especially at his workplace. "The program gave me the ability to understand why people operate the way they do—not just my wife, but people at work, too," he reported. "It's helped me to accept people and not be so judgmental."

With his new awareness, Eric was able to turn things around at work with one particularly difficult co-worker who'd been causing problems for the whole team. "This guy was clearly a Team Player and not getting appreciated for doing a good job, something important for that profile. The other guys were grinding on him, talking down about him, but I connected with him and showed him some appreciation and respect. Through my example, they saw they didn't have to be so negative, and they let up on him."

Eric is a typical Emotional Intelligence Specialist, someone who cares deeply about others and values the harmony that's possible in any environment. "That compassionate part of me was always there, but I didn't know how to express it . . . or even if I *should* express it," he said. "Now I've learned that the advantage of my having so few boundaries is my great empathy for people, how much I care when I'm at my best," he said. "If I can help people . . . wow . . . that's a huge thing—it makes my life worth living."

Eric's low self-esteem has started to turn around. "Standing up in front of people to talk would have been impossible for me before. I felt so self-conscious and judged by others," he confided. "But now it's no big deal. Still, I'm a work in progress, learning why I am who I am and how I can better myself."

Eric summarized the value of his experience with the profile program: "It all begins with knowing who you are and what you're doing here," he said, "and then having some structure for being supported so you can live it. For me, I don't feel so alone anymore—my whole world is one of being free to empathize with others. I can take my mask off and be seen as someone very different from who I thought was, and I'm able to express the deeper qualities that are in me in every moment."

Embracing Your Core Soul Qualities

As an Emotional Intelligence Specialist, your core soul quality is your *ability to feel love and beauty* as an infinite well within yourself to be shared unconditionally with everyone you meet.

You see beauty in everything that is alive, knowing that love is not something that can be withheld because it exists in everything that is conscious. You are in tune with its vibrations through all of your senses and know love through its smell, taste, and touch.

Because you live in love, you know that love is as plentiful as the air you breathe, and you show love by sharing your life openly and compassionately with everyone you know. You can see love in the eyes of children, lovers, and animals. You see it in every flower and tree. You see it in the sky, stars, clouds, and sunlight. In your natural state of being, you touch the hearts of everyone you come in contact with. You enjoy others so deeply and you share your love so unconditionally that others respond by opening their hearts and becoming childlike again. Even the sick or infirm can access their deepest source of self-love and healing just by experiencing your kindness and acceptance of them.

You can be very strong emotionally and even show compassion for those who have abused you in the past. You feel the intentions of others and love even the most wayward soul. This does not mean you put up with abusive behaviors in your relationships; you are clear that you won't be able to spend time with him or her if he or she insists on being abusive or critical of you and the people you love.

Once you own your core soul qualities, you will never be a victim again. The heart cannot be hurt; only self-image and ego can. Part of your life purpose is in realizing the unity of all people, and so you let go of the childish needs of your ego. Though your heart may break ten times a day, feeling the pain of every abused or neglected person and animal on the planet, you would not trade your ability to feel that hurt for anything. That same sensitivity allows you to feel the infinite pleasure and depth of a loving kiss, a hug from a small child, and tears of appreciation from those you touch with your heart, making it all worth it.

You are like the mouse that pulls the thorn from the paw of the ferocious lion. You remain humble and have a fluid self-image, never fixating on any rigid sense of self. You do not battle or strive but leave that to the Charismatic Leader–Charmers and Knowledgeable Achievers, preferring to live in a state of nonresistance and finding simple pleasures in all of life.

YOUR GIFT TO THE WORLD is your ability to help others love and trust themselves and others. Your inner gift of love flows out to the world one person at a time as you connect with and appreciate each of them. You can tap into universal love and so remind every person you meet that their deep desire for brotherly love is safe and understood by you.

In expressing your core soul self, you offer a view of a world in which people feel that they are enough just the way they are: no more struggling, no more wars—just love and acceptance of each other.

CORE SOUL QUALITIES OF THE EMOTIONAL INTELLIGENCE SPECIALIST

- Deep compassion for all
- Embodiment of universal love
- Appreciation of beauty in everything you see
- Feeling of depth of soul in yourself and in others
- Clairsentience and empathy
- Loving-kindness that heals
- Deep affinity for young children and the elderly
- Forgiveness for all people and all past transgressions

Extraordinary Power Process: Align with Your Profile Qualities

The Extraordinary Power Process, when repeated frequently in your daily life, supports you to align with your profile to live your unique life purpose. The activities below give you a chance to use the Emotional Intelligence Specialist/Poor Me profile to focus that process (as described in more detail in *Orientation to the Program* on page 117).

FEEL: Do the inner feeling work by identifying those core soul qualities and defensive patterns from the profile description that you feel most deeply. Then choose a few to work with that are the strongest. Write in your journal about what it is like to experience that quality or pattern in your life. Think of a specific situation at work, in your relationships, or regarding your health and well-being, and ask yourself the following questions about your core as well as your defense:

❖ How do I feel—physically, emotionally, and energetically?
❖ What am I saying to myself and to others?
❖ What am I attracting to myself?
❖ What am I rejecting or avoiding?

As you write, observe the power that is available from your core soul qualities and also the self-sabotage that results from being in your defense.

CHOOSE: Make conscious choices to create your future, no longer living in the self-sabotaging, knee-jerk reality of your defense. Select one core soul quality you felt the deepest from the reading. Sit quietly and visualize living in that core quality right now: How does it change your relationships, career, health, and finances? Project your life out one, five, and ten years into the future, and explore the same question. Write about your vision in your journal. Then come back to the present moment. Choose how you will do things differently based on living in your core soul qualities.

ACT: Align your actions with your core soul qualities in your career, relationships, health, or finances. Ask: *What would my Emotional Intelligence Specialist do in this area or situation? How would he or she respond and act right now?* Commit to taking action in this moment, even if it's a symbolic gesture of giving yourself time to simply sit and meditate on your feelings for just ten minutes a day, or start a feelings journal.

REPEAT THIS PROCESS and continue to *feel*, *choose*, and *act* in this way as you discover more and more about your unique Life Purpose Profile. Soon this simple process will become your default mode, overriding the knee-jerk programming you've been trapped in for most of your life, and you will be free.

Before You Go On . . .

Record aspects of your profile that you can align with on a Personal Profile Summary chart. Turn to page 204 and fill in the first two sections on the chart from your discoveries in Step 1: *My Core Soul Qualities (for this profile)* and *My Defensive Profile Patterns*. (You will have a chance to fill in the remaining sections of the chart in Step 2 and Step 3.) Your chart can then serve as a handy reference for the work you are doing to know yourself in this new way.

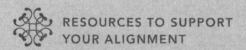

RESOURCES TO SUPPORT YOUR ALIGNMENT

The following are available at www.discoveryourpurposebook.com/members:

1. **Guided Meditation Audio Download.** *Your Secret Place.* This meditation not only helps you identify your profile but also shows you the difference between being in your core soul self and being in a defensive state.

2. **Crystal Bowls Audio Download.** Daily work with crystal bowls helps you to feel your alignment with your profile. Then you are called to your life purpose by energy resonance, not from force of mental will.

Step 2: Recognize Your Defenses

In Step 2, you use your profile as a lens to examine and then dismantle the defensive mask of your false self that is living in a virtual reality. You identify your core wounds and self-rejecting vows, as well as your negative pleasures, and you begin to replace these defensive behaviors with freeing statements and positive pleasures.

The Big Why story of my Emotional Intelligence Specialist student Rebecca illustrates how not living from your vows but being true to your core can impact the outcome of your life's most meaningful experiences.

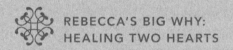

REBECCA'S BIG WHY: HEALING TWO HEARTS

Emotional Intelligence Specialist Rebecca, a thirty-six-year-old mother, entered the program because, as she told me, "it just felt right." Halfway through the first year of a three-year program, Rebecca became pregnant with her second son. She had no idea then of the terrifying ordeal she and her husband would go through in giving birth, and how being true to her life purpose would make the difference in how they would all grow from the experience.

Reflecting back on her life before she entered the program, Rebecca said, "I felt stuck and stagnant, like some piece of me was missing. Just below the surface was a sadness that I carried around with me all the time, but I didn't know why."

Rebecca knew that she was dealing with a troubled childhood in which her parents got divorced and she was sexually molested when she was very young. She had tried to find ways over the years to lessen the weight of her past. "All I could do was bury the pain deeper," she said. "For as long as I can remember, I was never comfortable in my own skin."

In the beginning of the program, Rebecca's history of difficult emotions started to unravel. "I'd always had my guard up against my feelings," she admitted. "It was as if my heart were literally outside of me, not in me, somewhere nearby but not part of me," she shared. "Then I discovered my defense in Rule Keeper, the secondary profile in which I lived most of my life. I saw how I'd vowed never to need love, never open my heart to love another fully. I judged myself as being weak for needing love."

Inside, Rebecca was in conflict: "At the same time I rejected my need for love, I longed for an intimate connection. But I was terrified of never being loved in a way that I needed to be."

Seventeen weeks into her pregnancy, Rebecca had a routine ultrasound and discovered her baby had Down syndrome. Further testing revealed severe heart defects. "The doctor told us we should consider terminating the pregnancy, because, in his opinion, our child had a one percent chance of benefiting from surgery. Even then, his quality of life would not be good."

Rebecca and her husband opted to go to term and then have heart surgery done on their son. "I could feel my inner critic, the Rule Keeper, attacking my decision, and, at the same time, my Emotional Intelligence Specialist side was feeling so much better."

In talking to other mothers with Down syndrome babies, she learned that the extra chromosome these babies carry is known as the "love chromosome," giving them the capacity to open hearts and transform all around them. "All that I'd been looking for, asking for, was love, love, love. And now I was getting this gift . . . hopefully for the rest of my life."

But further testing close to term showed the baby to have a worsening heart condition and that if he did survive, he would stop breathing as soon as the placenta separated from his mother's body. "I spent the rest of my pregnancy thinking that our baby was going to die," Rebecca confided. Because they thought they would only have a short amount of time with their son, she and her husband made the decision to give birth at home.

She delivered the baby at home with a midwife, and that's when a miracle happened. The newborn infant continued to breathe on his own. "Every time he drew another breath, I realized we weren't spending our last moments with him. I was flooded with the most incredible joy, love, and relief." Little Joseph had open-heart surgery at one week old and is scheduled for a few more surgeries to completely correct his defect.

After he was born, but before his first heart surgery, there were a few times when the tiny infant had turned blue. "I rushed to pick him up, thinking he was about to die, and as I held him in my arms, he instantly turned pink again," Rebecca told me. "I saw my love literally bring him back to life," she said, tearing up at the memory. "I know now that who I am and always have been is love. Nothing changed—I just became more of who I am. I accepted that, embraced my feelings, and both our hearts were healed."

Rebecca summed up what she had gained from the experience: "I would never have been able to go through any of this had I not understood that it is my life purpose to love—it is who I am—that missing piece I'd so longed for all my life. I experienced myself as the source of that love I thought was outside me, and now I'm able to feel love and share it freely."

Becoming Aware of Your Vows

Becoming aware of your vows—those hardwired beliefs that filter your every experience through a limited view—is critical for dismantling your defense. The source of all your vows is early life events that wounded you emotionally and energetically—your *core wounds*.

As an Emotional Intelligence Specialist, your core wounding experiences involved *emotional bonding*, *nurturance*, and *love relationships*.

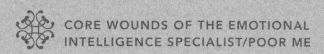

CORE WOUNDS OF THE EMOTIONAL INTELLIGENCE SPECIALIST/POOR ME

- Lack of nurturing or not being held sufficiently during infancy
- Abandonment trauma from a parent who was withholding or too busy
- Rejection by parent/caregiver, when you were told, *Just suck it up!* or threatened, *Just stop crying, or else.* Or told, *Don't be such a crybaby!*
- Realizing that no one could ever love you as much as you needed

As a result of your unique wounding experiences, you may have vowed never to abandon another the way you were abandoned. Or, having felt overwhelmed by others' pain, you vowed always to love helpless victims and not see how that can be enabling at times. You came to believe that love will solve all ills, and so you vowed always to be on the side of the poor, the young, and the old.

These vows support your Poor Me defense in which your heart bleeds for every victimized or abandoned person, and you see yourself as helpless in the faces of those who oppress you. You get overwhelmed by your feelings, so in your rejection you deny this core aspect of who you are as a sensitive person feeling his or her way through life in order to know what to do. When you don't let your feelings guide you, you become cut off from life and lost.

Vows become hardwired through unconscious statements that you say to yourself day in and day out. Read and allow yourself to feel the Vow Statements that typically form the Poor Me defense. Do you recognize any from the list on the next page that you've made in your life?

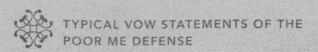

TYPICAL VOW STATEMENTS OF THE POOR ME DEFENSE

I vow always to be loving and compassionate, never mean (like my father/mother was).

I vow never to be critical and cold (like my mother/father was).

I vow never to suppress my feelings and always talk about them.

I vow always to feel what others are feeling, even if it's painful.

I vow always to hide my deep neediness and fear of being abandoned.

I vow always to be the victim of an uncaring world.

I vow always to help those who are abused and abandoned.

I vow never to ask for my needs to be met by others.

I vow to feel love only if I am loved by others.

I vow never to abandon another like I have been abandoned.

WRITE YOUR OWN: _____

Extraordinary Power Process: Release Your Vows

The activities below give you a chance to become aware of and release vows of the Poor Me defense.

FEEL: Choose those Vow Statements from the list that resonate most strongly for you. Mark them and add any of your own to the list. Then select one or more to work with in completing the following sentences:

1. A vow I made was always/never to _____

   _____.

2. How this vow is influencing my life right now: _____

   _____.

3. My self-talk that reinforces this vow: _____
_____.

EXAMPLE:

1. A vow I made was always to hide my need for love.
2. How this vow is influencing my life right now: I don't have a mate or romantic relationship. I'm shut down emotionally, always dissatisfied and alone.
3. My self-talk that reinforces this vow: "I don't need anyone to love me."

CHOOSE: Look at the vows you marked and, taking one at a time, ask yourself: *What would my life be like if I stopped honoring that vow?* Project out one, five, and ten years from now and ask: *How would not honoring that vow change my life?* Write your answers in your journal.

For example: *If I no longer honored the vow to hide my need for love, I could express myself to a partner and ask for what I want in the relationship.*

ACT: What action could you take to support your choice to no longer honor your vow? Decide to act based on your conscious choice, not a vow. Write in your journal about what happened when you did.

REPEAT THE PROCESS of *feel, choose,* and *act* every time you become aware that an ancient vow has been running your life. Vows are buried deep in your psyche, so it can take years to permanently release them. Be prepared to feel some amount of fear, guilt, and shame as you choose not to honor your vows; a vow is an unconscious promise, and you are breaking that promise when you choose to free yourself from your vows.

Before You Go On . . .

Record the Vow Statements you resonate with most strongly on your Personal Profile Summary chart on page 204. Fill in the section for *My Vow Statements* with statements from the list or some of your own.

Freedom Statements

Replace your Vow Statements with Freedom Statements, which are the solutions to your vows. Freedom Statements call forth your core soul qualities and support you to increasingly choose more consciously in every moment. Every time you consciously choose a Freedom Statement over a vow, you get back energy and open yourself to ever-growing life rather than stagnating as a wounded victim.

Use Freedom Statements as a bridge out of defense and onto the path of your truth. The following list offers you a variety of statements, but you can always add your own.

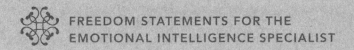

FREEDOM STATEMENTS FOR THE EMOTIONAL INTELLIGENCE SPECIALIST

I fully embody my feelings, love, and compassion.
I am open to being sensual and romantic; I feel intimacy through every cell in my body.
I effortlessly teach love, reverence, and forgiveness to each person I touch.
I am open to an infinite well of love filling me from deep within my soul that guides me as my life purpose.
I am a source of love and I share it effortlessly.
I see and honor the heart in every person I meet.

My power in the world is my amazing ability to embrace all of life and all people with nonresistance and gentle and loving acceptance.

I am open to asking for my needs to be met and saying, "I want what I want!"

I feel my guidance and direct connection to the creator through subtle feelings that most people don't even notice.

I am open to deserving love, simply because I exist.

WRITE YOUR OWN: _____

Extraordinary Power Process:
Become Free of Your Vows

The activities below give you a chance to replace your vows with Freedom Statements and live from your Emotional Intelligence Specialist soul qualities rather than your Poor Me defense.

FEEL: Read the list of Freedom Statements above, speaking each one aloud. Let yourself feel their truth as you sit quietly after speaking them. Notice those you may want to deny and then repeat those statements until you no longer have a negative reaction to them. Notice also which statements register strongly as *Yes, that's me!* Write those Freedom Statements in your journal.

CHOOSE: Speak your Freedom Statements out loud as often as possible to bring conscious choice to your vow-driven, knee-jerk defensive reactions. Tell others your Freedom Statements so that they can see your truth and support you in embodying it. Especially as an Emotional Intelligence Specialist, you will find that by speaking the words of love over and over, your feelings of being overwhelmed fade and begin to be replaced by the realization that your softness is a rare power on earth indeed.

Sit and inquire within about what your life will be like one, five, and ten years from now as you embody the truth in your Freedom Statements.

ACT: Explore how you would act differently in key areas of your life if your vows were replaced by Freedom Statements. Choose one action you can take that aligns you with the truth of your Freedom Statement, not your vow, and do it!

REPEAT THE PROCESS of *feel*, *choose*, and *act* often when dealing with your life's circumstances. You'll notice how your vow-driven actions begin to fade and you increasingly make choices and act based in the present of who you truly are rather than the past of your false and defended self.

Before You Go On . . .

Record the Freedom Statements you have chosen to replace your vows on the Personal Profile Summary chart on page 204. Fill in the section for *My Freedom Statements*.

Your Negative Pleasures

Living from your core soul qualities, not your vows, will empower you to embrace your life purpose. But without confronting your *negative pleasures*, real freedom will never be yours. Negative pleasures—those habits and behaviors you know you shouldn't do (or *don't* do but know you should!) yet justify in order to feel good about yourself—must be confronted and left behind if you are going to live your authentic purpose.

In the Poor Me defense, a common negative pleasure is feeling self-righteous about being the most emotional, sensitive, and loving person in any situation. This, in turn, justifies seeing life as emotionally overwhelming, since you are the only one who can feel how truly mean and callous other people are. Always being good and loving in a world of aggressive people can also lead to the negative pleasure of self-medication to numb the pain. This can set you up to become addicted to emotion-numbing substances that you justify because of "unmanageable" feelings of sadness, anger, or jealousy.

Another negative pleasure you may need to acknowledge is that you manipulate others with your emotions. For example, if someone around you is loud and boisterous, you take it so personally that you cringe or cry to make that person feel guilty, acting passive-aggressively in an attempt to force them to quiet down. A variation on this pattern is when you tell others or your children how much they drain you, playing the victim card as a way to stop them from saying or doing things that upset you or bother you.

The following list includes typical negative pleasures of the Poor Me defense. Feel free to add your own.

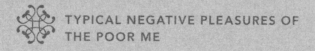
TYPICAL NEGATIVE PLEASURES OF THE POOR ME

Self-pity, dwelling on feelings of being unloved
Dramatizing feelings, good and bad, and regaling others with your latest dramas
Feeling superior to others who you judge as "numb"
Judging others as heartless and cruel
Having addictions to alcohol, smoking, food, or controlling loved ones emotionally

Talking on and on about your feelings to avoid taking action on
  those feelings
Complaining about being overtired, too emotional, and unloved
Pressuring others to express their feelings even if they don't feel
  safe
Avoiding public events and shopping malls so you don't have to
  worry about your appearance
Telling others that they drain you

WRITE YOUR OWN: _____

Extraordinary Power Process:
Diminish Your Negative Pleasures

The activities below give you a chance to become aware of your negative pleasures. The key to diminishing your negative pleasures is to become conscious of the poor substitutes they are for the real pleasures you could be having in your life.

FEEL: As you read the list of negative pleasures for the Poor Me defense, let yourself feel which ones resonate deeply to evoke *Yes, that's me!* Mark those and write them in your journal.

CHOOSE: Choose one negative pleasure from the list that you identified and are willing to let go of. Sit with all the pain that this behavior has caused you and others to date. Then visualize your life projected out ten years from now. If you don't change that behavior, what positive pleasure will it cost you?

To help you do this, fill in the following:

1. A negative pleasure that I have in my life is _____
_____.

2. Having that negative pleasure in my life costs me now and in the future: _____.

EXAMPLE:

1. A negative pleasure I have in my life is dwelling on self-pity when feeling unloved.
2. Having this negative pleasure costs me the energy I could use to love myself and others. It is keeping me trapped in a vicious cycle of misery and isolation and not getting what I really want. Ten years from now my health will be permanently affected and I will have done irreparable damage to my relationships.

Now write about a *positive pleasure*, one that comes from living in your core, and explain how experiencing that pleasure might look in your life. For example: *If I knew myself as always being filled with love, I would never feel unloved again. I could focus on giving the love I have to others.*

ACT: Having chosen a negative pleasure you are ready to let go of, the next time it comes up in your life, ask yourself: *What positive pleasure am I missing as I indulge this negative one? How would my Emotional Intelligence Specialist respond in this situation?* Then take action in accordance with your answer.

REPEAT THIS PROCESS OFTEN. As your negative pleasures become increasingly noticeable, see them as behaviors based on fears that you are now ready to grow out of. Don't beat yourself up. Go slow, get support, and let each negative pleasure go, one at a time. You will start to experience positive pleasures that come from accepting your life and the people in it. Soon, the unconscious habits and behaviors you've been substituting for real pleasure will no longer seem as attractive.

Every negative pleasure you successfully let go of allows you to bring back into your life all of the wasted energy that went into that defense. With that energy you can make powerful choices to live your life as a creative presence.

Before You Go On . . .

Record your negative pleasures on your Personal Profile Summary chart on page 204. Fill in the section for *My Favorite Negative Pleasures*.

In Transition . . .

As you transition out of the Poor Me defense and into your core self, you may find yourself stuck in frustrating old patterns. Your defenses have been supporting you to be someone you are not, or to be only half of who you truly are. Now newly aware of your defenses, you can make choices and set goals to act differently.

For the Emotional Intelligence Specialist, a good goal is to let those who you believe have not loved you enough know how much you appreciate their love.

ACTIVITY: Choose a family member, such as your spouse, grown child, or either of your parents. It could also be a lover or a friend. Feel in every cell of your body the truth of how much that person loves you. Then choose to tell that person you can feel his or her love, and that it feels good. See in your imagination how that person becomes more open in the relationship. Act by sharing with that person how much you appreciate the love. Say it from the place deep inside you where you know it to be true. Write in your journal about your experience and the outcome of your having taken that action.

Repeat this process with anyone who you believe doesn't love you enough. Watch your world of relationships transform as you accept the love they can give, which, in turn, lets them feel safer in giving even more.

RESOURCES TO SUPPORT YOUR TRANSITION

1. **Guided Meditation Audio Download.** *Calling Back Your Spirit* (available at www.discoveryourpurposebook.com/members).

2. **Recommended Reading List**
   - *Getting the Love You Want*, by Harville Hendrix
   - *Soul Mates*, by Thomas Moore
   - *The Mastery of Love*, by Don Miguel Ruiz
   - *Emotional Intelligence*, by Daniel Goleman
   - *Enchanted Love*, by Marianne Williamson

Step 3: Live Your Life Purpose

Having begun the process of dismantling your defenses in Step 2, you are now ready to integrate your profile's unique higher- and lower-self qualities. As you become less conflicted, and more whole and balanced, you can make choices and take courageous actions in your life, not just react automatically from your ancient vows. You are also able to use the

Law of Attraction to attract what best supports your unique life purpose as you create and live an extraordinary life.

Your Shadow: Lower- and Higher-Self Traits

Your shadow is made up of traits that you have rejected by vowing *always* or *never* to be or do something. Those traits can be seen as aspects of your higher self and your lower self. As you identify rejected higher- and lower-self traits, you can begin to accept and integrate them, and so achieve a state of inner balance and wholeness. Fully integrating your shadow allows your defensive mask to dissolve and your true core soul self to emerge.

The following chart contains a list of the lower- and higher-self traits *in matched pairs* that you must own and integrate to fully live your life purpose as an Emotional Intelligence Specialist.

LOWER- AND HIGHER-SELF TRAITS FOR EMOTIONAL INTELLIGENCE SPECIALISTS	
LOWER-SELF TRAITS	**HIGHER-SELF TRAITS**
Obsessively reactive	Acutely sensitive to environmental change
Codependent	Unconditionally loving
Needy	Guided by a deep desire for oneness
Demanding	Asking for your needs with no expectations
Helpless	Grounded in being your own inner resource of love
Emotionally excessive	Emotionally moved by all of life
Unstable	Flowing with changes in each moment, holding to nothing
Powerless	Peaceful and loving

Selfish	Nurturing and tender
Self-righteous victim	Unconditionally loving and supportive of those in need
Narcissistic	Honoring your unique quality of love and sharing it freely
Manipulative	Fearless in the face of emotional turmoil
Drama king/queen	Authentically expressing the fullness of emotions
Pathetic	Gentle and soft-spoken
Pollyanna	Wondrously innocent and open
Irrational	Grounded in your soul's guidance
Submissive	Spiritually surrendered
Self-absorbed	In open communion with all
Emotionally overwhelmed	Flowing with the universe
Empty, drained	Filled with love from within

Extraordinary Power Process: Integrate Your Shadow

The activities below give you a chance to integrate your shadow (rejected traits) with your higher-self light.

FEEL: As you read the list of matched-pair lower-/higher-self traits, reach deep into yourself to feel the full range of your raw, lower self at one end and your exalted, higher self at the other. Both are within you to varying degrees. Your raw power and personal needs are found in your lower-self traits, while how you consciously use that power and fulfill those needs is in your higher-self traits. When you can own both in any moment and still choose your higher-self traits, then everything you do will be aligned with your life purpose.

Put a check mark next to the lower- and higher-self traits you recognize as ones you exhibit. Also notice traits that elicit a powerful negative reaction and check them, too. These are traits you have rejected in yourself or in others. (In rejecting lower-self traits, you say to yourself, *I'd never do that—it's too negative, mean, or evil*; while in rejecting higher-self traits, you say, *I could never do that—it's too perfect, saintly, or godlike.*)

CAUTION: No higher-self trait can exist without the lower-self trait alongside it. To be whole and balanced, you must be conscious of both within you. Selecting only those traits you like will send you back to your vow-created life where only half of you exists.

Using your strongest traits checked, complete these statements for each:

1. A lower-/higher-self trait that I see as strong in me is
   _____.

2. My greatest fear of owning that trait is _____
   _____.

EXAMPLE:

1. A lower-self trait that I see as strong in me is being too easily emotionally overwhelmed.
2. My greatest fear of owning that trait is that others will perceive me as weak, and I will see myself as weak and helpless against a cold world.

AND:

1. A higher-self trait that is the partner to my lower-self trait is "flowing with the universe" and all the feelings and passions that go with it.

2. My greatest fear of owning that trait is that my being easy-going and full of love, acceptance, and happiness will be perceived as condoning others' bad behavior. Or, if I truly show how I feel in any moment, I might get rejected or abandoned.

CHOOSE: Now work with one set of lower- and higher-self traits that you identified as not being fully owned in their full range. Ask how your life would be different if you owned both higher- and lower-self traits equally, able to accept either freely but choosing the higher-self quality.

Visualize your life up to now and see how damaging it has been to express the lower-self trait unconsciously. Also feel how you have wanted to express the higher-self trait more often but don't, since the lower-self trait cannot be resolved. Now project out this pattern of behavior one, five, and ten years into the future and see what your life looks like with just this one conflict within you.

What would happen if you were able to embrace both at all times, rejecting neither, as part of your life purpose? Notice that if you did not stand in such judgment and fear of being who you actually are in your life and relationships one, five, and ten years into the future, you would instead reveal your true power and purpose.

For example: *If I accepted that I am easily overwhelmed by life, I would be able to accept and love my sensitivity and have the ultimate pleasure of living as very few can. This, I know, will be my inspirational message to those in the world who, like me, feel that they should not be overwhelmed by life and reject their own sensitivity.*

ACT: Take actions that align with your new state of inner balance and wholeness. Commit to one action you will take that reflects your new self-acceptance, and then do it. Write in your journal about what happened when you did.

REPEAT THE PROCESS! Once you've worked with one pair of higher- and lower-self trait in this way, repeat the process, covering more traits in both lists. Accepting both higher and lower selves as the whole of who you are is the most powerful spiritual work you can do.

Before You Go On . . .

Turn to page 204 and fill in the section for *Lower- and Higher-Self Traits* on your Personal Profile Summary chart.

Living Courageously

Living your life purpose means speaking and acting fearlessly from your core soul self. To remain in that state, you will need to step out of your comfort zone often and take the road less traveled, leaping over obstacles in your way. The following are some ways you as an Emotional Intelligence Specialist can do that.

Accept your need to merge deeply with the people you love.

You came into the world in a state of oneness, and your purpose is to bring to others the awareness that we are all connected in a deeply spiritual way. The closest thing human beings can do to experience universal oneness is to feel love, and that is what you help everyone do.

Overcome your tendency to isolate and be alone.

Merging in oneness is uncomfortable and foreign for all the other profiles, which means that you are always going to want a deeper connection in a relationship than your partner can give (unless your partner is also an Emotional Intelligence Specialist). You will have to accept this and recognize that you are the source of the love you long for, and no one person can ever give it to you.

Openly express your sensitivity.

You naturally feel your oneness with others, but admitting your sensitive nature can be seen as a form of weakness to be exploited and negated by others, especially if you are a male. Hiding your sensitivity and being obsessed with the injustice of it all is your Poor Me's way of distracting you from your living truth.

Recognize your true power.

Your capacity to connect from your heart and soul with others makes you among the most powerful people on earth. Until you can feel proud to be a "feeler" and admit that what you truly want is an emotional depth that frightens most people, you will stay in denial and defense. Recognize the power of your love in order to live fully in your core.

Before You Go On . . .

Turn to page 204 and fill in the section for *Actions to Take for Living Courageously* on your Personal Profile Summary chart.

Speak Your Truth

To remain in your Emotional Intelligence Specialist core, you must be willing to speak your truth to others, especially to those with whom you are in a close relationship. Practice by reading each of the Essential Word Statements below, visualizing that you are speaking directly to someone you love and feeling your words deeply as you read them.

Make a commitment to speak these essential words—not the automatic words dictated by your vows and defenses—to an important person in your life. Then act to call, write, or speak with that important person to share your truth.

ESSENTIAL WORDS FOR EMOTIONAL INTELLIGENCE SPECIALISTS TO SPEAK

- I love you, but you need to know that sometimes I may desire a union with you that is so deep that I cannot tell where I end and you begin.
- My greatest fear is that when I share my deepest needs for love with you in each moment, you will feel that it is too much and abandon me, and I will be alone in my need for your love.
- Please don't expect me to "toughen up" and hold back on my tears of joy or tears of hurt. I don't seem to be able to close my heart. Please honor this quality in me as I have been judged harshly for this my entire life.
- I know I am childlike and vulnerable, but I do not need protecting. Please just be with me in this amazing Technicolor life of mine, where I am constantly wide-eyed and in awe.

Before You Go On . . .

Turn to page 204 and fill in the section for *Speaking Your Truth* on your Personal Profile Summary chart.

The Law of Attraction

According to the Law of Attraction, like attracts like. It follows that you will always attract people and situations that are like you. As your alignment with your life purpose grows, your internal magnet for attracting who and what you want in your life is strengthened. If you are not aligned with your life purpose, no amount of visualizing will help you achieve your desires—in spite of what popular culture tells you about how constant visualizing will bring you what you want.

For example, as an Emotional Intelligence Specialist not congruent but stuck in the Poor Me defense, you love others but often with conditions, driven by your vow of *I'll always love you only if you love me back.* As a result, you only attract love into your life that comes with conditions. Similarly, if you live from the stance of being needy and empty, you only attract other needy and empty people, or people who are so dissociated, their presence in your life proves that your needs can never be fulfilled.

Only when you *are* love, having integrated all aspects of yourself, and are whole and complete within yourself, can you attract real love. Love comes from within us, and we are all connected to the source of infinite love, but some people radiate the heart vibration to remind us that we must unlock what we already have. Emotional Intelligence Specialists are the love bringers by innately being that love, not by anything they do or have.

ACTIVITY: EXPLORE THE GAP. The gap is the space between where you are now and where you know you will be when you fully embody your core soul profile qualities and live your life purpose. Looking in areas of life such as health, relationships, finances, and career or job, inquire about the following:

❖ What am I attracting in my life right now from living in my defenses?
❖ What do I want to attract in my life from living in my core soul self?

Are you attracting what supports your life purpose or what keeps you stuck in your defense? How can you act from your core soul qualities and not your defenses to close that gap and attract what you want to support your life purpose? Write your responses in your journal.

Before You Go On . . .

Turn to page 204 and fill in the section for *Law of Attraction* on your Personal Profile Summary chart.

Extraordinary Power Process: Your Personal Profile Summary Chart

Your Personal Profile Summary chart now holds what you have learned about yourself from the Emotional Intelligence Specialist Profile, either as your primary or your secondary Life Purpose Profile.

Once you have completed your charts for both primary and secondary profiles, use them as a tool to support you in living your life purpose. Follow the Extraordinary Power Process of *feel*, *choose*, and *act* as you refer to each section you've filled in on your chart:

1. Feel: Do the inner feeling work—don't just think.
2. Choose: Make conscious choices—don't automatically react based on your vows.
3. Act: Align your actions with your profile's core soul qualities—not with your defenses—to live your truth.

When you repeat this sequence as often as possible throughout your day, applying it to everything you do, then everything you do reveals the mystery of who you are rather than reinforcing who you already think you are. *Feeling, choosing,* and *acting* in accordance with your profile gives you access to your extraordinary power so you can effortlessly manifest your life purpose and live it in every area of your life.

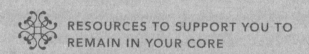 RESOURCES TO SUPPORT YOU TO REMAIN IN YOUR CORE

1. **Guided Meditation Audio Download.** *Your Subpersonalities.* Explore your higher- and lower-self traits through a guided meditation, available at www.discoveryourpurposebook.com/members.

2. **Bioenergetic Exercises for the Emotional Intelligence Specialist,** available on pages 205–206 and also on the same website.

Emotional Intelligence Specialist/Poor Me
PERSONAL PROFILE SUMMARY

Profile	☐ This is my PRIMARY PROFILE ☐ This is my SECONDARY PROFILE ☐ This is my THIRD, FOURTH, or FIFTH PROFILE
My Core Soul Qualities (for this profile)	1 _____ 2 _____
My Defensive Profile Patterns	1 _____ 2 _____
My Vow Statements (How I self-sabotage)	1 _____ 2 _____ 3 _____
My Freedom Statements (Solutions to my Vow Statements)	I am open to _____ I am open to _____ I am open to _____
My Favorite Negative Pleasures (How I self-sabotage)	Something I do that I shouldn't do but get pleasure from: _____ Something I get pleasure from not doing that I know I should do: _____
Lower- and Higher-Self Traits (matched pairs)	Lower: Higher: 1 _____ / _____ 2 _____ / _____
Actions to take for living courageously from your profile	1 _____ 2 _____
Speaking Your Truth (ESSENTIAL WORDS you must say to others)	1 _____ 2 _____
Law of Attraction (People, situations, etc. that I am attracting)	In defense, I attract _____ In my core, I attract _____

BIOENERGETIC EXERCISES FOR THE EMOTIONAL INTELLIGENCE SPECIALIST

Yoga, especially the Sun Salutation, is an excellent form of exercise for Emotional Intelligence Specialists. In addition, practicing the following emotional containment exercises can help you stop judging your feelings so you can "go for the ride," not put on the brakes, when feelings come up.

EXERCISE #1: HOLD THAT FEELING. Practice holding an emotion, such as sadness, elation, or fear, as it comes up during your day. Count to ten before judging or trying to change it. Let your deepest feelings build within you and notice your tendency to cry or talk about it in order to avoid whatever the emotion is calling you to do, such as asking for a need to be met or speaking your truth in some way.

EXERCISE #2: EMOTIONAL WORKOUT. Lie on a mat or on your bed and practice feeling the following emotions as deeply as you can: anger (clenching every muscle), fear (trembling), longing (reaching for a mother's love that is not there), sadness (collapse). Take a few minutes to feel those negative emotions when you express them. Then practice feeling alive (expanded and full of energy), love (radiating warmth), intimacy (sacred connection and union), power (your flowing energy that inspires others). At first when you do these exercises you will need to remember events that trigger these emotions. After you have mastered them, you just feel them for what they are and add to the list more complex emotions.

EXERCISE #3: HAVE A "TANTRUM." Lie on your back on a bed or couch and use your legs and arms to kick or hit while letting out angry words or screams. Notice how difficult it is to sustain energy and how easily you tire and go out of your body or into fear that you have committed a violent or unloving act.

EXERCISE #4: LET GO OF "IT'S JUST NOT ENOUGH!" Stand your ground and stamp your feet to feel your anger. This will help you acknowledge that you are misled in thinking that you never get what you need. Accepting that allows you to let go of that persistent complaint and negative pleasure: *It's just not enough!*

EXERCISE #5: EXTENDED HUG. Hold a partner in a standing hug. Feel love for the other person and relax fully.

CHAPTER 9

Profile #3: Team Player/People Pleaser

THE TEAM PLAYER

with People Pleaser defense

Welcome to the Team Player profile and its defense, the People Pleaser. You will find valuable information and activities here to help you access your extraordinary power to embody your life purpose.

If this is your secondary or other profile, or the profile of someone in your life, you can use what you learn to deepen your understanding of yourself and others.

 TEAM PLAYERS WE ALL KNOW

Historical: The silent supporters of every titleholder or headliner in history who remained in the background while others took the limelight. These often unsung heroes are the mothers, best friends, and loyal employees who showed up on time, stayed late, and always had a smile on their face. Florence Nightingale is one example, but many more go unnamed.

Contemporary: Ethel Kennedy, wife of Bobby; Mata Amritanandamayi (Amma, the Hindu "Hugging Saint"). Also actors in supporting roles, such as Kevin James as Doug Heffernan on *The King of Queens*, Alan Hale Jr. as the Skipper on *Gilligan's Island*, Charles Durning as the suitor of Dustin Hoffman's character in *Tootsie*, John Goodman as Dan Conner on *Roseanne*, Dom DeLuise as sidekick to Burt Reynolds in several '70s and '80s movies, Florence Henderson as Carol Brady in *The Brady Bunch*, Vivian Vance as Ethel in *The Lucy Show*, and Debra Jo Rupp as Kitty Forman in *That '70s Show*.

Step 1: Align with Your Profile

In this first step of the program, you learn all about your profile, including those core soul qualities that support you to live in your life purpose, as well as the defenses that cause you to sabotage your efforts. The Big Why story of Team Player Tim demonstrates how knowing your life purpose allows you to live a more authentic and empowered life.

About Your Profile

What follows is a general description of your profile, including how it looks when you are in defense as the People Pleaser. You will take a closer look at your relationships, your career or job, how you handle money, and your physical and energetic aspects.

GENERAL DESCRIPTION. As a Team Player, you are a compassionate and nurturing individual. You are capable of consistently putting your own needs aside in order to attend to the needs of those with whom you are in a relationship. Most people have a desire to support and care for others, but the Team Player has a capacity for compassion beyond that of any in the other profiles.

When not in defense as People Pleasers, Team Players are the glue that holds families and society together. Your level of social intelligence makes you readily accepted in any group; you reach out and connect in many ways.

You have a warm, nurturing energy, and may be known as a great hugger. You have the ability to be a devoted and loyal friend to everyone you meet. Befriending, supporting, and talking to others come so naturally to you that many people consider you their best friend.

In your highest potential, you can mother the world, whether you are female or male. As someone with such deep compassion and the ability to feel what others need, you are a natural healer. When you look into the eyes of others, they know you accept them unconditionally. You see the best in others, even when they are in defense, and you are often less conscious of your own good qualities.

You feel most comfortable in groups and love family get-togethers, team meetings, class reunions, parties, and the like. There are so many people in your life whom you appreciate deeply, you feel you never have time to connect with them all individually. In group gatherings, you go from person to person, connecting with each and finding out how they are doing in their lives. You have a great interest and respect for other people's journeys in life, and even if there are fifty people at a party, you will remember the details of what is going on in their families, marriages, jobs, and so on, and you will remember their children's names and birth dates.

Like the Emotional Intelligence Specialist, the profile closest to the Team Player, you feel for others deeply, but the difference is that you are often not in touch with your own feelings. Without an awareness of your own feelings, you must rely on the input of other people to help you understand how you are feeling. You are unlikely to come up with original ideas for your life until you first find out what others need; only then do you know your own purpose.

In your core, you are highly socially intelligent and you are fulfilled by having enjoyable and intimate relationships. You are not wired to have independent desires outside of relationships, as people in other profiles do. Because you discover who you are in relationships, you love to constantly expand your friend base, befriending everyone you meet.

IN PEOPLE PLEASER DEFENSE, you find yourself in self-sabotaging patterns that involve getting lost in your relationships, especially with those who mean the most to you, because you give more than you get in return. Furthermore, you measure your self-worth by how much you are doing for others and how much they appreciate what you do for them, leaving you feeling exhausted, unappreciated, and resentful.

You have a difficult time saying no in any relationship because you are never quite committed to the yes of your own personal needs. You would rather cancel your own plans than inconvenience anyone else. You have a hard time setting any personal boundaries and often feel like a victim with no choices in own your life.

Even though you are a wonderful friend to others, you would prefer more alone time because it is so exhausting to say yes to everyone. As you get older, you end up becoming more of a caretaker for your family and parents, rarely enjoying your time with them. *When do I get to live my life?* becomes a constant refrain. The idea of having more "takers" in your life makes you think you need to get away from people and spend more time on your own. But it's only those friends who take more than they give that you want to avoid, yet avoiding them would mean setting firm boundaries, which is your greatest challenge.

Your hope is always that if you love and support others, they, in turn, will do the same for you. You want to please the important people in your life; otherwise, you fear you'll lose your loving connection to them. But you sacrifice your individuality and your own needs to support these relationships. Over time, you become resentful and angry and start to withdraw from people, preferring to go solo in your life. However, when you withdraw from people, you lose your connection to your life purpose.

You often do things for others, even when they don't ask, and burn yourself out in the process. Or you complain and get resentful, feeling like a slave or martyr and saying to yourself, *but I have to . . .* Your defensive pattern is to feel like a slave to your life and the people in it rather than an active participant. You say yes to more obligations than you can handle and never finish your own to-do list without feeling the guilt or shame of neglecting others. This pattern of always putting others' needs before your own leaves you feeling trapped and exhausted much of the time. You can become brooding and resentful, hoping that others treat you as well as you've treated them.

You have a general dislike of being at the center of attention and often feel humiliated when you have to speak in public or stand up for yourself. Your low self-esteem may be derived from a lifetime of feeling like your efforts are taken for granted. You know innately that you are here to love and support others but get caught in the illusion that only the service you provide for others makes you valuable; you feel that if you stop serving others, you will have no value. As a result, you are always doing good things for others, even unappreciative people.

If you are in People Pleaser defense, you struggle with humiliation and anger as the primary negative forces in your life. You fear being humiliated and rejected if you stand up for what you want, but at the same time you also feel humiliated by complying with others' demands in order to keep peace in the relationship. You live between a rock and a hard place, and grow bitter at being caught in such a bind.

PRIMARY MATE AND SOCIAL RELATIONSHIPS. Team Players often find the Charismatic Leader–Charmer/Enforcer-Seducer as a primary mate. Being appreciated for all you do by a Charismatic Leader–Charmer partner makes you feel validated. Your natural compassion also makes the more volatile Charismatic Leader–Charmer feel unconditionally loved, giving them the confidence to trust in themselves and in the goodness that is within all people. Together, you make a powerful team, as exemplified by a successful politician who tirelessly campaigns while being supported by a loyal partner who loves him or her even in defeat. Ethel Kennedy provided that support both before and after Senator Robert Kennedy was killed; she was the glue that held her family together after the tragic death of her husband.

In defense, however, you self-sabotage by letting your Enforcer-Seducer spouse dictate your life, relinquishing any sense of self or personal power. You rarely end a relationship but grumble and hate that your life is not your own. You create excuses for your partner's inexcusable behavior by saying things like, *Oh, he's Italian, so that's how he learned to let off steam—he doesn't really mean it.* Or the excuse might be *Oh, she drinks and gets that way because of the terrible traumas she experienced in her childhood.* In this way, you may enable others in their detrimental behavior rather than push them to seek counseling or other help.

You may also be under the illusion that there are no relationships in which you will ever be fulfilled. Balanced, fifty-fifty, give-and-take relationships are not an option; you unconsciously set up all your relationships to be thirty-seventy, by giving more and asking for less, and then blaming your partner for victimizing you.

If you are not married, you have probably gotten into a situation where the person you care for is sick or an irresponsible substance abuser who never seems to improve. You feel trapped in the relationship because they need you.

CAREER OR JOB. You tend to do work that serves others, whether as a social worker, nanny, massage therapist, counselor, business consultant, or health attendant. You are the smiling face behind the counter in the store, the nurse who treats everyone with love and integrity, the beloved spouse who holds a family together so they can be their best. You could be a volunteer sports coach or a professional mediator, resolving conflicts and serving as an advocate for those who need help.

The one job you are not cut out to do is to be your own boss. You have a hard time making the choices necessary to keep a business afloat because your allegiance is solely to your clients. Team Player business owners aren't able to say no to clients and try to be everything to everyone. It is best to go into business with a Charismatic Leader–Charmer or Knowledgeable Achiever partner who can handle the tough money and service decisions.

You are dedicated and unafraid to work by the sweat of your brow, and you are not driven by personal ego. If there is a family business, you find your place in it and happily support it. You are a worker at heart and rarely will be without some kind of job. As long as you feel that you are contributing and that there is a sense of camaraderie, you are happy doing just about anything.

You are the heart and soul of any organization, since you are able to defuse volatile situations between co-workers, and you are happy to do extra work if you feel it is supportive of the business and the staff. You love your customers and the staff equally, and get any job done with a smile. You work well as a team player, not demanding the spotlight, but deeply recognizing your importance in helping your team succeed.

In defense, you self-sabotage by taking on a job that demands that you put yourself second in every situation, and you begrudgingly do so. You are constantly working and are never able to rest. Even if you are at home raising children, you may have a part-time job or do volunteer work to keep every minute of the day filled with some sort of service work. Then you wonder, *When is it ever going to be my turn to try yoga, treat myself, or go on a vacation?* You will often tell others that you are fine, but really you are resentful and tired, and simply don't want to burden them with your troubles.

HOW YOU HANDLE MONEY. As a Team Player, you generally don't focus on money or material security. Materialism goes against every fiber of your being. You have a hard time valuing your services, especially when you are doing business with friends. Friendship is always more important than remuneration, and so you will often accept less than you deserve.

Your inner mantra is: *I could never put a price on making someone else happy.* Even when others offer to pay you for help, you say, "No, you can pay me next time," but next time never comes. You value relationships over material wealth.

Because you are unconscious of this dynamic, you don't understand why you never seem to have enough money. But as you come into your core, that dynamic shifts, and you see that letting others pay you is a gift to them because it allows them to value your services, often in the only way they know how.

Your relationship with material possessions is such that you often have a hard time with clutter—you don't feel you have the right to decide what should be kept or thrown away. You see money the same

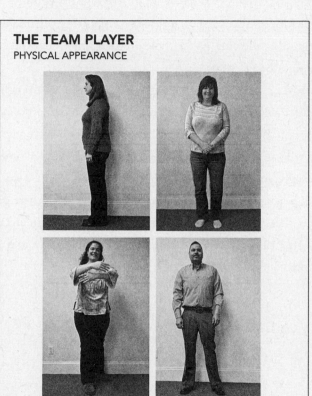

THE TEAM PLAYER
PHYSICAL APPEARANCE

When you are visually assessing a person's profile, notice that Team Players/People Pleasers carry their energy in the belly and heart areas, making them seem warm and inviting. They may also be carrying extra weight in those areas of the body. Team Players give great hugs and have broad, open faces, smiling easily when they greet you. When you talk with them, their eyes rarely stray, showing how much they are connected and care about you. These people have huge hearts, giving you the feeling that they are there for you, even more than they are for themselves. The Team Players' most salient traits are their solidly grounded compassion and attentiveness, making you feel deeply cared for by them as their very best friend.

way. Even if you earned it, it immediately goes into the family account, where it is no longer yours to spend. Or you become a hoarder, stashing money away but having no idea how much you have.

PHYSICAL AND ENERGETIC ASPECTS. Energetically, you are the most solid and stalwart of all the profiles. Your energy is dense, warm, and powerful but slow and plodding in moving through life. You may have a stocky body and short muscles, supporting an orientation to action but also allowing you to hold in your emotions when you feel they are unsafe to express.

With your strong, tight constitution, you have a hard time releasing negative energy from feeling controlled or underappreciated. Letting off steam could mean hurting others' feelings, which is not something you are willing to do. As a result, your negative energy comes out in passive-aggressive behavior. *After all I do for you, how dare you treat me this way!* is your common response. It is only when others get angry with you that you feel justified in your own anger, an unconscious strategy that often backfires because it creates conflict and distance from those you love most.

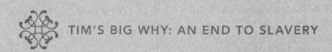

TIM'S BIG WHY: AN END TO SLAVERY

Tim, a forty-four-year-old bank teller, came to see me on referral from a friend.

"My friend tells me I need to deal with my anger," he said in our first session and then paused for a moment. "But my biggest problem is that I don't have any!" I chuckled at his joke but also recognized an early clue about his profile. The Team Player tends to stuff anger and brood with resentment instead of expressing angry feelings. "I need to learn to say no to all the people in my life that I've somehow agreed to support," he said.

As our session went on, Tim revealed his deeper concerns: "I used to be a great guy, easygoing, had great friends, but now I'm resentful all the time. All I want is one free moment to do what *I* want to do." When I asked him what he wanted to do, he gave me a blank stare and said, "I don't know . . . I've never had enough time to even think about it. But it's *gotta* be something that keeps all those demanding people out of my life."

When I told him that he needed more, not fewer, people in his life, he thought I was crazy. I explained that, instead of others choosing him to be in their lives, he needed to choose people who actually appreciated him and his giving nature. As I told him more about his Team Player profile and the People Pleaser defense, he could see how his relationships with people had him in a downward spiral of prioritizing their needs over his.

Tim looked back to his not-so-distant past when he'd enjoyed people and had many friends. Now he was taking care of everyone he knew instead of enjoying them as friends. He grew up not having any needs because, he told me, "My parents weren't going to give me what I wanted anyway, so why bother? It was their way or no way." He went on. "Later in life, I figured that by not expressing any personal needs, I was being nicer to my friends—pleasing them as I'd pleased my parents."

Of course, Tim was a "giver," so the "takers" monopolized all his time and energy. He made the mistake of assuming that, if he was available to others, they would eventually return the favor. But even at his age, he was living in denial of how others can be selfish. "Maybe I should be a bit more selfish myself," he told me.

In his sessions doing the profile work, Tim discovered the defensive pattern he was stuck in: telling people he didn't need anything from them and then being angry when they didn't give him what he needed. Tim realized that he loved doing kind things for others, but in his enthusiasm, he'd set up one-way relationships—his energy was always going out and away from him. He'd never considered that letting others know what his needs were could be a gift to them—he was denying others the gift of giving that he so enjoyed.

"The lesson I've learned," he told me, "is that having needs and expressing them lets your partner or friend see the real you, and that helps you both discover whether you have a compatible relationship." He was learning that expressing needs reveals the deeper aspects of a person. He added, "Any relationship in which one person only has needs and the other takes on the job of filling those needs is not really a relationship—it's a form of slavery."

Tim came to see me several times, each time reporting how he'd made peace in many of his problem relationships by telling friends and family members more of what he wanted in the relationship. "I looked at all the places I was resentful, like when my friend called me over to drive her to the doctor's. She was never ready on time and would keep me waiting and wasting my time. It was hard at first, but I started asking her to be ready when I arrived . . . that it meant she valued me for the favor I was doing. She agreed, and now we have a friendship that is more honest, even more fun. I don't feel like her chauffeur but like a real friend."

Tim had started slowly with his more casual friends and moved on to expressing his needs to more and more of the people in his life, including one infirm older relative who had come to rely on him as a free caretaker and dishwasher. In a frank conversation, Tim told his relative that he needed to be asked in advance to do certain chores and respected if he declined. Tim was learning to set boundaries that bolstered his self-esteem and kept him from feeling angry and resentful much of the time. He was also learning to distinguish between those who wanted to be in an equal relationship with him and those who wanted to use him. He was letting go of relationships that never supported him in being a Team Player but kept him continually in his People Pleasing defense.

"People who weren't able to meet me halfway have started to drop out of my life," he told me. "And you know what? I'm fine with that, because I have so much more time to enjoy with my friends who value and appreciate me for who I am."

Embracing Your Core Soul Qualities

As a Team Player, your core soul self is expressed through the following qualities: *attentiveness*, *perseverance*, and *compassion* for yourself and others. You have a warm disposition and rarely get angry with others. You see a tough situation and know how tough it is for everyone involved. You are humble and cooperative. You live in a win-win world where you treat your neighbor as you would treat yourself.

You are aware of the gift of compassion you give so freely to others but also have firm boundaries and integrity within all of your relationships. You will not be taken advantage of, abused, or disrespected by anyone. It may be difficult, but you walk away from anyone who makes you feel abused, knowing that your compassion is a wonderful gift and should be appreciated deeply. It saddens you if another doesn't appreciate you, but you accept it, knowing that there are many others deserving of your love and attention who will appreciate your gifts.

Your life purpose is to embrace compassion in all its forms, beginning with compassion for yourself. It may seem like you don't do much, but in your core, you value your contribution and know it makes a difference, however subtle. Others recognize your warmth and love, and often come to you when their lives are falling apart. By your nature, you are a mediator able to bring others to the realization that everything can be worked through and brought into balance. You have innate social intelligence, and if you are put in a room with two people in conflict, or with a person in conflict with him- or herself, you will know exactly what to say or do to resolve the issue.

Team Players live out the message of Martin Luther King Jr. to respect the solidarity and empowerment of every man, woman, and child, regardless of your connection to them. You believe that we are only as strong as the weakest among us, and that the strong must always lend a hand to uplift the weak.

YOUR GIFT TO THE WORLD is your friendship and love for your family and friends that supports all of society. Our greatest need is to be seen, heard, and understood, and while mystics will be happy with God seeing them, the rest of us need to be seen and acknowledged by people in our lives. You see each person truly and teach those in the other four profiles to reach beyond the egotistic self and share life with others. You offer the world a humble model for how to place the needs of others above the needs of the personal ego.

Building self-esteem in others is another valuable gift of the Team Player. You may live a simple life of service and support to others, but your highest purpose is to see and validate all for who they truly are, not for what they do, restoring and building self-esteem in each person you meet. You are that friend who sees strength in others, helping them to make the choice of trusting themselves enough to walk their often challenging path to their life purpose.

In your balanced state, you become a natural mediator for others in

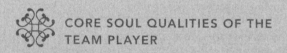

CORE SOUL QUALITIES OF THE TEAM PLAYER

- Supports others in achieving their greatness
- Compassionate as a caregiver, best friend, healer, helper
- Strongly bonded to those you are in relationship with
- Unpretentious and down to earth
- Warm and loving, a great communicator
- Capable of selfless commitment and devotion to people and organizations
- Shows that trust and intimacy are not only possible but essential for all people
- Hardworking, the backbone of progress in your community and in the world

disagreements because you can empathize with both parties and are therefore able to offer a compassionate compromise. You become a person who can negotiate any situation because your gift is feeling the needs of others before they are aware of them. In your strength, you don't work *for* others; you offer them support so they can do their own work.

Extraordinary Power Process: Align with Your Profile Qualities

This Extraordinary Power Process, when repeated frequently as you go through your daily life, supports you to align with your profile to live your unique life purpose. The activities below give you a chance to use the Team Player/People Pleaser profile to focus that process (described in more detail in *Orientation to the Program* on page 117).

FEEL: Do the inner feeling work by identifying those core soul qualities and defensive patterns from the profile description that you feel most deeply. Then choose a few to work with in which you are the strongest. Write in your journal about what it is like to experience that quality or pattern in your life. Think of a specific situation at work, in your relationship, or with regard to your health and well-being, and ask yourself the following about your core as well as your defense:

- ❖ How do I feel—physically, emotionally, and energetically?
- ❖ What am I saying to myself and to others?
- ❖ What am I attracting to myself by being in that quality?
- ❖ What am I rejecting or avoiding?

As you write, observe the power that is available from your core soul qualities and also the self-sabotage that results from being in your defense.

CHOOSE: Make conscious choices to create your future, no longer living in the self-sabotaging, knee-jerk reality of your defense. Select one core soul quality you felt the deepest from the reading. Sit quietly and visualize living in that core quality right now: How does it change your relationships, career, health, and finances? Project your life out one, five, and ten years into the future, and explore the same question. Write about your vision in your journal. Then come back to the present moment. Choose how you will do things differently based on living in your core soul qualities.

ACT: Align your actions with your core soul qualities in your career, relationships, health, or finances. Ask: *What would my Team Player do in this area or situation? How would he or she respond and act right now?* Commit to taking action in this moment, even if it's a symbolic gesture of calling a friend, not because your friend needs you but because you want to talk to your friend. Or practice replying to someone who wants your help by saying into a mirror, "I would really like to help you, but I need some time for myself now." This is not a no to them, but a yes to you.

REPEAT THIS PROCESS and continue to *feel*, *choose*, and *act* in this way as you discover more and more about your unique Life Purpose Profile. Soon this simple process will become your default mode, overriding the knee-jerk programming you've been trapped in for most of your life, and you will be free.

Before You Go On . . .

Record aspects of your profile that you can align with on a Personal Profile Summary chart. Turn to page 249 and fill in the first two sections on the chart from your discoveries in Step 1: *My Core Soul Qualities* and *My Defensive Profile Patterns*. (You will have a chance to fill in the remaining sections of the chart in Step 2 and Step 3.) Your chart can then serve as a handy reference for the work you are doing to know yourself in this new way.

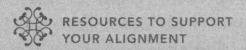

RESOURCES TO SUPPORT YOUR ALIGNMENT

The following are available at www.discoveryourpurposebook.com/members:

1. **Guided Meditation Audio Download.** *Your Secret Place.* This meditation not only helps you identify your profile but also shows you the difference between being in your core soul self and being in a defensive state.

2. **Crystal Bowls Audio Download.** Daily work with crystal bowls helps you to feel your alignment with your profile. Then you are called to your life purpose by energy resonance, not from the force of mental will.

Step 2: Recognize Your Defenses

In Step 2, you use your profile as a lens to examine and then dismantle the defensive mask of your false self that is living in a virtual reality. You identify your core wounds and self-rejecting vows, as well as your negative pleasures, and you begin to replace these defensive behaviors with freeing statements and positive pleasures.

The Big Why story of my client and Team Player Stephanie illustrates how living from your core, not your vows, can dramatically impact the outcome of your life's most meaningful experiences.

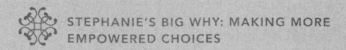

STEPHANIE'S BIG WHY: MAKING MORE EMPOWERED CHOICES

A mother of three, Stephanie was deeply entrenched in the People Pleaser defense when she came to see me. She loved her work as a part-time massage therapist and was very popular at one of the largest health spas in the area. Married to a lawyer who was a Charismatic Leader–Charmer, she juggled her work with raising children and keeping a nice home in the suburbs. She did not need to work for the money but felt she needed to be a productive member of society, so once the children were all in school full-time, she got her massage therapy license and started working.

She came to see me on her fortieth birthday. "I'm doing anywhere from fifteen to twenty massages a week, but this is the first time in two years that I've had a healing session for myself," she told me. Her complaint was that over the last five to ten years, she had lost her joy in working and in life in general. She hardly ever went out with friends, tended to be angry at everyone, and felt exhausted most of the time.

Stephanie could see that her anger was bringing demanding, controlling people to her. Still, she was in victim mode about how people treated her. "My boss regularly changes my schedule without consulting me and uses me as a filler whenever other therapists can't come in," she reported. "He just expects me to be there, even when it conflicts with my children's schedules." I asked her what it would be like if she said no to her boss, and she said, "If I said no, he'd tell me I have no option if I want to keep my job." Stephanie thought about leaving a number of times, but her clients depended on her, so she put up with it—the typical grin-and-bear-it response of a People Pleaser defense.

At home, her husband was confident, strong, and persuasive, and he rarely let her win even a minor argument. He always seemed to have a plan; Stephanie was often too busy to argue or come up with her own plans, but whenever she did, they were quickly shot down. Whenever she challenged her husband's demands or ideas, he aggressively argued his case. She wrote this off as what lawyers do but told me, "It reminded me a lot of my father, who was also a lawyer and treated my mom the same way." She added, "It's gotten so bad that when I don't want to do something, I'll agree to do it anyway, and then not find the time to get it done." Unsurprisingly, her husband reacts angrily to this pattern, but Stephanie feels justified in fighting with him because she feels that she has been a victim of his aggression.

As Stephanie got more familiar with her profile, she could see that she was setting up her relationships in a 20/80 ratio, where she had 20 percent of the say but did 80 percent of the work, and the other people had 80 percent of the say but did 20 percent of the work. She began to identify and release some of her core vows made in childhood to "never turn against any authority, like my dad" and "always give more than I get, like my mom."

Seeing the many layers of how she'd attracted her current life, Stephanie undertook finding one relationship in which she was able to have a fifty-fifty balance of giving and receiving by speaking up and asking for her needs to be met. She also practiced letting the other person do more for her. "It wasn't easy to let someone else give to me, but my girlfriend had been wanting to return my favors for quite a long time, so when I started graciously accepting her overtures to pick up the tab in a restaurant or give me a gift, she told me she felt so much better about our relationship."

Stephanie continued to work with me until she realized she was not willing to let go of a particularly unhealthy relationship— her marriage. She said she could see that what she was doing was bad for her and good for him, but she was willing to endure it for eight more years until the children were off to college. By acknowledging her situation and making a conscious decision about it, Stephanie was taking a step in the right direction and reclaiming her power. Many of us have made sacrifices similar to hers. Most important, Stephanie realized that she could make choices in her life, which was empowering.

Stephanie came back a few times until her husband told her it was costing too much and I was filling her head with silly stuff that everyone knows. But in her last session, she shared with me what she was learning:

"Since I've been more in charge of my decisions, even in doing something I don't want to do, both my husband and my boss have become more appreciative and somehow less demanding." When I asked her for examples of this in her life, she told me.

"Last week, I agreed to host a dinner for my husband's clients, but I didn't really want to. I sometimes feel like I'm the hired help in my own house! But right after I agreed to do it, I thought to myself, *You just chose that, so get it done without playing the victim.* My husband and his guests repeatedly complimented me on getting a terrific dinner together even though I'd worked hard all day, and they knew it. When my husband asked me for a repeat performance next week, he did it in a way that was respectful and considerate, and even though once again I said yes when I didn't want to, I did so knowing I was not a victim, but rather someone having a hard time speaking my truth and who would eventually get there."

Stephanie had had an important breakthrough. She was learning to be more compassionate with herself, the place where it all starts, and that was a valuable lesson for any Team Player/People Pleaser.

Becoming Aware of Your Vows

Becoming aware of your vows—those hardwired beliefs that filter your every experience through a limited view—is critical for dismantling your defense. The source of your vows are events early in life that wounded you emotionally and energetically—your *core wounds*.

For a Team Player, this core-wounding event may have occurred when your innate gift of compassion was belittled or ignored when you were a child. Unrecognized, your gift of caring for others became distorted into the defense of people-pleasing slavery and self-negation.

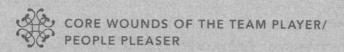

CORE WOUNDS OF THE TEAM PLAYER/ PEOPLE PLEASER

- Will-crushing parental control early in life
- Love withheld and core qualities rejected when you didn't comply with parental demands
- Severe control over all your bodily functions, such as potty training
- Being forced to care for an alcoholic, sickly, or irresponsible parent
- Punishment aggressively meted out for any attempts at personal autonomy
- Family dynamics that discouraged individuality or autonomy
- Public shaming for attempts to be independent from your family
- Sexual abuse that was never addressed, leaving you to feel as though the abuse were your fault
- Violation of your right to have your own opinion

As a Team Player, you have a life purpose of being compassionate and caring, so your vows focus on *supporting others, living selflessly in devotion and service*, and *being obedient to authority*.

For example, you may have vowed never to be selfish or mean, never to say no to the needs of others because your parents always said no to you. Or, as you grew older and you experienced being treated like a doormat, you vowed not to take on any new friends, since the family and friends you had were more than you could handle. These vows support your People Pleaser defense in which you focus on the needs of others and give to them freely but become resentful when they don't reciprocate. You may feel victimized when those you care about take you for granted, but because you've vowed always to be nice, they don't think you mind being treated that way. Having always to be the good and helpful one can be very degrading when you are unable to say no to abusers.

When people around you are self-abusing, you are often in the position of trying to save them from themselves because of your vow always to do your best for others. This creates codependent relationships in which you care more about another's health and well-being than they do. Such unhealthy relationships further entrench your vow of *I never have needs*, when your abusive partner ignores your needs because he or she is so much worse off than you are.

Your belief that giving your love and time to people can save them leaves you in a constant state of giving more than you can. Your unconscious need to be loved for your own good deeds attracts narcissistic "taker" types who are looking more for a slave than a mate, so they can focus solely on themselves. This situation may mirror an unresolved, wounded relationship with your parents who never appreciated your good nature, repeating that frustrating pattern.

Furthermore, a person who is caring, selfless, and giving will often be the default person in a family to be given the hand-me-downs, smallest room, and the last of the food on the dinner table because he or she doesn't make waves. A vow never to be a bother may give you some sense of self-definition but won't support your life purpose.

Vows become hardwired through unconscious statements you say to yourself day in and day out. Read and allow yourself to feel the Vow Statements that typically form the Poor Me defense. Do you recognize any from the list on the next page in your life?

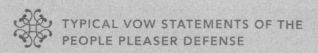

TYPICAL VOW STATEMENTS OF THE PEOPLE PLEASER DEFENSE

I vow never to be selfish (like my father/mother).

I vow always to be helpful and give unconditionally.

I vow never to let anyone feel I am better than they are.

I vow always to love and support my family forever—family comes first.

I vow always to let others go first.

I vow never to show anger or aggression toward another person.

I vow always to do what no one else will do. If it needs to be done, I have to do it.

I vow always to care for the sick and injured, and make a difference in their lives.

I vow never to stand out and be the center of attention—it's too embarrassing.

I vow always to hide my resentment, always suffering in silence.

WRITE YOUR OWN: _____

Extraordinary Power Process: Release Your Vows

The activities below give you a chance to become aware of and release vows of the People Pleaser defense.

FEEL: Choose those Vow Statements from the list that resonate most strongly for you. Mark them and add any of your own to the list. Then select one or more to work with in completing the following sentences:

1. A vow I made was always/never to _____

_____.

2. How this vow is influencing my life right now: _____
_____.

3. My self-talk that reinforces this vow: _____
_____.

EXAMPLE:

1. A vow I made was never to be selfish and always to put others before myself.
2. How this vow is influencing my life right now: I am caught in a never-ending cycle of doing what everyone else wants me to do and I never have time for me.
3. My self-talk that reinforces this vow: "What I want isn't as important as what someone else wants."

CHOOSE: Look at the vows you marked and, taking one at a time, ask yourself: *What would my life be like if I stopped honoring that vow?* Project out one, five, and ten years from now and ask: *How would not honoring that vow change my life?* Write your answers in your journal.

For example: *If I no longer honored this vow, I could have relationships that are more balanced and genuinely fulfill me.*

ACT: What action could you take to support your choice to no longer honor your vow? Decide to act based on your conscious choice, not a vow. Write in your journal about what happened when you did.

REPEAT THE PROCESS of *feel*, *choose*, and *act* every time you become aware that an ancient vow has been running your life. Vows are buried deep in your psyche, so it can take years to permanently release them. Be prepared to feel some amount of fear, guilt, and shame as you choose not to honor your vows; a vow is an unconscious promise, and you are breaking that promise when you choose anything other than your vow.

Before You Go On . . .

Record the Vow Statements you resonate with most strongly on your Personal Profile Summary chart on page 249. Fill in the section for *My Vow Statements* with statements from the list or that you wrote in.

Freedom Statements

Replace your Vow Statements with Freedom Statements, which are the solutions to your vows. Freedom Statements call forth your core soul qualities and support you to increasingly choose more consciously in every moment. Every time you consciously choose a Freedom Statement over a vow, you get back energy and open yourself to ever-growing life rather than stagnating as a wounded victim.

Use Freedom Statements as a bridge out of defense and onto the path of your truth. The following list offers you a variety of statements, but you can always add your own.

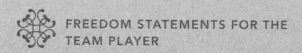 **FREEDOM STATEMENTS FOR THE TEAM PLAYER**

I am warm and real, and I give great hugs.
It is just as important to show compassion to myself as it is to show it to others.
I am open to having deep, loving relationships at every level.

I am open to saying no when I mean no and yes when I mean yes, based on how I feel in the moment, not on what I think I am supposed to do.
I am open to setting healthy boundaries with those I love.
I am open to letting others know my needs.
I see and support others in living their life purpose, just as I recognize my own life purpose.
I am a great mediator.
I value my selfless devotion to my family and community.
I work tirelessly but also support myself by getting the rest I need.

WRITE YOUR OWN: _____

Extraordinary Power Process:
Become Free of Your Vows

The activities below give you a chance to replace your vows with Freedom Statements and live from your Team Player soul qualities rather than your People Pleaser defense.

FEEL: Read the list of Freedom Statements above, speaking each one aloud. Let yourself feel their truth as you sit quietly after speaking them. Notice those that you may want to deny and then repeat those statements until you no longer have a negative reaction to them. Notice also which statements register strongly as *Yes, that's me!* Write those Freedom Statements in your journal.

CHOOSE: Speak your Freedom Statements out loud as often as possible to bring conscious choice to your vow-driven, knee-jerk defensive reactions. Tell others your Freedom Statements so that they can see your truth and support you in embodying it. Especially as a Team Player, you will find it difficult to share your deepest qualities with others, but when you share your mission of connecting deeply and supporting those you love, they will appreciate your generosity and sacrifice, and validate your efforts in life.

Sit and inquire within about what your life will be like one, five, and ten years from now as you embody the truth in your Freedom Statements.

ACT: Explore how you would act differently in key areas of your life if your vows were replaced by Freedom Statements. Choose one action you can take that aligns you with the truth of your Freedom Statement, not your vow, and do it!

REPEAT THE PROCESS of *feel*, *choose*, and *act* often when dealing with your life's challenges. You'll notice how your vow-driven actions begin to fade and you increasingly make choices and act based in the present of who you truly are rather than the past of your false and defended self.

Before You Go On . . .

Record the Freedom Statements you have chosen to replace your vows on the Personal Profile Summary chart on page 249. Fill in the section for *My Freedom Statements*.

Your Negative Pleasures

Living from your core soul qualities, not your vows, will empower you to embrace your life purpose. But without confronting your *negative pleasures*, real freedom will never be yours. Negative pleasures—those habits and behaviors you know you shouldn't do (or *don't* do but know you should!) because they make you feel better about yourself—must be confronted and left behind if you are going to live your authentic purpose.

In People Pleaser defense, you find your negative pleasure in feeling self-righteous. The pleasure you experience comes from holding on to your hidden anger and resentment toward people you serve. Whether they are a spouse, a child, or a boss, you find pleasure in being the better person because you sacrifice your own needs for the needs of others. The negative pleasure of not having any needs and being the one who always compromises justifies your brooding anger.

You also take pleasure in being passive-aggressive—saying you'll do something but then not getting it done on time or in the right way. In your People Pleaser defense, you are not allowed to openly show your anger and set boundaries because it wouldn't be "loving," so you resist and express anger in more subtle ways. The reward you get from this pattern is to see yourself as a victim when your partner gets mad at you. Then finally, you can blow up and vent the resentment that had been building up.

The following list includes typical negative pleasures of the People Pleaser defense. Feel free to add your own.

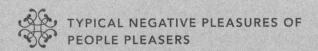

TYPICAL NEGATIVE PLEASURES OF PEOPLE PLEASERS

Being polite as a "good girl/boy" and feeling better than others as a result

Playing the martyr and being angry that you are always the one to sacrifice your needs for the family

Feeling superior because you care more about others than others do about themselves

Complaining about being overtired and overworked but never
  resting

Never asking for what you are worth, then feeling resentful when
  you get less than others

Doing favors for others when they haven't asked for your help,
  then being angry at them for not appreciating what you did

Feeling superior because you ask for nothing while everyone else
  is so needy

Not letting others pay you for work you did that they appreciated

Not having sexual needs in the bedroom as a form of control in
  the relationship

Letting your resentment build, then blowing up at the people
  you love, so you feel guilty and ashamed afterward

WRITE YOUR OWN: _____

Extraordinary Power Process:
Diminish Your Negative Pleasures

The activities below give you a chance to become aware of your negative pleasures. The key to diminishing your negative pleasures is to
become conscious of the poor substitutes they are for the real pleasures
you could be having in your life.

FEEL: As you read the list of negative pleasures for the People Pleaser
defense, let yourself feel which ones resonate deeply to evoke a response
of *Yes, that's me!* Mark those and write them in your journal.

CHOOSE: Choose one negative pleasure from the list that you identified and are willing to let go of. Sit with all the pain that this behavior
has caused you and others to date. Then visualize your life projected

out ten years from now. If you don't change that behavior, what positive pleasure will it cost you?

To help you do this, fill in the following:

1. A negative pleasure I have in my life is _____
_____.

2. Allowing that negative pleasure in my life costs me now and in the future: _____.

EXAMPLE:

1. A negative pleasure I have in my life is playing the martyr and being angry that I am always the one to sacrifice my needs for the needs of my family.
2. Allowing this negative pleasure costs me the deeper and more loving relationships with my family that I truly desire.

Now write about a *positive pleasure*, one that comes from living in your core, and how experiencing that pleasure might look in your life. For example: *When I know deep in my heart that I love to serve and be there for my family (which does not preclude me from living my life), I do not feel like a martyr. Instead, I feel blessed to be living my life purpose.*

ACT: Having chosen a negative pleasure you are ready to let go of, the next time it comes up in your life, ask yourself: *What positive pleasure am I missing as I indulge this negative one? How would my Team Player respond in this situation?* Then take action in accordance with your answer.

REPEAT THIS PROCESS OFTEN. As your negative pleasures become increasingly apparent, see them as behaviors rooted in fear that you are now ready to grow out of. Don't beat yourself up. Go slow, get support, and let each negative pleasure go, one at a time. You will start to experience positive pleasures that come from accepting your life and the people in it. Soon, the unconscious habits and behaviors you've been substituting for real pleasure will no longer seem as attractive.

Every negative pleasure you successfully let go of allows you to bring back into your life all of the wasted energy that went into that defense. With that energy, you can make powerful choices to live your life as a creative presence.

Before You Go On . . .

Record your negative pleasures on your Personal Profile Summary chart on page 249. Fill in the section for *My Favorite Negative Pleasures*.

In Transition . . .

As you transition out of People Pleaser defense and into your core self, you may find yourself stuck in frustrating old patterns. Your defenses have been making you someone you are not, or something less than who you truly are. Now awakened, you can make conscious choices and set goals to act differently.

For the Team Player, when you see no way out of your obligations to serve others, a good goal is to turn inward to get in touch with your own feelings. You have a great capacity for empathy and feeling for others, but until you are able to turn that empathy and love inward on yourself, your life will never be your own.

Here is an activity to support your transition out of People Pleaser defense into your core self as a Team Player.

ACTIVITY: As a Team Player, you protect yourself from the demands of people by going solo much of the time. To take back your autonomy, set a goal of choosing to help one person who is not family and not someone you "have to" care for. Make that person a priority over the demanding "takers" and "have to" people in your life. Give yourself a friend who is just for you.

When the two of you decide what you are going to do together, it is a fifty-fifty decision. This sets a boundary—not against giving your friend what he or she wants but against you automatically forgetting your needs. A real friendship will give you the opportunity to take back your autonomy and begin living your life purpose as a caring friend who has a great balance between serving others and serving your own needs in deeply enjoyable relationships.

Write in your journal about what happened when you did this.

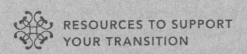

RESOURCES TO SUPPORT YOUR TRANSITION

1. **Guided Meditation Audio Download.** *Calling Back Your Spirit* (available at www.discoveryourpurposebook.com/members).

2. **Recommended Reading List**
   - *Codependent No More*, by Melody Beattie
   - *Healing the Shame That Binds You*, by John Bradshaw
   - *Soul Mates*, by Thomas Moore
   - *You Can Heal Your Life*, by Louise Hay

Step 3: Live Your Life Purpose

Having begun the process of dismantling your defenses in Step 2, you are now ready to integrate your profile's unique higher- and lower-self qualities. As you become less conflicted, and more whole and balanced, you can make choices and take courageous actions in your life, not just react automatically from your ancient vows. You are also able to use the Law of Attraction to attract what best supports your unique life purpose as you create and live an extraordinary life.

Your Shadow: Lower- and Higher-Self Traits

Your shadow is made up of traits that you have rejected by vowing *always* or *never* to be or do something. Those traits can be seen as aspects of your higher self and your lower self. As you identify rejected higher- and lower-self traits, you can begin to accept and integrate them, and so achieve a state of inner balance and wholeness. Fully integrating your shadow allows your defensive mask to dissolve and your true core soul self to emerge.

The following chart contains a list of the lower- and higher-self traits *in matched pairs* that you must own and integrate to fully live your life purpose as a Team Player.

LOWER- AND HIGHER-SELF TRAITS FOR TEAM PLAYERS	
LOWER-SELF TRAITS	**HIGHER-SELF TRAITS**
Resentful when serving others	Gracious friend and helper
Codependent	Uncompromising with good boundaries
Resistant	Open to all

Childish	Plays well with others
Spiteful	Fair and compassionate
Taking directions mindlessly	Choosing what to do to best serve others
Victim	Draws clear boundaries
Passive-aggressive	Follows through on a job to completion
Self-hating	Deeply compassionate for the oppressed
Self-punishing	Taking care of yourself
Self-sacrificing	Conscious surrender in loving relationships
Brooding	Openly sharing your needs and appreciation
Stubborn	Unbendable support for others
Obstinate	Driven and committed
Submissive	Lovingly and actively supportive of leaders
Dense and slow to respond	Taking time to lovingly care for others
Stuck mentally	Free from fixed mental views
Masochistic	Finds enjoyment in service
Feels abused	Is grateful but can say no
Spineless	Flexible to flow with all of life

Extraordinary Power Process: Integrate Your Shadow

The activities below give you a chance to integrate your shadow (rejected traits) with your higher-self light.

FEEL: As you read the list of matched-pair lower-/higher-self traits, reach deep into yourself to feel the full range of your raw, lower self at one end and your exalted, higher self at the other. Both are within you to varying degrees. Your raw power and personal needs are found in your lower-self traits, while how you consciously use that power and fulfill those needs is in your higher-self traits. When you can own both in any moment and still choose your higher-self traits, then everything you do will be aligned with your life purpose.

Put a check mark next to the lower- and higher-self traits you recognize as ones you exhibit. Also notice traits that elicit a powerful negative reaction and check them as well. These are traits you have rejected in yourself or in others. (In rejecting lower-self traits, you say to yourself, *I'd never do that—it's too negative, mean, or evil*; while in rejecting higher-self traits, you say, *I could never do that—it's too perfect, saintly, or godlike.*)

CAUTION: No higher-self trait can exist without the lower-self trait alongside it. To be whole and balanced, you must be conscious of both within you. Selecting only those traits you like will send you back to your vow-created life where only half of you exists.

Using your strongest traits checked, complete these statements for each:

1. A lower-/higher-self trait that I see as strong in me is

   _____.

2. My greatest fear of owning that trait is _____

   _____.

EXAMPLE:

1. A lower-self trait that I see as strong in me is being spiteful when my grown children don't appreciate all I do for them.
2. My greatest fear of owning that trait is they will judge me as immature or selfish and will not want to spend time with me.

AND:

1. A higher-self trait that is the partner to my lower-self trait is my ability to be fair and compassionate, even toward those who have abused me or taken advantage of me.

2. My greatest fear of owning that trait is that people continue
   to take advantage of my good nature and compassion.

CHOOSE: Now work with one set of lower- and higher-self traits that
you identified as not being fully owned in their full range. Ask how
your life would be different if you owned both higher- and lower-self
traits equally, able to accept both but choosing the higher-self quality.

Visualize your life up to now and see how damaging it has been to
express the lower-self trait unconsciously. Also feel how you have
wanted to express the higher-self trait more often but don't, since the
lower-self trait cannot be resolved. Now project out this pattern of
behavior one, five, and ten years into the future and see what your life
looks like with just this one conflict within you.

What would happen if you were always able to embrace both lower-
and higher-self traits, rejecting neither, as part of your life purpose?
Notice how, if you did not stand in such fear of being who you actually
are in your life one, five, and ten years into the future, you would
instead reveal your true power and purpose.

For example: *If I accept that I get resentful toward my children and
withhold my love and attention from them, destroying what I want the
most in my life, then I can be fair with them. I don't have to let them abuse
me, but rather be compassionate for where they are in their lives, knowing
that I was there, too, not long ago.*

ACT: Take actions that align with your new state of inner balance and
wholeness. Commit to one action you will take that reflects your new
self-acceptance, and then do it. Write in your journal about what happened when you did.

REPEAT THE PROCESS! Once you've worked with one pair of higher-
and lower-self traits in this way, repeat the process, covering more traits

in both lists. Accepting both higher and lower selves as the whole of who you are is the most powerful spiritual work you can do.

Before You Go On . . .

Turn to page 249 and fill in the section for *Lower- and Higher-Self Traits* on your Personal Profile Summary chart.

Living Courageously

Living your life purpose means speaking and acting fearlessly from your core soul self. To remain in that state, you will need to step out of your comfort zone often and take the road less traveled, leaping over obstacles in your way. Following are some ways you as a Team Player can do that.

Owning your purpose to serve unconditionally.

Your greatest challenge is to face the fact that you were born to put the needs of others above your own, the definition of unconditional love. Our deepest spiritual purpose is to find the face of God on earth. For you, God is the human being standing right in front of you, not a vision, feeling, inspiration, or knowledge, as it is for those in other profiles.

Saying no and meaning it.

As a Team Player, you never reject someone in need or someone whom you respect as an authority, but your challenge is to learn that you, too, are human and must take care of yourself.

Speaking up for yourself.

You are wired to see the sincerity of others, so people always feel seen, heard, and understood by you. But in any relationship, you must claim your right to have half the say, and since others don't generally give that permission, you have to ask for it. Know that what you do for others is your creative self-expression, a valuable contribution to them and to you equally.

Accepting that you can't be everything to everyone.

Your purpose is to serve others but not to surrender your integrity. You came into the world prepared to make others' lives better and happy, but true integrity comes when you figure out how to give while not being everything to everyone.

Participating in groups and making new friends.

Because you tend to attract people who want something from you, you stay away from joining groups where you will be sharing yourself with people and possibly making new friends. *I don't do groups* is your response when invited to a class, workshop, or program. But it is in group activity and in relating to people that you find yourself and your greatest life purpose, so you will never be happy avoiding groups.

Embracing your role in evolving humanity.

As a Team Player, you are faced with the daunting task of disarming the Enforcer-Seducers and Rule Keepers of the world who amass their power in corporations, governments, and churches, preying on the other three profiles and on each other. You are here to teach them compassion as the path to evolution, not extinction, on planet earth. When you do this, you are the embodiment of Christ's words, *Love thy neighbor as thyself.*

Before You Go On . . .

Turn to page 249 and fill in the section for *Actions to Take for Living Courageously* on your Personal Profile Summary chart.

Speak Your Truth

To remain in your Team Player core, you must be willing to speak your truth to others, especially to those with whom you are in an intimate relationship. Practice by reading each of the Essential Word Statements below, visualizing that you are speaking directly to someone you love and feeling your words deeply as you read them.

Make a commitment to speak these essential words—not the automatic words dictated by your vows and defenses—to an important person in your life. Then act to call, write, or speak with that important person to share your truth.

ESSENTIAL WORDS FOR TEAM PLAYERS TO SPEAK

- Sometimes I am so happy for you and so involved in your life that I lose myself and don't feel any purpose beyond being in your life.

- I know I am supposed to be an individual, but it is when I am part of your life that I feel the most like me.
- If you reject my love or criticize what I give so freely, it will hurt more than anything in the world.
- I am here to love you, and I only know how to love me through loving you, so please be kind because what you think of me is that important.
- To be appreciated and loved by you is what gives me my deepest purpose.

Before You Go On . . .

Turn to page 249 and fill in the section for *Speaking Your Truth (Essential Words)* on your Personal Profile Summary chart.

The Law of Attraction

According to the Law of Attraction, like attracts like. It follows that you will always attract people and situations that are like you. As your alignment with your life purpose grows, your internal magnet for attracting who and what you want in your life is strengthened. If you are not aligned with your life purpose, no amount of visualizing will help you achieve your desires—in spite of what popular culture tells you about how constant visualizing will bring you what you want.

For example, as a Team Player stuck in the People Pleaser defense, you are naturally solid energetically, so you easily magnetize those elements in the material world you need to create your life. But because you have so little sense of your own self and your own needs, you attract people more than you attract material elements throughout your life.

In your power, the people you attract will bring you money in exchange for services you provide. But you do not attract money or material goods directly, since those are not highly valued by you. You care more about people, and so you will always attract resources in the form of people who will pay you or provide opportunities for income.

In defense, you may see yourself as a Good Samaritan, attracting those who are the most in need but have little or nothing to pay for your services. To ask for what you are worth in the world often creates guilt and shame that you are somehow asking too much for something you would give away willingly. This reinforces your low self-worth and leads to a lifetime of resentment in which you never get the monetary or material confirmation of your good work in the world.

ACTIVITY: EXPLORE THE GAP. The gap is the space between where you are now and where you know you will be when you fully embody your core soul profile qualities and live your life purpose. Looking in areas of life such as health, relationships, finances, and career or job, inquire about the following:

- ❖ What am I attracting in my life right now from living in my defenses?
- ❖ What do I want to attract in my life from living in my core soul self?

Are you attracting what supports your life purpose or what keeps you stuck in your defense? How can you act from your core soul qualities and not your defenses to close that gap and attract what you want to support your life purpose? Write your responses in your journal.

Before You Go On . . .

Turn to page 249 and fill in the section for *Law of Attraction* on your Personal Profile Summary chart.

Extraordinary Power Process:
Your Personal Profile Summary Chart

Your Personal Profile Summary chart now holds what you have learned about yourself as a Team Player, either as your primary or your secondary Life Purpose Profile.

Once you have completed your charts for both primary and secondary profiles, use them as a tool to support your life purpose. Follow the Extraordinary Power Process of *feel*, *choose*, and *act* as you refer to each section you've filled in on your chart:

1. Feel: Do the inner feeling work—don't just think.
2. Choose: Make conscious choices—don't automatically react based on your vows.
3. Act: Align your actions with your profile's core soul qualities—not with your defenses—to live your truth.

When you repeat this sequence as often as possible throughout your day, then everything you do will reveal the mystery of who you are rather than reinforcing who you think you are but are not. *Feeling, choosing,* and *acting* in accordance with your profile gives you access to your extraordinary power so you can effortlessly manifest your life purpose and live it in every area of your life.

Team Player/People Pleaser
PERSONAL PROFILE SUMMARY

Profile	☐ This is my PRIMARY PROFILE ☐ This is my SECONDARY PROFILE ☐ This is my THIRD, FOURTH, or FIFTH PROFILE
My Core Soul Qualities (for this profile)	1 _____ 2 _____
My Defensive Profile Patterns	1 _____ 2 _____
My Vow Statements (How I self-sabotage)	1 _____ 2 _____ 3 _____
My Freedom Statements (Solutions to my Vow Statements)	I am open to _____ I am open to _____ I am open to _____
My Favorite Negative Pleasures (How I self-sabotage)	Something I do that I shouldn't do but get pleasure from: _____ Something I get pleasure from not doing that I know I should do: _____
Lower- and Higher-Self Traits (matched pairs)	Lower: Higher: 1 _____ / _____ 2 _____ / _____
Actions to take for living courageously from your profile	1 _____ 2 _____
Speaking Your Truth (ESSENTIAL WORDS you must say to others)	1 _____ 2 _____
Law of Attraction (People, situations, etc. that I am attracting)	In defense, I attract _____ In my core, I attract _____

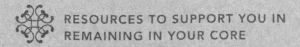

RESOURCES TO SUPPORT YOU IN REMAINING IN YOUR CORE

1. Guided Meditation Audio Download. *Your Subpersonalities.* Explore your higher- and lower-self traits through a guided meditation, available at www.discoveryourpurposebook.com/ members.

2. Bioenergetic Exercises for Team Players, available below and also on the same website.

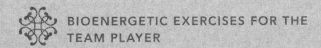

BIOENERGETIC EXERCISES FOR THE TEAM PLAYER

The following exercises help you to establish your right to say no *in* your life, not *to* your life, in order to deal with the invasion you've allowed others.

EXERCISE #1: STAND YOUR GROUND. Work with your voice to speak your true feelings and needs, including screaming and yelling just for the fun of it, not against anyone.

Clench your fists, stamp your feet, and punch downward while saying "NO!" to punctuate each physical punch and stomp. Next, punch out in front and say "No!" Stop and feel what it is like to say no and define your own space in a downward, rooting way.

Then move your energy into freedom by jumping up and saying "Yes!" You must learn how to say no first if you are ever going to say yes to yourself.

EXERCISE #2: RELEASE THE SHOULDERS AND NECK. Often the Team Player/People Pleaser has a submissive forward head tilt and slumped shoulders. Energetically, this is from shouldering too many of other people's burdens. Deep tissue and chiropractic work is helpful, but the real issue is that you must free yourself from having to submit to others' needs.

In this exercise, you stand up straight, hold your head high, and jab your elbows backward at shoulder level, one at a time with a slight twist as you say, "Get off my back!" The twisting motion will open your pelvis as well.

EXERCISE #3: RELEASE YOUR HIPS. Now that the neck and shoulders are released, the hips are next. Put your hands on your hips and drive your hips forward in a sexual way. You can grunt as you drive your hips forward and back. Alternate the back-and-forth movement to feel heat in your hips and pelvis. Feel your passionate sensuality and the deepest needs of your body and being. The goal is to free up your energy from the earth to heaven and then from heaven to the earth, and experience being safe doing it.

CHAPTER 10

Profile #4: Charismatic Leader–Charmer/ Enforcer-Seducer

THE CHARISMATIC LEADER–CHARMER

with Enforcer-Seducer defense

W elcome to the Charismatic Leader–Charmer profile and its defense, the Enforcer-Seducer. You will find valuable information and activities here to help you access your extraordinary power and embody your life purpose.

If this is your secondary or other profile, or the profile of someone in your life, you can use what you learn here to deepen your understanding of yourself and others.

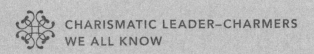

CHARISMATIC LEADER–CHARMERS WE ALL KNOW

Historical: John F. Kennedy, Martin Luther King Jr., Margaret Thatcher, Adolf Hitler, Napoleon Bonaparte, Julius Caesar, Queen Elizabeth I, Catherine the Great, Alexander the Great, and Queen Victoria

Contemporary: Nelson Mandela, Bill Clinton, Angela Merkel, Tony Soprano (as played by James Gandolfini), Angelina Jolie, Harrison Ford, Beyoncé, Morgan Freeman, Sean Connery, Jack Nicholson, Sonia Sotomayor, Oprah Winfrey, and Steve Jobs

Step 1: Align with Your Profile

In this first step of the program, you learn all about your profile, including those core soul qualities that support you to live in your life purpose and those defenses that cause you to sabotage your efforts. The Big Why story of my student Martina demonstrates how knowing your life purpose can help you give your gifts and expand your career.

About Your Profile

What follows is a general description of your profile, including how it looks when you are in defense as an Enforcer-Seducer. You will consider your current life situation, including your relationships, career or job, how you handle money, and the physical and energetic aspects of your profile.

GENERAL DESCRIPTION. The Charismatic Leader–Charmer is the most energetic, dynamic, and capable of all the profiles. We are all called to our life purpose by the feelings that arise within us, but as a Charismatic Leader–Charmer, you demonstrate how to trust your gut and act on those feelings. You are sensitive like the Emotional Intelligence Specialist, but your feelings are not something that you spend a lot of time mulling over. Rather, your feelings call you to instant and sometimes impetuous action.

As a Charismatic Leader–Charmer, you exhibit strength and charisma from the moment you are born until the moment you die. You come into the world knowing that others are here to serve you. Then, when you actually step into your life purpose, you find how your massive energy can serve the world.

You are a born leader and don't feel comfortable taking orders that go against your own sense of truth. Your leadership can take many forms—the most obvious of which include the warrior, politician, and actor. But you can also be a great lover, charmer, the family protector and caretaker, or a rebellious entrepreneur or pioneer. Because your life purpose is to lead, no matter what situation you get into, you find a way to gain control and achieve your highest directive, influencing others and leading them to their highest potential in the process. You can become a great motivational role model by following your own inner conscience and leading others to do the same in their own lives.

At times, your leadership takes the form of challenging authority, as Martin Luther King Jr.'s did, but even when you're not challenging anyone, you are a magnifier of energy. Whether in sports, business, relationships, acting, or politics, you find a way to take charge. Your desire to win is fierce and innate.

As you fearlessly take action, you rarely experience remorse for the consequences because you consider inaction and lost opportunity to be the greatest crimes. Critics don't bother you. You do not regard your actions as good or bad, as a Knowledgeable Achiever would, but your main concern is whether you achieved your desired goal. You rarely try to justify your actions, because they are extensions of your nervous system, hardwired and instinctual.

You often act as part of some larger cause that you believe fully justifies your actions, and you stand innocent of any wrongdoing in your own mind, even if the outcome negatively affects others. In this way, you do not nurse memories of failure, as people in the other profiles tend to do, and you can keep pushing on until you achieve your goals. The other profiles all have a difficult time taking the leap and putting everything on the line to live their life purpose, but you show us that, at some point, we must put ourselves first and fight for what we truly believe in.

IN ENFORCER-SEDUCER DEFENSE, you are still a leader, but you find yourself mistrusting others and being self-centered. You fight for causes that feed your ego, such as ascending the corporate or institutional ladder regardless of the greater good. For you, the ends can always justify the means, and taking the needs of others into account is rarely part of your plan.

You can be a master manipulator, using your considerable charm to influence others. Your favorite manipulation techniques are seduction, aggression, acting like a victim to justify victimizing others, lying, and instilling fear in others to gain control and influence their choices. The people you control don't understand the power you have over them because you can be so charming and make them feel wonderful (although you will turn on them if they fall out of line for whatever reason).

As an Enforcer-Seducer, you can self-sabotage through addictions. This happens when your hypersensitive nature has you believe that everyone is against you, that there is only a never-ending stream of bad parents, teachers, bosses, and partners who are in constant battle with you. Being a victim seems to justify self-medicating and the reckless use of alcohol and drugs.

A high percentage of people who frequent rehab facilities are in Enforcer-Seducer defense but use their leadership qualities in destructive ways. You may be able to tolerate levels of alcohol and drugs that would kill others, but rarely will you admit that addiction is a problem for you. Ironically, you seem to know unconsciously that destroying your own life with alcohol and drugs is the greatest damage you can do to people close to you.

As a Charismatic Leader–Charmer, you are fearless in battle, but when in defense you make battles personal, often being motivated by revenge. You can self-righteously destroy opponents and have no remorse. You are wired as a warrior, always seeking the chink in the armor of any opponent, aiming to exploit their weakness so you can survive. In daily interactions, you use these same tactics to control family and friends.

A primary defense that you are willing to admit is your lack of trust in others, but, more fundamentally, your problem is that you cannot trust yourself. You know you have betrayed yourself in the past by not standing up for what you believe. As much as you do not forgive others for their transgressions, you are equally severe with yourself. Since you don't trust others, your warrior or inner victim is hypervigilant in protecting yourself, never letting anyone get close enough to hurt you.

Because you fear betrayal, you go it alone in life and never let others into your world for long. Or you may go in the opposite direction and trust others but are unforgiving and feel that you've made the biggest mistake of your life when they disappoint you. You feel helpless and angry when others hurt you. People may wonder why you have such a chip on your shoulder.

You use your natural inner strength, dynamic nature, and persuasive willpower to gain control over others' decisions and your environment, justifying your actions because you are making it safe for yourself and your loved ones. A grandiose sense of self and your commitment to succeed give you the passion to persevere, but in defense you feel that the ends always justify the means. Then, you will use any tactic—forcefulness, aggression, charm, seduction, depression, illness, or infirmity—to get your way and create an environment that you know is safe.

You were born to lead, but in your Enforcer-Seducer eyes, both positive and negative behaviors that lead to gaining full control are equally valid. When taken to an extreme, this attitude can become psychopathic, as evidenced by Adolf Hitler.

When you are in your defense mode, you don't take criticism well. You may try to hide your power, but not letting it flow naturally can cause disease and mental disorders ranging from chronic pain to obsessive-compulsive behavior.

You may think you understand people's personalities when you first meet them, but your perceptions of their motives or behaviors are based on your warrior's paranoia about being attacked or criticized. You recognize others' strengths and weaknesses because this understanding is necessary for your own survival.

Charismatic Leader–Charmers have a powerful presence and often become actors. You hear people say "You should get an Academy Award for that performance" even when you don't think you are acting. With this talent in Enforcer-Seducer defense, you can mimic any of the other profiles, playing them so well and for so long that you forget your true nature and make whatever profile you are exhibiting into your identity.

When you live in Enforcer-Seducer defense, your life often feels broken, filled with disasters such as divorce, failed businesses, and other causes of self-hatred. You may become depressed and take medication, experiencing life as a constant battle with the world, your weight, your spouse, your boss, or your children. Such derailment is a complete reversal of your life purpose, which is to act instinctively for the good of all. When that is impeded, your life is filled with self-defeat, anger, and continual exhausting drama.

PRIMARY MATE AND SOCIAL RELATIONSHIPS. As a Charismatic Leader–Charmer, you find the Team Player as your primary mate. Through the Team Player's patience and willingness to be flexible and dependable, you learn about compassion and trust in a relationship. Learning to trust that someone else can see and understand you is important for you to come into your life purpose of standing behind a cause greater than yourself. Your life purpose often begins when you simply learn to trust and love someone.

You empower your Team Player partner to set boundaries and choose the life he or she truly wants. The Team player sees your greatness and encourages you to expand your message, business, and influence out into the world, and you are able to trust that, at the end of the day, you can come home to a loving and supportive spouse. This relationship teaches you to see the importance of balance in relationship and to honor the paths that others are on.

Charismatic Leader–Charmers are the archetypal Don Juan or femme fatale who are wonderful lovers with a strong sexual presence but also extremely attentive to the needs of their partner. You are deeply in touch with your body and the need for union, enjoying the time after sex as much as the time before and during. With the right partner, you can enjoy wild, dynamic sex. When undefended, you are a sexual dynamo who can comfortably go wherever your partner desires and enjoy it all.

In defense, your sexual encounters support unhealthy patterns. You may treat sexual encounters as conquests and have many partners in a lifetime but never feel fully connected to any of them. Fantasy and the power dynamic of dominance and submission are far more important than intimacy. Your goal is not intimacy but to affirm your own desirability. You enjoy playing the role of the dominator/dominatrix or seducer/seductress.

In your primary relationships, you demand that others give up their outside relationships and support systems because you want them to focus on you, depend on you, need you, and be there for you when you need them. You are the one who is always telling others what to do, needing their support on your mission. Those who do not conform to your expectations get unceremoniously kicked out of your life.

Over time, you become isolated, no longer surrounded by minions or adoring fans, having burned every bridge with family and friends, and leaving only the most superficial of relationships to fill your life.

Socially, you make friends fast but only stay in relationships that do not challenge your dominance. When meeting you for the first time, people may feel like they have known you their entire life, and within a few hours you have a best friend. This is because in defense you are a master at creating rapport by mirroring the qualities of others. But once you find out that others have a strong will of their own and can't be manipulated by you, the relationship ends.

For that reason, your world is full of superficial friends and acquaintances, with few truly close friends. You often feel alone, afraid you'll be victimized whenever you open up to others. You may be a member of a social club or a political or religious group, or you may be a regular at the local bar, where you are popular.

In defense, you see that your only recourse is to create a safe and controlled environment in an unsafe world. In your relationships, you may deny others the right to their own space and invade every aspect of their lives to "keep tabs" on them, even controlling which friends they have.

CAREER OR JOB. You are naturally inspiring, using your deep ability to sense others' gifts and bring out those qualities in them. You excel in areas such as leadership, sales, and acting, always bringing your dynamism into whatever you do. You have the energy to become a great athlete, actor, lawyer, law enforcement officer, politician, or business executive, or you may be a social darling who influences others with your beauty and charm. You can be a powerful leader/manager who can effectively take charge of large projects and many employees, and you delegate effortlessly. You can also be the greatest mom, dad, volunteer, lover, world traveler, or guru.

You are a hero or heroine by nature, so the job of firefighter, soldier, or champion of causes comes naturally to you. Movie heroes and heroines who rise above victimhood to fight back and become victorious are Charismatic Leader–Charmers.

You often experience chaos and conflict in your life that others find overwhelming, but you thrive on this as a powerful motivator. You are so dynamic that others will ask you to lead their organization or group even when your life seems to be a mess. In business, you may enter a company and make it to the top faster than others. But if you don't feel special in that position, you create conflict with higher-ups and may quit or get fired. You tend to work and be in relationships in three-to-four-year cycles, creating something amazing in that amount of time, then getting bored and looking for another conquest; in defense, you unconsciously sabotage your relationships so that you can leave in a battle of some kind, blaming the other party.

When you are in defense, you also get to the top in business but burn bridges along the way due to your need to win rather than compromise. *Get them before they get you* is an adage you embrace after being burned in previous interactions. You think that everyone is out to get you, your family, or your job.

Your purpose in life is to be a leader, to be the best at something. When you can't be the best at what you do, you may become the best at being a failure. Creating chaos in your life is the shadow aspect of the leader. It may take the form of frequently changing jobs or having no job, being lazy or not doing work you are asked to do because you don't like your boss, using a physical or mental disability as an excuse not to work and to get lifelong disability checks, letting yourself get overweight, or getting into massive debt. The more energy and power you have for the good, the more you can turn it against yourself in defense.

Charismatic Leader–Charmers are here to mobilize and inspire the masses. In Enforcer-Seducer defense, you mobilize the masses in a negative way, getting people to fight your battles for you. If you have a strong warrior in you, you can feel like you're walking onto a battlefield every time you leave your house or go to work.

HOW YOU HANDLE MONEY. As a Charismatic Leader–Charmer, you are on the planet to manage resources and people with the highest integrity. You see money and the people in your life as resources that you are responsible for. You empower others and show them how to make money to support themselves, and, in so doing, you give each person the ability to choose his or her own path.

You know how to make money by offering products and services that are valuable to many. You are careful with money and will pay up front for everything, knowing that the level of initial investment will force you to be responsible for your actions going forward. You invest in your vision and will gamble with what you have rather than borrow from others. You have so many resources and so much raw energy and charisma that you easily obtain whatever you set your mind to.

In defense, you see the money and people in your life as property that you can do what you want with. You use the resources of others, having no remorse when the big get-rich-quick scheme you got them into fails dismally. Or you marry into money, knowing that you never wanted to work for a living. You may also ask for far more than you deserve in a divorce settlement, citing your perceived victimhood as justification.

THE CHARISMATIC LEADER–CHARMER
PHYSICAL APPEARANCE

When you are visually assessing a person's profile, notice that Charismatic Leader–Charmers/Enforcer-Seducers have a dynamic energy that is magnetic. They can be sensually seductive and alluring, and often love to be in front of a camera or on stage. Their body shape will often take the form of their secondary profile, so they can be overweight or underweight, depending on what that profile is. Their skin and musculature often have an elastic quality, allowing them to go from being out of shape to in shape in a matter of weeks. Charismatic Leader–Charmers often have hourglass bodies with wide shoulders and a thin waist. They are eye-catching in appearance, even if not classically beautiful (which they often are) and have a charisma that captivates your attention. Their most salient traits are their fearlessness and sensuality and their ability to inspire you just by being around them.

PHYSICAL AND ENERGETIC ASPECTS. The energetic signature that distinguishes you from all other profiles is the high amount of energy you have. You are generally attractive, and even if you are not conventionally handsome/beautiful, you have a striking appearance that draws others to you.

In defense, you hold most of your energy in your head, shoulders, and neck, as you use your will and words to control and influence or pressure others.

Your Charismatic Leader–Charmer body is elastic and responds to whatever profile you choose to express the most. This means that, physically, you come in every shape and size and can experience drastic weight gain and loss over your lifetime.

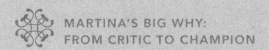

MARTINA'S BIG WHY: FROM CRITIC TO CHAMPION

Martina, a forty-four-year-old healing practitioner and spiritual counselor, took the questionnaire and got the expected results for Charismatic Leader–Charmers: All five profiles came up with an equal count.

"I was surprised," she told me, "because Charismatic Leader–Charmer was the one profile that felt foreign to me." Martina's reaction is typical for the Charismatic Leader–Charmer, who can identify with all the profiles, causing some confusion at first. "If I were to pick a secondary, it would be Creative Idealist, because I recognize my defensive pattern to be like the Thinker. I used to hide, to play small, and be 'above it all,' always criticizing people who are more outgoing than me as doing it all wrong."

Before she took the three-year training, Martina had a healing practice that was successful, but she couldn't deal with certain kinds of people. "Before I knew my profile, I would avoid people who had aggressive energy, those I later knew to be

Enforcer-Seducers," she recounted. "I hated politicians, always questioning their motives, and also sports players, who I judged to be all brawn and no brain." Martina now recognized that her defense kept her in control to avoid getting sucked into traps. "I was critical and skeptical, which is how I protected myself and stayed safe and small."

It never occurred to her that this pattern was a problem until she looked back on her earlier career. "When I was still working in the corporate world, I was smug and cut off, thinking I didn't have a problem. I was often forced to interact with aggressive energy, and at times I flat out refused. It harmed my career because I wouldn't suck up to the boss. I was naive and arrogant, and dismissed stuff I should've been able to deal with."

After going through the Life Purpose Profile Program, Martina discovered that those people she'd had a problem with had aspects of her own shadow, and by rejecting them she'd rejected her power as a Charismatic Leader–Charmer. She found there was an Enforcer-Seducer in her, not one that was physically threatening but one that was invasive in a different way.

"I didn't threaten people myself, but in an instant I could know someone's weaknesses," she said. "I used my intuition to figure them out even before they walked into the room. Psychically, I stripped them naked to see exactly what their defenses were. It's an Enforcer skill, but before, I thought that it was normal, that everyone did the same thing."

Martina still figures her clients out before they come through the door, but now she uses that skill to relate more deeply to them, letting her clients know that they are seen for who they are. "Knowing the profile system, I now understand what I'm dealing with when a client is in defense, and I can talk to them about it," she said. "I can also speak directly to their core, which makes them comfortable and builds trust."

Martina has a new ability to help people in situations that would have frightened her before. "I'm especially interested in helping people who've had illnesses that the usual medical approach can't help. My neighbor's child was diagnosed with a rare cancer, and even though I didn't know the woman very well, I felt like I should offer my support. Up until then, I'd been hiding behind my Thinker paranoia, worried that if people around me knew what I did—how really 'out there' I am—they would treat me and my family differently."

But empowered by the knowledge that she was a Charismatic Leader–Charmer, Martina offered the neighboring family her support and healing services. "It was scary, my 'coming out' as a Charismatic Leader–Charmer. I had to leave behind my tendency to hide, which at first was extremely frightening."

Not surprisingly, Martina became a huge support for the whole family in their ordeal. The cancer-stricken child died soon after she got involved, but Martina continued to support the mother, becoming her champion to see her through a very rough time. "I could see a Charismatic Leader–Charmer in the mother, too, waiting to emerge," she said. "As I worked with her, she grew and was empowered from the tragedy that had happened to her child."

Martina has since had many clients who've lost children to cancer. "I talk to their core, not just to the grieving or anxious person they appear to be, and champion their spiritual development as they go through the sometimes terrifying medical experience," she said. "It's about caring for the souls of the relatives, not just the children who are dying."

Knowing who she is and coming into alignment with her core self has helped Martina to embrace her work in a new, empowered way. "Because I have strong Creative Idealist qualities, I am connected to the spiritual realm, and now in my power as a Charismatic Leader–Charmer, I can guide and lead people out of their dark places."

She's also had personal benefits. "I've always had a great gift for healing and did well in business," she said. "But I wouldn't have been as fulfilled as I am now, because I wouldn't have come into the power that I actually have. Now I grow as I help others grow."

Embracing Your Core Soul Qualities

As a Charismatic Leader–Charmer, your highest core soul qualities are *truth*, *justice*, and *integrity*. You may not easily recognize these qualities in yourself, but as you dismantle your defensive mask, your narcissistic worldview shifts to put you in the role as leader for the good of all.

Your life's mission is supporting other people to follow their own journey, and, in surrendering to that, you become a great motivational icon. In some of the world's greatest actors, politicians, athletes, business leaders, and executives, we see an incredible integrity and willingness to fight for truth and justice for all. That is the hallmark of the Charismatic Leader–Charmer.

To free people from the repression of other Enforcers, your greatest weapon is your unwillingness to back down in standing for your truth. Martin Luther King Jr., Gandhi, and Nelson Mandela all demonstrated this quality.

You possess the ability to think on your feet and respond instantly to any situation. You trust your intuition and go with your gut, and you are usually right. Since all the world's a stage to you, you can play any role—the great hero warrior or the victim seeking justice, and everything in between. For the Charismatic Leader–Charmer, it is only a matter of choosing what you want to do.

You take full responsibility for everything in your life. Of all the profiles, there is no greater difference between core soul qualities and the defense because Enforcers don't trust anyone and take little responsibility for their actions.

If all the world is a stage for you, life may not be easy, but it will be dynamic and over the top. Every event in your life is an opportunity for you to play your greatest role, testing the very fiber of your being and inspiring all those you come in contact with. While controlling others is your defense, empowering them by being a living example of strength, grace, and willpower is your core soul quality.

YOUR GIFT TO THE WORLD is to make a difference by putting yourself first and leading by example. Once awakened to your purpose, you will die for your cause and become the ultimate model for the rest of us to do the same.

You are grounded by your passion and drive to make a positive and dramatic change in the world. To see you in your core is to see a shining star that energizes everyone you come in contact with. Your primary life task is to transcend your personal needs and realize that your mission is to lead by example and unify groups of people to make a difference in the world. No matter what you do, you carry the leadership energy to be CEO of a household, a business, a sports team, or any group you are in charge of. You are grounded and in your element when you are making a difference in the world.

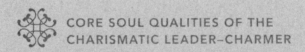

CORE SOUL QUALITIES OF THE CHARISMATIC LEADER–CHARMER

- Warrior, leader, motivator, and fierce champion of others
- Goddess/god quality of grace and leadership
- Willing to die for a cause you find worthy
- Role model with passion and commitment
- Fearless in battle, no matter what shape the battle takes
- Open to the challenges of life
- Sensual, seductive power in relationships
- Protective love
- Untiring loyalty and spotless integrity to a person or cause

Extraordinary Power Process:
Align with Your Profile Qualities

This simple process, when repeated frequently as you go through your daily life, supports you in aligning with your profile and living your unique life purpose. The activities below give you a chance to use the Charismatic Leader–Charmer Profile to focus that process (described in more detail in *Orientation to the Program* on page 117).

FEEL: Do the inner feeling work by identifying those core soul qualities and defensive patterns from the profile description that you feel most deeply. Then choose a few to work with that are the strongest. Write in your journal about what it is like to experience that quality or pattern in your life. Think of a specific situation at work, in your relationship, with regard to your health and well-being, and ask yourself, when in your core or in your defense, the following questions:

* ❖ How do I feel—physically, emotionally, and energetically?
* ❖ What am I saying to myself and to others?
* ❖ What am I attracting to myself by being in that quality?
* ❖ What am I rejecting or avoiding?

As you write, observe the power that is available from your core soul qualities and also the self-sabotage that results from being in your defense.

CHOOSE: Make conscious choices to create your future, no longer living in the self-sabotaging, knee-jerk reality of your defense. Select one core soul quality you felt the deepest from the reading. Sit quietly and visualize living in that core quality right now: How does it change your relationships, career, health, and finances? Project your life out one, five, and ten years into the future, and explore the same question. Write about your vision in your journal. Then come back to the present moment. Choose how you will do things differently based on living in your core soul qualities.

ACT: Align your actions with your core soul qualities in your career, relationships, health, or finances. Ask: *What would my Charismatic Leader–Charmer do in this area or situation? How would he or she respond and act right now?* Commit to taking action in this moment, even if it's a symbolic gesture of writing down your most inspired message that you are going to share with your staff at work, or listing all the people who have been supporting you in life and thanking them personally.

REPEAT THIS PROCESS and continue to *feel, choose,* and *act* in this way as you discover more and more about your unique Life Purpose Profile. Soon this simple process will become your default mode, overriding the knee-jerk programming you've been trapped in for most of your life, and you will be free.

Before You Go On . . .

Record aspects of your profile that you can align with on a Personal Profile Summary chart. Turn to page 297 and fill in the first two sections on the chart from your discoveries in Step 1: *My Core Soul Qualities* and *My Defensive Profile Patterns.* (You will have a chance to fill in the remaining sections of the chart in Step 2 and Step 3.) Your chart can then serve as a handy reference for the work you are doing to know yourself in this new way.

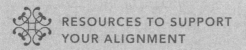

RESOURCES TO SUPPORT YOUR ALIGNMENT

The following are available at www.discoveryourpurposebook .com/members:

1. **Guided Meditation Audio Download.** *Your Secret Place.* This meditation not only helps you identify your profile but also shows you the difference between being in your core soul self and being in a defensive state.

2. **Crystal Bowls Audio Download.** Daily work with crystal bowls helps you to feel your alignment with your profile. Then you are called to your life purpose by energy resonance, not from force of mental will.

Step 2: Recognize Your Defenses

In Step 2, you use your profile as a lens to examine and then dismantle the defensive mask of your false self that is living in a virtual reality. You identify your core wounds and self-rejecting vows, as well as your negative pleasures, and you begin to replace these defensive behaviors with freeing statements and positive pleasures.

The Big Why story of my student and Charismatic Leader–Charmer Angelo illustrates how living from your core, not your vows, can dramatically impact your life.

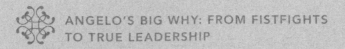

ANGELO'S BIG WHY: FROM FISTFIGHTS
TO TRUE LEADERSHIP

Referred by a friend, Angelo came to see me because he felt his life was spiraling out of control. He was a handsome man, despite the extra weight he carried, and he exuded a kind of charm that women like.

Angelo appeared competent and successful: he was a financial adviser in his forties with his own business, a wife, and two children, ages eight and eleven. But underneath, his life had all the signs of a Charismatic Leader–Charmer in defense: chaos, violence, and a history of being sexually molested.

"I feel as if life is happening to me—like I'm the passenger and someone else is driving the car," he told me. "I'm good at performing my duties, but inside I'm depressed and anxious." Angelo had been diagnosed with depression and anxiety, suffered from insomnia, and took prescription meds. At the same time, he was doing recreational drugs and drinking excessively.

The depression, drinking, and drug abuse were affecting his marriage, and at work he was involved in several lawsuits. "Life is a constant battle," he remarked. "Not just verbally, but I even get into physical confrontations and end up in fistfights way too often." Angelo had consulted several psychologists but felt that none of what they did was working for him. He felt it was a weakness to be in therapy and didn't like talking about himself.

He showed up one day in my office with a fat lip, a black eye, and scratches and bruises all over his arms. He'd been in a fight at work, and his wife had asked him to leave the house, no longer wanting to put up with his violent, aggressive behavior.

"That was the bottom of the barrel for me—to not be together with my family," he said. "I knew I had to do something." Angelo enrolled in the classes I was offering through my institute, despite the difficulty he had with trusting people in a group setting. He wanted to solve his problems quickly, and I assured him that committing to a class would get him the results he wanted.

"One of the biggest lessons I got is that I am in charge of me, and no one else is," he commented. "Before I took the class, I could never understand why people did the things they did, but learning about the profiles gave me insights that helped me react less dramatically. I came to understand that everyone is different energetically, and it made sense how I react the way I do."

Angelo discovered that his experience of being molested by a neighbor when he was eight had been hugely impacting his life. "That event led to vows that created the Enforcer in me, someone who would never surrender, would fight to the death. I became hypervigilant, always on guard, and would never allow myself to be dominated by anyone."

Angelo's secondary profile is Team Player/People Pleaser, which put him in direct conflict with his Enforcer energy. "All I really wanted to do was to give you a big hug," he said. "Then, after ripping your head off, I'd feel so guilty, so full of remorse."

Because he buried the molestation trauma and never shared it with anyone in his life, he grew to believe that he didn't need anyone's help. But when that didn't work out, he felt stuck and hopeless. "I hated myself for being weak and was ashamed of allowing something like that to happen to me."

The healing process for Angelo started when he began to share his early experience, first in the class and then with important family members, including his wife. "I was terrified, but without sharing the experience, keeping it locked away and buried, it only ate me up inside."

In class, Angelo did a meditation that took him back in time to that early wound and all the guilt and shame surrounding it. "I saw that little boy I had been and walked up to him and gave him a hug, letting him know he was going to be all right," he said. "This was especially powerful for me, having an eight-year-old son now myself. If this had happened to my son, I would have put my arms around him, too. I needed that, and I gave it to myself."

Things at work started to improve with this shift in Angelo's acceptance of himself. As CEO of his own financial services company, he often had to give feedback to his five employees. "Rather than chew people out, I now approach them from a different angle, as a leader, helping them to do things better," he said. "I deserve to be followed, because I'm not the Enforcer that everyone's afraid of any longer. I'm back in the driver's seat, able to have meaningful conversations with people instead of holding my resentments in and then exploding, screaming and yelling."

On the family front, Angelo returned to the home he'd shared with his wife and two kids. Drinking and drug abuse were no longer an issue. While he'd suffered some setbacks in his physical health—high blood pressure and precancerous esophageal complications—he took these conditions as a wake-up call and got into a fitness program, exercising daily and losing forty-five pounds.

"That vicious cycle of feeling depressed and eating to fill the hole inside me got broken when I started to live from my profile, not just from my ancient vows," he said. "Today, my life is worth fighting for. I'm worth fighting for, and so is the welfare of my family and my employees."

Angelo had this to say about his participation in the program: "When I started learning about the profiles, I thought I was supposed to change who I was. But it turned out that I was called to be more of who I already am in my core. Now I can recognize when I'm slipping into defense and can choose to be a leader instead. This has been transformative for me and has given me my energy and my life back."

Becoming Aware of Your Vows

Becoming aware of your vows—those hardwired beliefs that filter your every experience through a limited view—is critical for dismantling your defense. The source of all your vows is early life events that wounded you emotionally and energetically—your *core wounds*.

As someone with an Enforcer-Seducer defense, you've had at least one experience of trusting but being betrayed by someone who had authority over you.

Because sexual energy and passion are part of your life purpose, you will probably have wounds in this area, too. Your early interest in the sensations of your genitals may have been noticed by predator adults, giving them a justification, in their minds, to molest you. Or you may have connected to your parents' sexual energy at a young age, causing an Oedipal complex with a parent. You may have been put to sleep in your parents' bed and exposed to them making love right next to you. All such sexual inappropriateness is wounding to a young child and can be at the source of many vows made at that time and later in life.

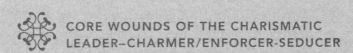

CORE WOUNDS OF THE CHARISMATIC LEADER–CHARMER/ENFORCER-SEDUCER

- Betrayal by someone you trusted, such as a parent who couldn't handle your challenging personality
- Being emotionally, sexually, or physically abused
- Being Momma's boy or Daddy's girl, in a bond used for control by one parent against the other parent
- Growing up in a volatile home where aggression was a tool everyone used
- Being told you were a liar or having parents who lied to you all the time
- Being told you were born gifted and are better than everyone else
- Using seduction or rage to get what you want
- Getting attention by being or faking sickness or injury
- Having your true power suppressed, so you must live by exhibiting any of the other profile defenses—Thinker, Poor Me, People Pleaser, or Rule Keeper

As a Charismatic Leader–Charmer, you have a life purpose of being powerful and influential in the world, so your core vows are focused on protecting those forms of self-expression.

Charismatic Leader–Charmers often vow never to conform or comply with other people's rules in life, unless it suits their own needs, too. For example, you comply with all of the inane and silly rules in your new job to build rapport with your boss, but as soon as you have some leverage, you change the rules or find a way around them.

Your core vows are never to be weak or compliant like your mother or father, never to trust what others tell you, or never to surrender to authority. These are devastating vows for a Charismatic Leader–Charmer, because in order to live your life purpose and find your place in the world, you must work through the elements of power and vulnerability. Your vows will prevent you from doing this.

Your gift of championing a just cause in the world will never have the energy needed until your early vows are addressed and released. Before you can fight injustice in the world, you must deal with the injustice of not being understood and seen for who you truly are. Once the vows that limit your truth are addressed, you will feel your willingness to fight *for* a cause, not only *against* other people.

Read and allow yourself to feel the Vow Statements that typically form the Enforcer-Seducer defense. Do you recognize any from the list in your own life? If not, add some of your own.

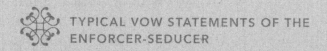

TYPICAL VOW STATEMENTS OF THE ENFORCER-SEDUCER

I vow never to trust others and get screwed (like my father did).
I vow never to be a wimp (like my mother who was cowed by my father).

I vow always to protect my family, even if it means controlling them.

I vow never to get so deep in a relationship that I can't reject the other before they reject me.

I vow never to let my guard down with anyone, showing people only what I want them to see.

I vow always to get what I deserve, because life is about the survival of the fittest.

I vow never to show others how much I need their attention and approval.

I vow never to get emotionally attached to anyone, so I can cut ties if needed.

I vow never to forgive myself for the evil things I've done, going it alone and preventing anyone from ever knowing the true me.

I vow always to resist anyone who has power over me in any way.

WRITE YOUR OWN: _____

Extraordinary Power Process: Release Your Vows

The activities below give you a chance to become aware of and release vows of the Enforcer-Seducer defense.

FEEL: Choose those Vow Statements from the list that resonate most strongly for you. Mark them and add any of your own to the list. Then select one or more to work with in completing the following sentences:

1. A vow I made was always/never to _____

   _____.

2. How this vow is influencing my life right now: _____

   _____.

3. My self-talk that reinforces this vow: _____

_____.

EXAMPLE:

1. A vow I made was never to be vulnerable and weak like my mother, who always caved in to my father's demands.
2. How this vow is influencing my life right now: It keeps me from being able to share my deepest feelings and passions, and from being vulnerable in my closest relationships.
3. My self-talk that reinforces this vow: "No one will ever dominate me and make me a victim, and they will be sorry if they do."

CHOOSE: Look at the vows you marked and, taking one at a time, ask yourself: *What would my life be like if I stopped honoring that vow?* Project out one, five, and ten years from now and ask: *How would not honoring that vow change my life?* Write your answers in your journal.

For example: *If I no longer honored this vow, I could have a relationship in which I can let down my guard and trust that I can defend myself if needed, and my deepest needs and desires will possibly get fulfilled.*

ACT: What action could you take to support your choice to no longer honor your vow? Decide to act based on your conscious choice, not a vow. Write in your journal about what happened when you did.

REPEAT THE PROCESS of *feel*, *choose*, and *act* every time you become aware that an ancient vow has been running your life. Vows are buried deep in your psyche, so it can take years to permanently release them. Be prepared to feel some amount of fear, guilt, and shame as you choose not to honor your vows; a vow is an unconscious promise, and you are breaking that promise when you choose something other than your vow.

Before You Go On . . .

Record the Vow Statements you resonate with most strongly on your Personal Profile Summary chart on page 297. Fill in the section for *My Vow Statements* with statements from the list or that you wrote in.

Freedom Statements

Replace your Vow Statements with Freedom Statements, which are the solutions to your vows. Freedom Statements call forth your core soul qualities and support you in increasingly choosing more consciously in every moment. Every time you choose a Freedom Statement over a vow, you get back energy and open yourself to ever-growing life rather than stagnating as a wounded victim.

Use Freedom Statements as a bridge out of defense and onto the path of your truth. The following list offers you a variety of statements, but you can always add your own.

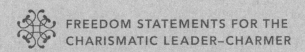

FREEDOM STATEMENTS FOR THE CHARISMATIC LEADER–CHARMER

I am open to trusting myself and seeing myself as a born leader and motivator.

I am open to leading by example in my unique way.

I am open to letting others make their own choices to follow me or to follow their own guidance.

I am open to being a hero and leader who fights to protect those I love and those who cannot help themselves.

I love that I am a rebel and live my life on my terms.

I trust in myself and my abilities to do good in the world.

I am open to lead through example but never force others to follow.

I am not only unique in the world but unique in every moment, constantly transforming—alive, fresh, new, and different every day.

I take full responsibility for all of my actions and choices, never denying my power by blaming others.

I am open to loving myself and will never lie or compromise for fame, money, sex, or safety.

WRITE YOUR OWN: _____

Extraordinary Power Process:
Become Free of Your Vows

The activities below give you a chance to replace your vows with Freedom Statements and live from your Charismatic Leader–Charmer soul qualities rather than your Enforcer-Seducer defense.

FEEL: Read the list of Freedom Statements above, speaking each one aloud. Let yourself feel their truth as you sit quietly after speaking them. Notice those you may want to deny and then repeat those statements until you no longer have a negative reaction to them. Also notice which statements register strongly as *Yes, that's me!*

CHOOSE: Speak your Freedom Statements out loud as often as possible to bring conscious choice to your vow-driven, knee-jerk defensive reactions. Tell others about your Freedom Statements so that they can see your truth and support you in embodying it. Especially as a Charismatic Leader–Charmer, you will want to use your Freedom Statements to be the foundation of the inspirational message that you share with others and the world.

Sit and inquire within about what your life will be like one, five, and ten years from now as you embody the truth in your Freedom Statements.

ACT: Explore how you would act differently in key areas of your life if your vows were replaced by Freedom Statements. Choose one action you can take that aligns you with the truth of your Freedom Statement, not your vow, and do it!

REPEAT THE PROCESS of *feel*, *choose*, and *act* often when dealing with your life's obstacles. You'll notice how your vow-driven actions begin to fade as you increasingly make choices and act based on who you truly are rather than the past of your false and defended self.

Before You Go On . . .

Record the Freedom Statements you have chosen to replace your vows on the Personal Profile Summary chart on page 297. Fill in the section for *My Freedom Statements*.

Your Negative Pleasures

Living from your core soul qualities, not your vows, will empower you to embrace your life purpose. But without confronting your *negative pleasures*, real freedom will never be yours. Negative pleasures—those habits and behaviors you know you shouldn't do (or *don't* do but know you should!) because they make you feel better about yourself—must be confronted and left behind if you are going to live your authentic purpose.

Negative pleasures in the Enforcer-Seducer defense will always involve getting others to bend or comply with your will; using your beauty, cleverness, or charm to get special treatment; or self-sabotaging your success and relationships. In short, you find your negative pleasures in battling and beating others to get on top, or battling and beating yourself to be your own worst enemy.

When visiting family or exposed to certain social situations, you may dominate the conversation, cleverly hiding behind your words and seeding conversation with gossip, misinformation, or accusations. After all is said and done, you take no responsibility for the damage because you tell yourself that you were just the messenger.

If there isn't someone to battle outwardly, you turn your anger inward, sometimes leading to depression. Self-medication through drinking, smoking, or doing drugs helps you deal with the stress and anxiety of trying to maintain control. Your strong constitution protects you from some degree of bodily abuse (but obviously not all).

If you can't be the best and most loved, feared, wealthy, influential, or beautiful/handsome, then you choose the negative pleasure of being the biggest catastrophe. This can happen through any form of self-sabotage—whether it's anger, manipulation, theft, laziness, or addiction.

Enforcer-Seducers who have not created power or wealth in their lives often find negative pleasure in getting a free ride from government subsidies for a fabricated or self-imposed disability.

A person in full Enforcer-Seducer defense is simply a survivalist, and any opportunity to gain control is fair game. They will even say, *It's nothing personal!* after their destructive behavior has impacted others.

The following list includes typical negative pleasures of the Enforcer-Seducer defense. Feel free to add your own.

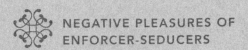

NEGATIVE PLEASURES OF ENFORCER-SEDUCERS

Being special and more important than others
Being the winner no matter what, but not even caring what you
  are fighting for
Lying pathologically
Always getting your way
Never saying *I'm sorry* or saying it only to get someone off your
  back
Using seduction to get others to comply with your will
Using bullying to get others to comply with your will
Dominating conversations and cutting others off
Keeping secrets and never letting the whole truth be told
Being a self-righteous victim who vilifies others

WRITE YOUR OWN: _____

Extraordinary Power Process: Diminish Your Negative Pleasures

The activities below give you a chance to become aware of your negative pleasures. The key to diminishing your negative pleasures is to become conscious of the poor substitutes they are for the real pleasures you could be having in your life.

FEEL: As you read the list of negative pleasures for the Enforcer-Seducer defense, let yourself feel which ones resonate deeply to evoke a response of *Yes, that's me!*

CHOOSE: Choose one negative pleasure from the list that you identified and are willing to let go of. Sit with all the pain that this behavior has caused you and others to date. Then visualize your life projected out ten years from now. If you don't change that behavior, what positive pleasure will it cost you?

To help you do this, fill in the following statements:

1. A negative pleasure I have in my life is

   _____.

2. Allowing that negative pleasure in my life costs me now and in the future: _____.

EXAMPLE:

1. A negative pleasure I have in my life is never trusting any-one, so I don't ever share anything personal about myself.
2. Allowing this negative pleasure costs me any ability to be a trusted leader or truly to inspire others, and leaves me iso-lated and defended, thinking that others are *against* me more than *for* me.

Now write about a positive pleasure, one that comes from living in your core, and describe how experiencing that pleasure might look in your life. For example: *By trusting in myself and my intuition to share my deepest passions and inspirations in life, I will become the leader I was born to be.*

ACT: Having chosen a negative pleasure you are ready to let go of, the next time it comes up in your life, ask yourself: *What positive pleasure am I missing as I indulge this negative one? How would my Charismatic Leader–Charmer respond in this situation?* Then take action in accordance with your answer.

REPEAT THIS PROCESS OFTEN. As your negative pleasures become increasingly noticeable, see them as behaviors based on fear and a limited point of view that you are now ready to grow out of. Don't beat yourself up. Go slow, get support, and let each negative pleasure go, one at a time. You will start to experience positive pleasures that come from accepting your life and the people in it. Soon, the unconscious habits and behaviors you've been substituting for real pleasure will no longer seem as attractive.

Every negative pleasure you successfully let go of allows you to bring back into your life all of the wasted energy that went into that defense. With that energy, you can make powerful choices to live your life as a creative presence.

Before You Go On . . .

Record your negative pleasures on your Personal Profile Summary chart on page 297. Fill in the section for *My Favorite Negative Pleasures*.

In Transition . . .

As you transition out of Enforcer-Seducer defense and into your core self, you may find yourself stuck in frustrating old patterns. Your defenses have been making you someone you are not, someone less than who you really are. Now awakened, you can make conscious choices and set goals to act differently.

As the Charismatic Leader–Charmer core quality awakens, you begin to trust your instincts and become a warrior of light and consciousness. You know what atrocities people are capable of. The shift from Enforcer-Seducer to Charismatic Leader–Charmer happens when you no longer need to trust others because you fully trust yourself and your own mission in life. You trust that you are capable of taking the high road and surrendering to what you are called to do and be in the world, letting others do the same rather than trying to control them.

A shadow warrior in defense goes it alone and trusts no one. On the other hand, a hero fights against injustice and joins others in making a difference.

Here is an activity to support your transition out of Enforcer-Seducer defense into your core self as a Charismatic Leader–Charmer.

ACTIVITY: To counter your tendency to hide and isolate out of mistrust, set a goal of sharing some aspect of yourself with another person each day. Begin with something small, like telling a co-worker about your favorite pastime. Gradually build up to sharing more of yourself. You may find that you can share your greatest desires or wildest dreams, but decide beforehand that if you don't get the response you want,

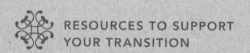

RESOURCES TO SUPPORT YOUR TRANSITION

1. **Guided Meditation Audio Download.** *Calling Back Your Spirit* (available at www.discoveryourpurposebook.com/members).

2. **Recommended Reading List**
   - *The Art of War*, by Sun Tzu
   - *Loving What Is*, by Byron Katie
   - *Unlimited Power*, by Anthony Robbins
   - *In Search of the Warrior Spirit*, by Richard Strozzi-Heckler
   - *Full Catastrophe Living*, by Jon Kabat-Zinn
   - *Comfortable with Uncertainty*, by Pema Chödrön
   - *The Psychopath Test*, by Jon Ronson

you won't become deflated or take another's opinion personally in any way.

Write in your journal about what happened when you did this.

Step 3: Live Your Life Purpose

Having begun the process of dismantling your defenses in Step 2, you are now ready to integrate your profile's unique higher- and lower-self qualities. As you become less conflicted and more whole and balanced, you can make choices and take courageous actions in your life, not just react automatically from your ancient vows. You are also able to use the Law of Attraction to attract what best supports your unique life purpose as you create and live an extraordinary life.

Your Shadow: Lower- and Higher-Self Traits

Your shadow is made up of traits that you have rejected by vowing *always* or *never* to be or do something. Those traits can be seen as aspects of your higher self and your lower self. As you identify rejected higher- and lower-self traits, you can begin to accept and integrate them, and so achieve a state of inner balance and wholeness. Fully integrating your shadow allows your defensive mask to dissolve and your true core soul self to emerge.

The following chart contains a list of the lower- and higher-self traits *in matched pairs* that you must own and integrate to fully live your life purpose as a Charismatic Leader–Charmer:

LOWER- AND HIGHER-SELF TRAITS FOR
CHARISMATIC LEADER–CHARMERS

LOWER-SELF TRAITS	HIGHER-SELF TRAITS
Pathological liar	Teller of inconvenient truths
Selfish	Self-sacrificing for a worthy cause
Self-righteous abuser	Fights for truth
Irrational and impulsive	Never a slave to a system
Cheater	Breaks rules that oppress others
Fighter who hurts others	Fearless warrior-hero
Narcissistic	Encourages others to be the "one and only"
Angry	Passionately motivated to change
Shape-shifter	Able to create rapport with anyone
Seductive	Charming
Controlling	Leads by example
Hypervigilant against others	Deeply protective of loved ones
Ruthless need to win	Creates a win-win
Overbearing, controlling	Strong and committed
Chronic disability	Never taking charity
Addict	Loving pleasure of every kind
Depressed and self-hating	Strong sense of self and ego
Violent	Able to walk away from a fight
Victim, justifying victimizing others	Never a victim, always victorious
Faking emotions to manipulate	World-class actor/actress

Extraordinary Power Process: Integrate Your Shadow

The activities below give you a chance to integrate your shadow (rejected traits) with your higher-self light.

FEEL: As you read the list of matched-pair lower-/higher-self traits, reach deep into yourself to feel the full range of your raw, lower self at one end and your exalted, higher self at the other. Both are within you to varying degrees. Your raw power and personal needs are found in your lower-self traits, but how you consciously use that power and fulfill those needs is in your higher-self traits. When you can own both in any moment and still choose your higher-self traits, then everything you do will be aligned with your life purpose.

Put a check mark next to the lower- and higher-self traits you recognize as ones you exhibit. Also notice traits that elicit a powerful negative reaction, and check them, too. These are traits you have rejected in yourself or in others. (By rejecting lower-self traits, you say to yourself, *I'd never do that—it's too negative, mean, or evil*; while in rejecting higher-self traits, you say, *I could never do that—it's too perfect, saintly, or godlike*.)

CAUTION: No higher-self trait can exist without the lower-self trait alongside it. To be whole and balanced, you must be conscious of both within you. Selecting only those traits you like will send you back to your vow-created life where only half of you exists.

Using your strongest traits checked, complete these statements for each:

1. A lower-/higher-self trait that I see as strong in me is

_____.

2. My greatest fear of owning that trait is _____

_____.

EXAMPLE:

1. A lower-self trait that I see as strong in me is being a shape-shifter who acts like a different person with everyone I know, and none of them are the real me.
2. My greatest fear of owning that trait is that in lying to everyone and not even knowing why, I will be considered a liar and will be rejected.

AND:

1. A higher-self trait that is the partner to my lower-self trait is that I can empathize and build rapport with anyone in an instant.
2. My greatest fear of owning that trait is that, with this higher-self gift, I cannot hide anymore, and I must have the highest integrity in how I influence others.

CHOOSE: Now work with one set of lower- and higher-self traits that you identified as not being fully owned in their full range. Ask how your life would be different if you owned both higher- and lower-self traits equally, able to accept either freely but choosing the higher-self quality.

Visualize your life up to now and see how damaging it has been to express the lower-self trait unconsciously. Also feel how you have wanted to express the higher-self trait more often but don't, since the lower-self trait cannot be resolved. Now project this pattern of behavior out into your life one, five, and ten years into the future and see what your life looks like with just this one conflict within you.

What would happen if you were able to embrace both higher and lower traits at all times, rejecting neither, as part of your life purpose? Notice that, if you did not stand in such fear of being who you really are one, five, and ten years into the future, you would instead reveal your true power and purpose.

For example: *If I accept that I can read people and influence them so easily, then I can also accept that when I reveal my true self to the world, I will inspire others through that expression and possibly move the masses for the good.*

ACT: Take actions that align with your new state of inner balance and wholeness. Commit to one action you will take that reflects your new self-acceptance, and then do it. Write in your journal about what happened when you did.

REPEAT THE PROCESS! Once you've worked with one pair of higher- and lower-self traits in this way, repeat with more traits in both lists. Accepting both higher and lower selves as the whole of who you are is the most powerful spiritual work you can do.

Before You Go On . . .

Turn to page 297 and fill in the section for *Lower- and Higher-Self Traits* on your Personal Profile Summary chart.

Living Courageously

Living your life purpose means speaking and acting fearlessly from your core soul self. To remain in that state, you will need to step out of your comfort zone often and take the road less traveled, leaping over obstacles in your way. What follows are some ways you as a Charismatic Leader–Charmer can do that.

Accept your selfish instincts in relationships.

You instinctually compete for power and control, and need to dominate others and use them for your own narcissistic purposes. By accepting that you enjoy control, you become conscious of the negative pleasure of being who you are. You begin your path to enlightenment by understanding the pleasure you get from manipulating others and the truth.

Bring honesty and trust into your relationships.

Most Charismatic Leader–Charmers/Enforcer-Seducers find themselves as double agents in their lives, with an internal world that does not match their external reality or relationships. You never reveal your real identity, but as you get deeper into a relationship, the need for honesty and intimacy becomes greater, and the pressure forces you to leave that relationship. You may have failed relationships, as well as jobs, because you can't be honest up front in your relationships. You will only stay in a relationship if the story of who you are and why you do what you do is never questioned.

Profiles are designed for relationship mastery. Whatever is true within us that we can't share is what ultimately destroys the relationship. As a Charismatic Leader–Charmer, you don't believe you can ever trust another person because you can never trust yourself. That is your greatest secret, and it drives you to dominate and control everyone in your life.

Before You Go On . . .

Turn to page 297 and fill in the section for *Actions to Take for Living Courageously* on your Personal Profile Summary chart.

Speak Your Truth

To remain in your Charismatic Leader–Charmer core, you must be willing to speak your truth to others, especially to those with whom you are in an intimate relationship. Practice by reading each of the Essential Word Statements below, visualizing that you are speaking directly to someone you love and feeling your words deeply as you read them.

Make a commitment to speak these essential words—not the automatic words dictated by your vows and defenses—to an important person in your life. Then act to call, write, or speak with that important person to share your truth.

ESSENTIAL WORDS FOR CHARISMATIC LEADER–CHARMERS TO SPEAK

- I love you so much that you need to know that I can be selfish and may hurt you sometimes.
- I need you to trust that I will always do my best in every situation to be aware of your needs as well as mine, but often I can see only mine.
- A relationship with me will be passionate and exciting, and I am a person who needs major change every couple of years.
- Please be strong with me and do not let me manipulate you, for it is in my nature to do that.

- I need you to treat me like a king or a queen but also make me treat you in the same way.
- I have a very important mission to achieve, so I need you to support me in every way you can, and I will support you in being all you can be in your life.
- Please never buy my story that I am broken or weak in any way, for I am truly the strongest person you or I will ever know. I am a survivor.

Before You Go On . . .

Turn to page 297 and fill in the section for *Speaking Your Truth (Essential Words)* on your Personal Profile Summary chart.

The Law of Attraction

According to the Law of Attraction, like attracts like. It follows that you will always attract people and situations that are just like you. As your alignment with your life purpose grows, your internal magnet for attracting who and what you want in your life is strengthened. If you are not aligned with your life purpose, no amount of visualizing will help you achieve your desires—in spite of what popular culture tells you about how constant visualizing will bring you what you want.

As a Charismatic Leader–Charmer, you have huge reserves of energy, so you naturally magnetize large amounts of material wealth and resources to you when in your core. In defense, when you reject your true self, you attract financial devastation in equal proportions. You are born to take the resources that are at hand and turn them into something greater, as you see how they can best serve your purpose. In defense, you have an expectation that life should serve you and your purpose, and the deeper you go into defense, the more you believe that others owe you.

This sense of entitlement can go two ways. You might be a wealthy investment banker who wants a house on Long Island and another in Key West, and buys them both on credit, assuming your position will somehow manifest the funds needed to pay for it all—until it doesn't. Or if you were not brought up with money or were manipulated through money, you may rebel and live in abject poverty, forcing family, friends, and the government to support you because you can't make enough on your own. In either case, you are left feeling like a victim and justify any means to get or reject money. In your core and undefended self, your sense of entitlement still exists but becomes transformed into generosity and wealth creation for the benefit of many.

ACTIVITY: EXPLORE THE GAP. The gap is the space between where you are now and where you know you will be when you fully embody your core soul profile qualities and live your life purpose. Examining areas of life such as your health, relationships, finances, and career, consider the following:

- ❖ What am I attracting in my life right now from living in my defenses?
- ❖ What do I want to attract in my life from living in my core soul self?

Are you attracting what supports your life purpose or what keeps you stuck in your defense? How can you act from your core soul qualities, and not your defenses, to close that gap and attract what you want to support your life purpose? Write your responses in your journal.

Before You Go On . . .

Turn to page 297 and fill in the section for *Law of Attraction* on your Personal Profile Summary chart.

Extraordinary Power Process: Your Personal Profile Summary Chart

Your Personal Profile Summary chart now holds what you have learned about yourself from the Charismatic Leader–Charmer profile, either as your primary or your secondary Life Purpose Profile.

Once you have completed your charts for both primary and secondary profiles, use them as a tool to support you in living your life purpose. Follow the Extraordinary Power Process of *feel*, *choose*, and *act* as you refer to each section you've filled in on your chart:

1. Feel: Do the inner feeling work—don't just think.
2. Choose: Make conscious choices—don't automatically react based on your vows.
3. Act: Align your actions with your profile's core soul qualities—not with your defenses—to live your truth.

When you repeat this sequence as often as possible throughout your day, then everything you do reveals the mystery of who you are rather than reinforcing who you think you are—but are not. *Feeling*, *choosing*, and *acting* in accordance with your profile gives you access to your extraordinary power so you can effortlessly manifest your life purpose and live it in every area of your life.

Charismatic Leader—Charmer/Enforcer-Seducer
PERSONAL PROFILE SUMMARY

Profile	☐ This is my PRIMARY PROFILE ☐ This is my SECONDARY PROFILE ☐ This is my THIRD, FOURTH, or FIFTH PROFILE
My Core Soul Qualities (for this profile)	1 _____ 2 _____
My Defensive Profile Patterns	1 _____ 2 _____
My Vow Statements (How I self-sabotage)	1 _____ 2 _____ 3 _____
My Freedom Statements (Solutions to my Vow Statements)	I am open to _____ I am open to _____ I am open to _____
My Favorite Negative Pleasures (How I self-sabotage)	Something I do that I shouldn't do but get pleasure from: _____ Something I get pleasure from not doing that I know I should do: _____
Lower- and Higher-Self Traits (matched pairs)	Lower: Higher: 1 _____ / _____ 2 _____ / _____
Actions to take for living courageously from your profile	1 _____ 2 _____
Speaking Your Truth (ESSENTIAL WORDS you must say to others)	1 _____ 2 _____
Law of Attraction (People, situations, etc. that I am attracting)	In defense, I attract _____ In my core, I attract _____

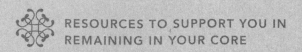

RESOURCES TO SUPPORT YOU IN REMAINING IN YOUR CORE

1. **Guided Meditation Audio Download:** *Your Subpersonalities.* Explore your higher- and lower-self traits through a guided meditation, available at www.discoveryourpurposebook.com/members.

2. **Bioenergetic Exercises for Charismatic Leader–Charmers,** available below and also on the same website.

BIOENERGETIC EXERCISES FOR THE CHARISMATIC LEADER–CHARMER

Exercises that bring you into balance involve trust, which is your profile's primary issue. Charismatic Leaders–Charmers become hypervigilant through their eyes, so any activity done with a blindfold can help to break the pattern of distrust.

EXERCISE #1: OWNING ANGER. Express aggressive energy downward through stamping your feet and kicking, not through punching and yelling. This gets you out of the vertical energy flow that projects your anger at others. Realize that your anger and rage are always yours. Then you can channel them for good, not against yourself or others. To be fully in relationship, you cannot hide your anger, but you must learn to channel it into what unifies you and others, not go into battle and isolation. Being genuine and vulnerable in the present moment, rather than always being on the attack, will change your life.

EXERCISE #2: STATUES. Let a friend or therapist move you through physical positions and sculpt you like a statue. Hold the position, no matter how silly or strange, until you feel what it is like to live in the world they created for you. Then go back to your normal stance. Do this two or three times. Letting others guide you is key to trust.

EXERCISE #3: BLINDFOLD "FRIEND OR FOE." To begin this exercise, you will need to be blindfolded and wearing boxing gloves. A friend or therapist can provide a punching pad. Begin by just standing and feeling vulnerable. The person with the pad pushes you hard enough to make you fall off balance but not hard enough to knock you down, or touches you gently with the pad. When the person pushes you hard, you fight with all you have and say "Get away from me!" or anything you might come up with. When the person touches you gently, you let down your guard and hug the person lovingly. The pad holder should randomly do one or the other, with the emphasis more on the push that forces you to fight back. This teaches you what it feels like to constantly be on guard and how difficult it can be to let down your guard to experience love and trust when you are so often defended against attack.

CHAPTER 11

Profile #5: Knowledgeable Achiever/Rule Keeper

THE KNOWLEDGEABLE ACHIEVER

with Rule Keeper defense

Welcome to the Knowledgeable Achiever profile and its defense, the Rule Keeper. You will find valuable information and activities here to help you access your extraordinary power and embody your life purpose.

If this is your secondary or other profile, or the profile of someone in your life, you can use what you learn here to deepen your understanding of yourself and of others.

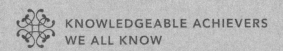

KNOWLEDGEABLE ACHIEVERS WE ALL KNOW

Historical: Socrates, Thomas Edison, William Blake, Indira Gandhi
Contemporary: Bill Gates, Hillary Clinton, Barack Obama, the Venerable Dalai Lama, Timothy Cook (Apple's chief operating officer)

Step 1: Align with Your Profile

In the first step of the program, you learn all about your profile, including those core soul qualities that support you to live in your life purpose and those defenses that cause you to sabotage your efforts. You will read the Big Why story of my student Sue, who discovered her life purpose by aligning with her Knowledgeable Achiever profile.

About Your Profile

What follows is a general description of your profile, including how it looks in defense as a Rule Keeper. Here you take a closer look at your current life situation, including your primary mate and relationships, your career or job, how you handle money, and your physical and energetic aspects.

GENERAL DESCRIPTION. As a Knowledgeable Achiever, you are highly driven, strongly self-disciplined, and well organized. You exhibit mastery and intelligent action on the way to accomplishing any task or project, knowing what to do and how to do it. You also have an ability to see the bigger picture in any endeavor, keeping an eye on the greater good.

You push yourself to levels of achievement that boggle the minds of people in the other profiles. You can organize and run projects, oversee tens of thousands of employees, and effortlessly get to the heart of every situation. Or you can spend twenty years on research to create a product that will change the way all of humanity functions, as in the case of Thomas Edison and the lightbulb. You have the mental discipline to master a martial art, climb the highest mountains, map the most treacherous terrain, and use mathematics to ensure a seventy-story skyscraper will not fall down.

Everything you do is practical and useful to others, as well as graceful. You are relentlessly thorough, whether you are spending time with family or pursuing a spiritual discipline. You most likely got straight As in school and are now highly qualified in your field. You tend to be at the top of your field due to your strong work ethic and willingness to study ideas until you master them. It's not unusual for you to be more knowledgeable than those considered experts in their field, and you often leave a workshop or seminar thinking, *Those teachers don't understand what they are teaching—I should be teaching that course!*

IN RULE KEEPER DEFENSE, you live by the belief *What I do is who I am.* Your focus is on *doing* at the expense of *being.* Even in defense you are hardworking and effective in the world, but you also become rigid and machinelike, often achieving goals in ways that others would think are heartless.

Emotions are rarely expressed publicly. You understand the world mentally but don't need to feel it like others do. You can be cool under pressure but at the cost of not being in touch with your emotions. Feelings that might distract you from your goals are kept at bay. You fully understand cultural and social norms, and express emotions that are functional, such as contentment, sadness, frustration, and detachment. You appear focused and interested, but you don't become overwhelmed by emotions such as rage and depression. The Tin Man character in *The Wizard of Oz* is an example of a Rule Keeper—all function and no heart.

Life in Rule Keeper defense is all work. You know that if you practice a sport every day, lift weights every other day, and take a lesson twice a week, you could become a national champion in less than five years. So often, in defense, the fun of the game is lost to the rules of achievement. Playing and freedom have fallen to the wayside, while self-improvement and work rule the day. You run your life like a competition, always pushing yourself to do more, as if you were a machine.

Your list of achievement-oriented activities, rigidly followed, only leads to more of the same, never to any real happiness or satisfaction because you can never stop; you must always do better. In everything you do, your inner voice is a ruthless tyrant that gives you few rewards and often reminds you that you could have done better.

You are a terminal perfectionist and have little tolerance for flaws or failure on any level. This intolerance is expressed through criticism, judgment, and disappointment in yourself and others.

In the Rule Keeper defense, you will often feel disappointed in yourself, no matter how "good" you perceive your life to be. You strive to achieve your ideal, whether as the perfect mother, business owner, or volunteer for a favorite charity. You work diligently to be the best at whatever you do, always aiming to appear independent and self-sufficient.

In defense, your self-sabotaging patterns revolve around being highly self-critical, never feeling that you have done enough—even if you are at the top of your field. You hold a personal bar just out of your own reach but strive for it daily. You tend to organize your life around practicality and efficiency rather than emotional needs. People, events, jobs, and other aspects of life are efficiently compartmentalized, so you don't waste time wondering how to deal with them.

In your conversations with others, you will often say the words *Yes, but* . . . for example, *Yes, you have a point there, but you really don't fully understand what you are talking about.* Or *Yes, I won the match, but I could have played better.* When you are in defense, perfection is the only thing you will be happy with, so you are left disappointed in life, even when life is good.

You tend to judge and see the world impersonally, in black or white, good or bad, right or wrong, truth or lie. This "instant knowing" can leave you disconnected from anyone who feels deeply or likes to sit on things to process how they feel. Once you make up your mind about the right way to do things, you can become stuck in tunnel vision. You don't compromise when working with others because there is only one true and right way. Often, you decide it is better to go it alone.

PRIMARY MATE AND SOCIAL RELATIONSHIPS. Knowledgeable Achievers often find themselves romantically paired with the Emotional Intelligence Specialists/Poor Me as a primary mate. Undefended, the two profiles are a match made in heaven. From the Emotional Intelligence Specialist, you learn how to open your heart; you teach the Emotional Intelligence Specialist how to set boundaries and safely enjoy the core gifts of their sensitive nature. You see the value of your partner's ability to live with an open heart and feel unconditionally accepted and loved by him or her. Your partner forgives you for your hard and critical nature, which in turn helps you to forgive yourself for being imperfect and human.

In defense, as a Rule Keeper relating to your partner's Poor Me, you try to stem his or her frequent emotional outpourings because they seem unproductive. Common Rule Keeper responses are *You are being overly emotional and irrational! We can deal with this easily, if you just stop crying long enough to do something!* The Poor Me partner counters with *You never listen to me or try to understand how I feel!* Eventually, you judge your Poor Me partner as pathetic and leave the relationship with parting words such as *When you get over this, I'll be happy to talk about a plan for the future.* Your partner feels abandoned and unloved, and you avoid your own emotions.

You have lots of friends and frequently join social clubs, expressing your love outwardly with actions, gifts, and direct support of others rather than sentimental gestures. You abide by the rules of social and cultural norms.

In Rule Keeper defense, you may have many acquaintances at your gym or club, but you rarely have close friends to confide in on a deeper, emotional level. This is because the perfect front you present to the world is very different from who you really are. While people in any profile can have public lives that don't resemble their private ones, this occurs to a greater extreme in the Rule Keeper defense. You must have the perfect home with perfectly behaved children, often controlling appearances by saying to your children *We don't act that way in our family,* or *We don't show anger,* or *We don't talk about your father/mother's drinking.*

As a Rule Keeper, there is little room for passion or adventure in your strict home environment, so you may take your passions outside the home in the form of an extramarital affair or drinking and using drugs on business trips. Inside the home, however, you will lecture your spouse and other family members on the dangers of having multiple sexual partners and on the evils of alcohol and drugs.

CAREER OR JOB. Achievement and perfection are ingrained aspects of your defense, and you create your identity based on what you do. You may be a doctor, lawyer, philanthropist, naturalist, feminist, or guru, but all of these identities are only coats of armor that protect you from simply being human.

Whatever your profession, you always try to make life fit your profession, limiting the true bounty you could be receiving if you opened to the flow of life. If you are trained in accounting, you see everything in your life as a problem of balanced payables and receivables. Trained in psychology, you analyze the behaviors of others and yourself. A Rule Keeper lawyer thinks that all disputes need to be litigated or settled.

In Rule Keeper defense, you easily get stuck in doing the same thing over and over again, believing that there is only one right way of doing things. If something worked before, then you stick to it, even if it means working with paper and pencil when others have moved on to computers.

When you are out of defense, aligned with your life purpose and living from your core, your intuition and gut instinct win over your rigid inner Rule Keeper. In this state, you are open to the realm of infinite possibilities and see everything in your life as a resource to be integrated into a grand plan. Family, ideas, books, time, and material resources all factor into your every decision. You treat people who work under you not as employees only but as partners in your greater purpose, avoiding the bottom-line, get-it-done-yesterday style of management.

In your long-term view, you balance work with home life both for yourself and also for your employees. You are capable of working twenty-four hours a day when you choose to, but you are also just as likely to work the perfect nine-to-five workday and take regular vacations, since you are efficient and get your work done quickly. Yoga and meditation may become a part of your general approach to life, not just as a means of de-stressing after your work.

HOW YOU HANDLE MONEY. Knowledgeable Achievers have high integrity around money and are diligent in assessing what they can afford and what is a gamble, doing some of each. You are an excellent long-term planner and can see the value of using money to make money. You invest in both your vision and your understanding of the market forces. You know that knowledge is the most important commodity in the world, and so you keep your own knowledge current.

Knowledgeable Achievers are known as the highest achievers in the world, pooling and managing massive resources and money with precision and elegance. It may take Charismatic Leader–Charmer Steve Jobs to start a huge, world-changing company like Apple, but it is the Knowledgeable Achiever chief operating officer Timothy Cook who keeps the company up and running as smoothly as a Swiss watch.

In Rule Keeper defense, you may be a penny pincher and live an austere life with a tight budget and limited way of seeing how to make money or value your work.

PHYSICAL AND ENERGETIC CONDITION. You keep your body fit and often push it to its limits when training or exercising. You usually look younger than you are and have a strong and lean body. You are generally well coordinated, hold your head up, and sit up straight, making the statement that you have everything under control. You dress well; women color coordinate, and men feel more comfortable in suits than in sweats. Energetically, you appear solid and contained with a strong presence.

In Rule Keeper defense, you view your body as a performance machine to be pushed to the extreme, which can become unhealthy. For example, you might work at your job eighty hours a week, work out on a StairMaster in your office, train and compete in five triathlons a year, and then force your four-year-old to do martial arts. You can have chronic lower-back stiffness and hip and knee problems, caused by muscle tension from striving to be perfect. You may have heart problems, but, more often, your health issues come from your stiff and rigid muscles, stopping the natural flow of energy and creating an imbalance in your body.

On an energetic level, your heart is protected by a three-foot-thick cement wall, a comfort zone to buffer you against any emotional pain. When a person stands too close to you, you get uncomfortable

THE KNOWLEDGEABLE ACHIEVER
PHYSICAL APPEARANCE

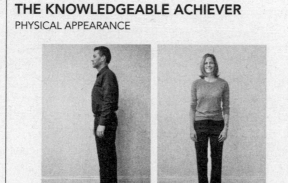

When you are visually assessing a person's profile, notice that Knowledgeable Achievers/Rule Keepers have perfect posture and an evenly balanced energy. They tend to be physically coordinated and rarely carry extra fat on their bodies. Knowledgeable Achievers look you straight in the eye and are not afraid of you looking as directly at them. They are proud of their bodies, displaying a self-confidence you can feel. These people are not huggers in general, but you sense they can meet you intellectually on almost any subject. Their most salient trait is their ability to manage their energy internally, making you feel safe in their presence.

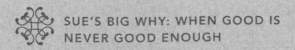

SUE'S BIG WHY: WHEN GOOD IS NEVER GOOD ENOUGH

Sue was a participant in my energy medicine certification program and currently works as a consultant for a management consulting firm. Previously, she worked from her home and authored three books on parenting teens while single-handedly raising her own two children. A double Knowledgeable Achiever (both as her primary and secondary profile), Sue knows about life both in defense as a Rule Keeper and in the freedom of aligning with her profile to live her life purpose.

"Before I discovered my profile, I had all the defensive qualities of a Rule Keeper," she reported. "I worked hard all the time to make my book business successful and felt no joy. I'd forgotten what fun was like and could literally feel the rigidity in my body. I'd dragged myself down into this place of misery where I could barely recognize myself and had no idea how to get out of it."

Sue suffered what many Rule Keepers endure: the isolation that comes from being single-mindedly focused on achieving success. "If you can't have fun and let things go, people don't want to be around you," she said. "But it was the excessive working that put me over the edge."

Not surprisingly, Sue also had a strong inner judge that constantly criticized others and thus pushed them away. Even though she wasn't shy, she kept to herself among new people unless she found someone with common interests. As a result, she often felt left out and jealous of others who easily formed bonds.

"Working with the Life Purpose Profile system, I saw how my vows and negative pleasures had me judge and be viciously unkind to myself, and it was keeping me apart from others."

Overwork and harsh self-judgment were indicators of an even deeper issue that had been plaguing Sue most of her life: low self-esteem.

"I'm a fairly accomplished person, so no one would believe I've suffered from low self-esteem and low self-confidence," she commented. "But when I was publishing my first book, my designer showed me the cover with my name printed boldly at the top, and I just shrank into a little ball. 'You have to make my name smaller,' I told her, pointing at the larger-than-life letters of my name. She looked at me as if I had three heads. 'Are you kidding me?' she said. 'No one has ever asked me for their name to be smaller!'

"But I did, because back then, I was afraid of being criticized by the experts. My area is communication, but many psychologists think I'm not qualified to write about relationships, so to put my name on the cover of a book on parenting made me feel extremely vulnerable."

Sue took classes at the institute over a period of three years. "As I gradually let my defenses down, dismantled my virtual reality, and awakened into living from my life purpose, I experienced a major shift in my comfort level with just being me. I learned that I was the one responsible for my low self-esteem. Yes, I was critical of others, but even more critical of myself.

"Now I can see myself through others' eyes and be comfortable with it, not have to hide and shrink for fear of exposure. I've learned to accept myself, both my strengths and my challenges. That intense self-consciousness, where I had to be so perfect in everything I did, is gone. I'm more comfortable in my own skin now than I ever have been."

Sue recently reaped the benefits of her new self-esteem when it came time to find a new job. "My kids were grown and I wanted to reenter the corporate world where I'd worked before becoming an author. But how on earth was I going to go from being self-employed to working for a big corporation?"

At first, she couldn't see the connection but kept focused on her life purpose, which she'd discovered was to bring out the best in people—holding on to the big picture and helping others find their place in it. "That's what I'd done in the parenting arena, and now I looked for a way to do it in the corporate world," she said.

Sue soon found the perfect job. "I now work as a consultant with a company that helps businesses be more successful by focusing on their human capital. I spend my days empowering individuals to use their skills and talents in a win-win situation for themselves and for the companies they work for.

"And to think, at one time, my life was all about me and pushing others away. I no longer shrink in fear of others' judgment, and I accept myself for who I am and who I am not," she said. "My life has changed and I'm having so much more fun now."

and move away. You tend to turn your energy inward and rarely project it out, requiring enormous discipline to stay so contained because energy, by its nature, flows outward into the world. You become an island unto yourself, trapped inside your self-made prison of protection.

Embracing Your Core Soul Qualities

As a Knowledgeable Achiever, your core soul qualities are *mastery* and *intelligence*. Your mission in life is to bring awareness, order, and unity to whatever endeavors you engage in for the purpose of benefiting all of humankind.

When you release your strict drive for perfection, you find that what your soul truly loves is mastery. Mastery happens when you let go of all control and see how everything has perfection, even in chaos. You let go of the Rule Keeper's constant striving and expectations that never match reality, clearly see what you can do to influence others, and take full responsibility for that. As this shifts, your experience goes from competitiveness to enthusiasm for infinite possibilities that are expressed through both failure and success.

You realize that your gift of being able to achieve and manifest has the higher purpose of awakening others to a broader perspective of life. You relate to people in their core soul self and life purpose in every moment. If you employ people, you act as their guide in expressing their core soul qualities, and you match the job to their gifts rather than arbitrarily assigning them a job for which they don't have skills and then criticize or fire them for poor performance. The once all-important goals that pitted you against the world give way to a flowing sense of oneness with the universe. By getting in touch with the more delicate needs of your heart and feelings, you awaken a passion and love, and find that your heart longs for romance, tenderness, and intimacy.

Being vulnerable and open to the gentle universal heart that holds all of creation together, you see that you have a soul that is perfect. In Rule Keeper defense, you try to be perfect in action to justify your existence and block any feelings that don't support your actions, but in your soul self, you let the feelings of your heart be your greatest guide.

Once you are connected to your more subtle feelings, you bring a compassionate worldview to previously empty achievement-oriented tasks. You let go of your drill sergeant ways and enjoy *being* as much as *doing*. Your life becomes playful and balanced. You inspire others with your incredible knowledge and achievement and raise the bar by showing them their potential. By releasing your strict self-boundaries and self-criticism, you free energy frozen at the core of your being. When this happens, you become real, empathizing and guiding others along their paths as individuals rather than seeing them as statistics. By getting in touch with your true feelings, you can honor others' feelings and paths with an equal level of enthusiasm. As you do this, you connect to your true mission, which is to lead others to all they can be by giving them direction and confidence. That confidence comes from knowing who you are at your core. You are deeply aware of your own and other people's life purpose as not what they do but who they are.

Knowledgeable Achiever William Blake, the great seventeenth-century English poet, wrote, "To see a World in a Grain of Sand / And a Heaven in a Wild Flower, / Hold Infinity in the palm of your hand / And Eternity in an hour." He was referring to "felt knowledge" that Knowledgeable Achievers can experience and express, in contrast to knowledge that comes less directly, from memory or analysis.

YOUR GIFT TO THE WORLD is your ability to see the big picture and influence others in a positive way through your speaking, writing, and action. You are the one who shows the laborer that he is not just laying bricks but building a cathedral.

In leadership positions, you see the oneness of humanity, and therefore never belittle or judge the importance of any one individual. You see the importance and interrelatedness of each of the cells in a complex organism, knowing it is only as strong as its weakest cells. You accept how everything in the world is perfectly in harmony and part of a larger universal order.

Knowledgeable Achievers are sages in training, ultimately becoming the wise masters we go to when we have lost our way in life. You may be the guru who gets a failing business back on track or the experienced marriage therapist who has helped thousands of couples turn their relationships around. You live your life discovering what works best for yourself and for others, and what does not. You are the wise and intuitive scientist and engineer who is always trying to figure out what makes things tick and how to fix what's broken.

Only when the Knowledgeable Achiever realizes that we are all here to love and have compassion can their true gift be revealed (thus their attraction to the Emotional Intelligence Specialist as a partner). You become the leaders for reform in government and foster harmony among nations and all humanity. You clearly see the devastating path that humans are on and do all you can to steer that careening oil tanker away from the rocks.

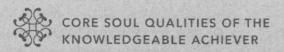

CORE SOUL QUALITIES OF THE KNOWLEDGEABLE ACHIEVER

- Holder of the big picture for humanity
- Wise teacher, sage in training, the Zen Master
- Natural authority with benevolent king or queen energy
- Mental brilliance and ability to execute your plans
- Impeccable in word and deed
- Loves mastery, becoming an expert in physical and mental disciplines
- Internally disciplined, externally graceful
- Manifester, able to effortlessly bring ideas into fruition
- Loving, knowing, and free

Extraordinary Power Process: Align with Your Profile Qualities

This simple Extraordinary Power Process, when repeated frequently as you go through your daily life, supports you in aligning with your profile so you can live your unique life purpose. The activities below give you a chance to use the Knowledgeable Achiever/Rule Keeper profile to focus the process (described in more detail in *Orientation to the Program* on page 117).

FEEL: Do the inner feeling work by identifying those core soul qualities and defensive patterns from the profile description that you feel most deeply. Then choose a few to work with that are the strongest. Write in your journal about what it is like to experience that quality or pattern in your life. Think of a specific situation at work, in your relationship, or with regard to your health and well-being, and ask yourself the following questions about your core and your defense:

❖ How do I feel—physically, emotionally, and energetically?
❖ What am I saying to myself and to others?
❖ What am I attracting to myself by being in that quality?
❖ What am I rejecting or avoiding?

As you write, observe the power that is available from your core soul qualities and also the self-sabotage that results from being in your defense.

CHOOSE: Make conscious choices to create your future, no longer living in the self-sabotaging, knee-jerk reality of your defense. Select one core soul quality you felt the deepest from the reading. Sit quietly and visualize living in that core quality right now: How does it change your relationships, career, health, and finances? Project your life out one, five, and ten years into the future, and explore the same question. Write about your vision in your journal. Then come back to the present moment. Choose how you will do things differently based on living in your core soul qualities.

ACT: Align your actions with your core soul qualities in your career, relationships, health, or finances. Ask: *What would my Knowledgeable Achiever do in this area or situation? How would he or she respond and act right now?* Commit to taking action in this moment, even if it's a symbolic gesture of saying in the mirror, *My best is never going to be perfect, and I am okay with that.* Or sign up for an emotional healing class so you can begin to feel more deeply and more often.

REPEAT THIS PROCESS and continue to *feel*, *choose*, and *act* in this way as you discover more and more about your unique Life Purpose Profile. Soon this simple process will become your default mode, overriding the knee-jerk programming you've been trapped in for most of your life, and you will be free.

Before You Go On . . .

Record aspects of your profile that you can align with on a Personal Profile Summary chart. Turn to page 343 and fill in the first two sections on the chart from your discoveries in Step 1: *My Core Soul Qualities* and *My Defensive Profile Patterns*. (You will have a chance to fill in the remaining sections of the chart in Step 2 and Step 3.) Your chart can then serve as a handy reference for the work you are doing to know yourself in this new way.

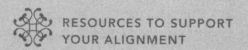

RESOURCES TO SUPPORT YOUR ALIGNMENT

The following are available at www.discoveryourpurposebook .com/members:

1. **Guided Meditation Audio Download.** *Your Secret Place.* This meditation not only helps you identify your profile but also shows you the difference between being in your core soul self and being in a defensive state.

2. **Crystal Bowls Audio Download.** Daily work with crystal bowls helps you to feel your alignment with your profile. Then you are called to your life purpose by energy resonance, not from force of mental will.

Step 2: Recognize Your Defenses

In Step 2, you use your profile as a lens to examine and then dismantle the defensive mask of your false self that is living in a virtual reality. You identify your core wounds and self-rejecting vows, as well as your negative pleasures, and you begin to replace these defensive behaviors with freeing statements and positive pleasures.

The Big Why story of my student and Knowledgeable Achiever Ryan illustrates how living from your core, not your vows, can dramatically impact your life.

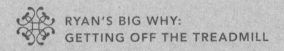

RYAN'S BIG WHY: GETTING OFF THE TREADMILL

Ryan began the energy healing program at my institute when his wife convinced him that taking the classes would help him in his career. He was working in the IT department for a major insurance company, and, while he loved his job, he was starting, at the ripe young age of thirty-two, to become a workaholic.

"My wife came home from a class one day and showed me a handout about something called a Knowledgeable Achiever/ Rule Keeper," he said. "'That's you,' she told me. 'You fit the description perfectly!' I had no idea what she was talking about and was kind of averse to the whole idea."

A year later, I met Ryan when he joined his wife at an introductory evening about the profile program. He appeared physically solid and grounded but emotionally he was rigid and tense, fidgeting a lot and not being present in the conversation. He signed up for the course anyway. Later he told me, "There's only been a few times in my life when a message from inside was so loud and clear: *Do it!*"

Listening to the crystal bowls helped while he did an exercise holding his wife's hands and being guided to tune into her energy. "I didn't care about becoming a healer; I just wanted to have more of that ability to know what to do," he said. "I tended not to make decisions easily." Later, Ryan realized he'd tapped into his intuition, a capacity he developed over the next two years of the course.

At work, Ryan kept his eye on the goal of improving online services for customers, using the skills he'd acquired through a certification process and his MBA. He was promoted from help desk to business analyst quickly, rising in the ranks to a problem-solving position that involved statistical analysis. "I went from solving the problems of individual users to solving problems that impacted forty thousand people across the United States," he said. "It was kind of a euphoric time—I really believed in what I was doing, and I was part of a team of really smart people."

But Ryan's company went through a leadership change and most of the people in his department were cut. He found himself working longer hours. This meant not going to the gym for his regular workout and having less time for his favorite sport, snowboarding.

In the program, Ryan's scores showed his profile to be Knowledgeable Achiever/Rule Keeper with a strong secondary as Team Player/People Pleaser. "I was relieved, even proud, because I'd worked hard to achieve things in my life," he said. Ryan had a fairly balanced blend of the other profiles, but initially he wanted to dismiss these others as "not me." It made him anxious not to have certainty about who he was, and he preferred to put everyone, including himself, into neat little boxes so there'd be no surprises.

"Learning more about the five profiles showed me that there's no right or wrong way to be." That insight gave him some much-needed breathing room, and he was able to explore a different side of himself that he'd never before considered.

"I thought I was someone who was considerate of others and could walk in their shoes, but I found that I interacted with people only if I felt safe and could play by my own rules," he confided. "I was actually very dismissive of people, at times even cold and aloof."

Things started to shift in Ryan's relationships. "The profiles taught me that there's nothing fixed about a person's identity—there's a bit of everyone in each of us," he said. "It helped me to stop judging people, dismissing them so easily, and feeling superior because of my achievements and credentials."

Ryan discovered that he had lots of rules for relating to people. He started to examine the vows he'd made and challenged himself to break some of them. "Immediately, I felt guilty, but instead of caving in to the guilt, I am now aware that guilt is the price I pay for breaking out of my box, and I don't let it stop me."

Recently, Ryan took some time off and went snowboarding with his wife. "I had to break my rule to do it, because I had a conflicting commitment," he said. "But I now know that it's part of my growth to be more flexible and sometimes break a rigid rule."

He still strives to do more and improve in his career, but lately he has refocused. "I was checking off lots of things on my list, but I started to wonder if what I was doing was really important," he said.

Then, on a business trip to Indonesia, Ryan realized he could ask different questions and solve bigger problems at work, instead of staying nose to the grindstone, day in and day out. The Knowledgeable Achiever core had awakened in him and he now knows he is here to do more. Putting himself back on the same old treadmill at work was no longer a choice.

"When I realized how restricted my constant striving had made me, I decided to stop and set no goals for the next few years," he said. "I'll wait and see what comes my way as far as the next step in my career. It's been tough not having a goal, but I recommend it for major overachievers like myself. Take a break, have some fun, and trust your intuition more!"

Becoming Aware of Your Vows

Becoming aware of your vows—those hardwired beliefs that filter your every experience through a limited view—is critical for dismantling your defense. The source of all your vows is early life events that wounded you emotionally and energetically—*your core wounds.*

Because you came into life as a Knowledgeable Achiever with the purpose of seeing the bigger picture in any situation and using your intelligence to take action and inspire others with that vision, your core wounds will involve being loved for what you do, not for who you truly are.

As a child who was recognized for your intelligence and talents, you began to base your self-worth on perfectionism and hid any perceived weaknesses or needs. You weren't perfect, though. For example, you weren't able to control your emotions and concentrate in school like an adult, which was your parents' expectation. The few times you may have soiled your underwear after getting out of diapers or blurted out something spontaneous and inappropriate led to your being punished and lectured to impersonally.

 **CORE WOUNDS OF THE KNOWLEDGEABLE ACHIEVER**

- Receiving love and attention only when you were good or perfect
- Having an alcoholic or ill parent, making you the only responsible one in the family
- Expectations that you be independent and never show weakness
- Shaming for expressing your sexuality

- Rejection by parents/caregivers due to your outbursts of emotion; being made to contain your emotions and be incredibly disciplined in order to succeed
- Traumatic incidents when you looked stupid, unprepared, or incompetent, possibly in school or in front of other children

As a Knowledgeable Achiever, your life is about being right and being perfect, so you made vows always to be prepared. The fear of being wrong is great. In Rule Keeper defense, you must "know," or you have no purpose in life.

For example, as a student, your vows drive you to study harder than anyone else and understand the function and form of everything so you are never seen as unprepared or stupid. You vow that you must have everything completely covered before you can relax and enjoy life.

Your vows always to be right and perfect protect you, but they can also isolate you from others, making you critical, dismissive, and aloof. You become your own authority, which keeps you separate and gives you a sense of superiority. You avoid any "messy" intimacy in your primary and work relationships in order to keep those relationships functional and solid, but you let out your wilder and steamier side in extramarital affairs or with drinking buddies.

Vows become hardwired through unconscious statements you say to yourself, day in and day out. Read and allow yourself to feel the Vow Statements that typically form the Rule Keeper defense. Do you recognize any from the list on the next page as your own?

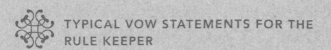

TYPICAL VOW STATEMENTS FOR THE RULE KEEPER

I vow always to be responsible (unlike my alcoholic mother/father who could never properly care for the family).

I vow always to be perfect.

I vow always to be my own biggest critic.

I vow always to keep my feelings separate from my job and goals.

I vow always to keep my body fit and disciplined.

I vow always to be in control emotionally and do my best to achieve success.

I vow never to allow chaos into my daily life.

I vow never to relax (until maybe when I'm retired).

I vow never to look or act stupid, or to appear a victim.

I vow never to take on something that I'm not already good at.

WRITE YOUR OWN: _____

Extraordinary Power Process: Release Your Vows

The activities below give you a chance to become aware of and release vows of the Rule Keeper defense.

FEEL: Choose those Vow Statements from the list that resonate most strongly for you. Mark them and add any of your own to the list. Then, select one or more to work with in completing the following sentences:

1. A vow I made was always/never to _____.

2. How this vow is influencing my life right now: _____

_____.

3. My self-talk that reinforces this vow: _____

_____.

EXAMPLE:

1. A vow I made was to be perfect and never let others see that I don't always know what I am doing.
2. How this vow is influencing my life right now: It makes me see people as critical judges who never let me be genuine or let myself off the hook.
3. My self-talk that reinforces this vow: "You are such an idiot! You should have known better! How could you be so stupid!"

CHOOSE: Look at the vows you marked and, taking one at a time, ask yourself: *What would my life be like if I stopped honoring that vow?* Project out one, five, and ten years from now and ask: *How would not honoring that vow change my life?* Write your answers in your journal.

For example: *If I no longer honored that vow, I could enjoy my life and relationships more, and step out of my self-imposed box that keeps me isolated from others until I somehow create perfection in my life.*

ACT: What action could you take to support your choice to no longer honor your vow? Decide to act based on your conscious choice, not a vow. Write in your journal about what happened when you did.

REPEAT THE PROCESS of *feel*, *choose*, and *act* every time you become aware that an ancient vow has been running your life. Vows are buried deep in your psyche, so it can take years to permanently release them. Be prepared to feel some amount of fear, guilt, and shame as you choose not to honor your vows; a vow is an unconscious promise, and you are breaking that promise when you choose something other than your vows.

Before You Go On . . .

Record the Vow Statements you resonate with most strongly on your Personal Profile Summary chart on page 343. Fill in the section for *My Vow Statements* with statements from the list or that you wrote in.

Freedom Statements

Replace your Vow Statements with Freedom Statements, which are the solutions to your vows. Freedom Statements call forth your core soul qualities and support you to increasingly choose more consciously in every moment. Every time you consciously choose a Freedom Statement over a vow, you get back energy and open yourself to ever-growing life rather than stagnating as a wounded victim.

Use Freedom Statements as a bridge out of defense and onto the path of your truth. The following list offers you a variety of statements, but you can always add your own.

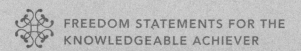

FREEDOM STATEMENTS FOR THE KNOWLEDGEABLE ACHIEVER

I am open to working toward mastery with enthusiasm and joy.
I am open to seeing my feelings and relationships as an integral part of the success I have achieved.
I am open to knowing the mystery of unconditional love, feeling the interdependence of all things in the world, not their separateness.
I am open to trembling like a child as I feel love again in every cell of my body.
I embrace my human imperfections, as well as the imperfections of others.

I am open to appreciating the very things I used to criticize in other people.

I synthesize information and actions, accepting both the ambiguous and the pragmatic.

I see the universal order of all things and how every action and event is in perfect harmony with the world.

I am open to deserving love and respect just because I exist, not for anything I have ever done.

I no longer assume that I know everything and am humbled in knowing a tiny part of the mystery of life.

WRITE YOUR OWN: _____

Extraordinary Power Process:
Become Free of Your Vows

The activities below give you a chance to replace your vows with Freedom Statements and live from your Knowledgeable Achiever soul qualities rather than your Rule Keeper defense.

FEEL: Read the list of Freedom Statements above, speaking each one aloud. Let yourself feel their truth as you sit quietly after speaking them. Notice those statements you may want to deny and then repeat them until you no longer have a negative reaction to them. Notice also which statements register strongly as *Yes, that's me!*

CHOOSE: Speak your Freedom Statements out loud as often as possible to bring conscious choice to your vow-driven, knee-jerk defensive reactions. Tell others your Freedom Statements so that they can see your truth and support you in embodying it. Especially as a Knowledgeable Achiever, your willingness to share your heart's deeper needs, rather than relying on your accomplishments, opens the door to a greater respect.

Consider what your life will be like one, five, and ten years from now if you embody the truth in your Freedom Statements.

ACT: Explore how you would act differently in key areas of your life if your vows were replaced by Freedom Statements. Choose one action you can take that aligns you with the truth of your Freedom Statement, not your vow, and do it!

REPEAT THE PROCESS of *feel*, *choose*, and *act* often when dealing with your life's circumstances. You'll notice how your vow-driven actions begin to fade and you increasingly make choices and act based in the present of who you truly are rather than the past of your false and defended self.

Before You Go On . . .

Record the Freedom Statements you have chosen to replace your vows on the Personal Profile Summary chart on page 343. Fill in the section for *My Freedom Statements*.

Your Negative Pleasures

Living from your core soul qualities, not your vows, will empower you to embrace your life purpose. But without confronting your *negative pleasures*, real freedom will never be yours. Negative pleasures—those habits and behaviors you know you shouldn't do (or *don't* do but know you should!) but justify because they make you feel better about yourself— must be confronted and left behind if you are going to live your authentic purpose.

In Rule Keeper defense, some of your negative pleasures are preferring to be right rather than happy, finding fault in others, worshipping the rules, and judging others for being too emotional.

A negative pleasure that is hard for you to admit to is that you would rather be right than happy. It doesn't matter if the topic of conversation is religion or politics—others must come around to seeing it your way, or you will dismiss them rather than compromise your position. You find satisfaction in the negative pleasures of being in control and looking good, showing extreme discipline in how you treat your body, diet, home, and work environment. This behavior is so second nature that it often escapes your notice, even while leading a double life through the negative pleasure of an extramarital affair.

JUDGING OTHERS FOR BEING EMOTIONAL. In your relationships, you love to give advice to a Poor Me to just "suck it up" and get on with his or her day, or to a Charismatic Leader–Charmer to just calm down and be more rational. You feel negative pleasure in acting like your partner's critical parent, saying, *You do see how you brought this on yourself, don't you?* The Rule Keeper loves to judge anyone who experiences any depth of emotion.

The following list includes typical negative pleasures of the Rule Keeper defense. Feel free to add your own.

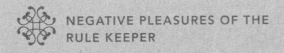

NEGATIVE PLEASURES OF THE RULE KEEPER

Being aloof, withholding, and "above it all"
Feeling frustrated about others' incompetence and justified in
   dismissing them
Being ruthlessly self-critical and never perfect enough

Knowing better than others about everything

Preferring to be right rather than happy in relationships

Living in perpetual dissatisfaction with your achievements

Asserting that what you do is who you are

Being the most responsible one in any situation, preferring to do things yourself because you think you are the only one who can do it right

Being the strongest and least emotional one in any volatile situation

Being compulsively neat

WRITE YOUR OWN: _____

Extraordinary Power Process: Diminish Your Negative Pleasures

The activities below give you a chance to become aware of your negative pleasures. The key to diminishing your negative pleasures is to become conscious of the poor substitutes they are for the real pleasures you could be having in your life.

FEEL: As you read the list of negative pleasures for the Rule Keeper defense, let yourself feel which ones resonate deeply to evoke a response of *Yes, that's me!* Mark those and write them in your journal.

CHOOSE: Choose one negative pleasure from the list that you identified and are willing to let go of. Sit with all the pain that this behavior has caused you and others to date. Then visualize your life projected out ten years from now. If you don't change that behavior, what positive pleasure will it cost you?

To help you do this, fill in the following statements:

1. A negative pleasure I have in my life is _____
_____.

2. Allowing that negative pleasure in my life costs me now and
in the future: _____.

EXAMPLE:

1. A negative pleasure I have in my life is always feeling like I
could have done it better or should have done more.
2. Allowing this negative pleasure costs me the feeling of fulfillment through my work and accomplishments. I am
never able to relax and enjoy the fruits of my labors because
I am a workaholic.

Now write about a positive pleasure, one that comes from living in
your core, and how experiencing that pleasure might look in your life.
For example: *I could enjoy my life more, and take more time to celebrate
my accomplishments and honor my gifts and family, rather than punish
myself for my imperfections.*

ACT: Having chosen a negative pleasure you are ready to let go of, the
next time it comes up in your life, ask yourself: *What positive pleasure
am I missing as I indulge this negative one? How would my Knowledgeable
Achiever respond in this situation?* Then take action in accordance with
your answer.

REPEAT THIS PROCESS OFTEN. As your negative pleasures become
increasingly noticeable, see them as behaviors based on fears that you are
now ready to grow out of. Don't beat yourself up. Go slow, get support,

and let each negative pleasure go, one at a time. You will start to experience positive pleasures that come from accepting your life and the people in it. Soon, the unconscious habits and behaviors you've been substituting for the real thing will no longer seem as attractive.

Every negative pleasure you successfully let go of allows you to bring back into your life all of the wasted energy that went into that defense. With that energy, you can make powerful choices to live your life as a creative presence.

Before You Go On . . .

Record your negative pleasures on your Personal Profile Summary chart on page 343. Fill in the section for *My Favorite Negative Pleasures*.

In Transition . . .

As you transition out of Rule Keeper defense and into your core self, you may find yourself stuck in frustrating old patterns. Your defenses have made you into someone you are not, or less than who you truly are. Now awakened, you can make conscious choices and set goals to act differently.

In transitioning to your core soul self, you can call forth your greatest strength of discipline to reverse old patterns. When you use your discipline to notice when you are going into defense, you begin the process of becoming a sage. You realize that your deeper gut feelings, passions, and needs are important guides for being real in your relationships. You throw caution to the wind and no longer postpone your gratification until you've had your children, achieved success in your career, bought a second home, put $500,000 in the bank, or reached retirement. You learn to live and enjoy life right now. You are not *less* responsible—the Knowledgeable Achiever is the most responsible of the profiles—but rather you are *more* responsible as a human *being*, not a human *doing*.

Here is an activity to support your transition out of Rule Keeper defense into your core self as a Knowledgeable Achiever.

ACTIVITY: Because Knowledgeable Achievers tend to isolate through perfectionism and overwork, try not to set any goals for a period of twenty-four hours, and simply let each moment unfold. Listen to your inner guidance for what to do from moment to moment rather than the demands of your mental to-do list. If this proves too difficult, then set one goal that is an anti-goal, such as lying around on the couch for one hour and reading a trashy novel or watching an old movie.

Then, write about what happened in your journal. Was it difficult at first? Did any fears come up? Did you experience any positive emotions or events that may have surprised you?

RESOURCES TO SUPPORT YOUR TRANSITION

1. **Guided Meditation Audio Download.** *Calling Back Your Spirit* (available at www.discoveryourpurposebook.com/members).

2. **Recommended Reading List**
   - *The Four Agreements*, by Don Miguel Ruiz
   - *The 7 Habits of Highly Effective People*, by Stephen R. Covey
   - *Love and Will*, by Rollo May
   - *The Marriage of Sense and Soul*, by Ken Wilber
   - *Comfortable with Uncertainty*, by Pema Chödrön

Step 3: Live Your Life Purpose

Having begun the process of dismantling your defenses in Step 2, you are now ready to integrate your profile's unique higher- and lower-self qualities. As you become less conflicted, and more whole and balanced, you can make choices and take courageous actions in your life, not just react automatically from your ancient vows. You are also able to use the Law of Attraction to attract what best supports your unique life purpose as you create and live an extraordinary life.

Your Shadow: Lower- and Higher-Self Traits

Your shadow is made up of traits that you have rejected by vowing *always* or *never* to be or do something. Those traits can be seen as aspects of you higher self and your lower self. As you identify rejected higher- and lower-self traits, you can begin to accept and integrate them, and so achieve a state of inner balance and wholeness. Fully integrating your shadow allows your defensive mask to dissolve and your true core soul self to emerge.

The following chart contains a list of the lower- and higher-self traits *in matched pairs* that you must own and integrate to fully live your life purpose as a Knowledgeable Achiever:

LOWER- AND HIGHER-SELF TRAITS FOR KNOWLEDGEABLE ACHIEVERS	
LOWER-SELF TRAITS	**HIGHER-SELF TRAITS**
Narcissistic	Esteeming self in balance
Selfish	Sets healthy boundaries
Perfectionist	Compassionately accepting and discerning

Withholding emotion	Understanding
Dismissive	Ability to have selective focus
Aloof	Wise witness
Hypocrite	Integrity in all actions
Cruel about others' deficits	Seeing the strength and gifts in others
Dissociating from events/ people	Letting go of what is over
Passionless and robotic	Enthusiastic and motivated
Abusively self-disciplined	Self-disciplined in a balanced way
Judgmental	Discerning
Know-it-all	Sage
Pigheaded	Committed to purpose
Hard-nosed	Fair but tough negotiator
Rock-hard ego self	Impeccable leader
Coldhearted	Tender heart revealed
Has no needs	Wants to be seen and understood
Competitive with others	Doing your personal best
Feeling superior mentally or spiritually	Humbly surrenders to the human condition

Extraordinary Power Process: Integrate Your Shadow

The activities below give you a chance to integrate your shadow (rejected traits) with your higher-self light.

FEEL: As you read the list of matched-pair lower-/higher-self traits, reach deep into yourself to feel the full range of your raw, lower self at one end and your exalted, higher self at the other. Both are within you to varying degrees. Your raw power and personal needs are found in your lower-self traits, while your conscious use of that power to fulfill those needs is in your higher-self traits. When you can own both in any moment and still choose your higher-self traits, then everything you do will be aligned with your life purpose.

Put a check mark next to the lower- and higher-self traits you recognize as ones you exhibit. Also notice traits that elicit a powerful negative reaction, and check them, too. These are traits you have rejected in yourself or in others. (In rejecting lower-self traits, you say to yourself, *I'd never do that—it's too negative, mean, or evil*; while in rejecting higher-self traits, you say, *I could never do that—it's too perfect, saintly, or godlike*.)

CAUTION: No higher-self trait can exist without the lower-self trait alongside it. To be whole and balanced, you must be conscious of both within you. Selecting only those traits you like will send you back to your vow-created life where only half of you exists.

Using your strongest traits checked, complete these statements for each:

1. A lower-/higher-self trait that I see as strong in me is

   _____.

2. My greatest fear of owning that trait is _____

   _____.

EXAMPLE:

1. A lower-self trait that I see as strong in me is being a perfectionist.
2. My greatest fear of owning that trait is that others will feel judged by me as I point out their imperfections.

AND:

1. A higher-self trait that is the partner to my lower-self trait is being accepting and discerning.
2. My greatest fear of owning that trait is that I will be too accepting of my own and others' limitations, and as a result I will accomplish nothing of merit.

CHOOSE: Now work with one set of lower- and higher-self traits that you identified as not being fully owned in their full range. Ask how your life would be different if you owned both higher- and lower-self traits equally, able to accept either freely but choosing the higher-self quality.

Visualize your life up to now and see how damaging it has been to express the lower-self trait unconsciously. Also feel how you have wanted to express the higher-self trait more often but don't, since the lower-self trait cannot be resolved. Now project this pattern of behavior out into your life one, five, and ten years into the future and see what your life looks like with just this one conflict within you.

What would happen if you were able to embrace both lower- and higher-self traits at all times as part of your life purpose? Notice that, if you did not stand in such judgment and fear of being who you actually are in your life one, five, and ten years into the future, you would instead reveal your true power and purpose.

For example: *If I accept that I can be punishing to myself and others with my judgments, then I will learn to embrace joy rather than perfectionism.*

ACT: Take actions that align with your new state of inner balance and wholeness. Commit to one action that reflects your new self-acceptance, and then do it. Write in your journal about what happened when you did.

REPEAT THE PROCESS! Once you've worked with one pair of higher- and lower-self trait in this way, repeat the process, covering more traits in both lists. Accepting both higher and lower selves as the whole of who you are is the most powerful spiritual work you can do.

Before You Go On . . .

Turn to page 343 and fill in the section for *Lower- and Higher-Self Traits* on your Personal Profile Summary chart.

Living Courageously

Living your life purpose means speaking and acting fearlessly from your core soul self. To remain in that state, you will need to step out of your comfort zone often and take the road less traveled, leaping over obstacles in your way. The following are some ways that you as a Knowledgeable Achiever can do that.

Acknowledge your judgmental nature.

Your biggest challenge is to recognize that your judgmental nature prevents you from having genuine relationships. Being able to admit that you wrongfully stand in judgment of those you love is the beginning of your transformation from Rule Keeper to Knowledgeable Achiever.

Accept that you have a tender heart.

You must admit that under your well-muscled and fit chest is a heart so afraid of getting hurt that you cut others off before they can get too close. You will walk away from a twenty-year relationship or job and feel nothing. Until you feel your heart connect with love, and respect others, you are on a deserted island all alone.

The lesson you must learn is that when you are loved, you become real. You think you are real only when you accomplish something—*I am what I do* is the motto of a closed heart. Learning to be real means being seen for your softer and more vulnerable side.

Be willing to be the wise sage.

By your nature, your life purpose is to teach all the other profiles. You are the wise sage, unbending in your intent, seeing the essence of all life and guiding others to see the same. You must overcome the hurdle of seeing yourself only as useful for your achievements.

Let go of what you are certain is the truth.

The discovery that nothing you believed was true defeats your striving ego. Education is the hope for the future, and, as the wise teacher, you show us the truth that cannot be seen with the naked eye.

Ask for help to solve your problems.

In defense, you get stuck in rigid patterns of right and wrong and having to be perfect. Recognize that your true purpose is to experience the daily mystery of life, to make choices and take actions based on who you are. To be perfectly human is to be flawed, humble, and clueless in so many ways. You become the sage only when you realize that life is unknowable but must be felt through your emotions, not your thoughts. Step out of your emotional cave and ask others for help in solving your problems.

Develop relationships that have no utilitarian purpose.

Build relationships with people because you like them and they awaken a spark in you. If you have a strong Rule Keeper defense, you are probably part of many success- and outcome-driven groups that push you to achieve your goals but don't help you feel more connected to life. Your likelihood of befriending people in the other profiles is slim, but it's the Creative Idealists, Emotional Intelligence Specialists, Team Players, and Charismatic Leader–Charmers who have the most to teach you.

Before You Go On . . .

Turn to page 343 and fill in the section for *Actions to Take for Living Courageously* on your Personal Profile Summary chart.

Speak Your Truth

To remain in your Knowledgeable Achiever core, you must be willing to speak your truth to others, especially to those with whom you are in an intimate relationship.

Practice by reading each of the Essential Word Statements on the next page, visualizing that you are speaking directly to someone you love and feeling your words deeply as you read them. Make a commitment to speak these essential words—not the automatic words dictated by your vows and defenses—to an important person in your life. Then act to call, write, or speak with that important person to share your truth.

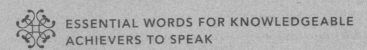

ESSENTIAL WORDS FOR KNOWLEDGEABLE ACHIEVERS TO SPEAK

- Show me you see a real person in me because sometimes I cannot. Help me out of the prison that I make for myself.
- I tend to hide my heart, but I love you so much that sometimes it is easier for me to judge you and protect myself.
- I see your light and how it touches mine, and there is no difference between you and me. When you suffer, I suffer. So if I am standing in judgment, come get me. Touch me. Help me feel again.
- When I feel our hearts touch, that is when the entire universe opens up for me. I know who I am and who you are.
- I am deeply afraid that life is passing me by as I work myself to the ground. Help me play and be fully in my life with you.

Before You Go On . . .

Turn to page 343 and fill in the section for *Speaking Your Truth* on your Personal Profile Summary chart.

The Law of Attraction

According to the Law of Attraction, like attracts like. It follows that you will always attract people and situations that are like you. As your alignment with your life purpose grows, your internal magnet for attracting who and what you want in your life is strengthened. If you are not aligned with your life purpose, no amount of visualizing will help you achieve your desires—in spite of what popular culture tells you about how constant visualizing will bring you what you want.

Knowledgeable Achievers are by nature life purpose manifesters. You have the strongest and most disciplined energy of all the profiles and so will naturally attract material wealth and resources. The Law of Attraction works well with your unstoppable energy, which makes you a magnet for resources. You create possibility and unify people around a group cause, seeing the big picture and knowing how to efficiently guide others to resources.

As a Knowledgeable Achiever, you are on the planet to manage resources and people in the most intelligent way. You are a model for how to attract abundance. You empower others and show them how to make money in a sustainable way and, in so doing, give others the ability to choose their own path.

ACTIVITY: EXPLORE THE GAP. The gap is the space between where you are now and where you know you will be when you fully embody your core soul profile qualities and live your life purpose. Looking in areas of life such as health, relationships, finances, and career or job, inquire about the following:

❖ What am I attracting in my life right now from living in my defenses?
❖ What do I want to attract in my life from living in my core soul self?

Are you attracting what supports your life purpose or what keeps you stuck in your defense? How can you act from your core soul qualities and not your defenses to close that gap and attract what you want? Write your responses in your journal.

Before You Go On . . .

Turn to page 343 and fill in the section for *Law of Attraction* on your Personal Profile Summary chart.

Extraordinary Power Process:
Your Personal Profile Summary Chart

Your Personal Profile Summary chart now holds what you have learned about yourself from the Knowledgeable Achiever profile, either as your primary or your secondary Life Purpose Profile.

Once you have completed your charts for both primary and secondary profiles, use them as a tool to support your life purpose. Follow the Extraordinary Power Process of *feel*, *choose*, and *act* as you refer to each section you've filled in on your chart:

1. Feel: Do the inner feeling work—don't just think.
2. Choose: Make conscious choices—don't automatically react based on your vows.
3. Act: Align your actions with your profile's core soul qualities—not with your defenses—to live your truth.

When you repeat this sequence as often as possible throughout your day, then everything you do reveals the mystery of who you are rather than reinforcing who you think you are—but are not. *Feeling, choosing,* and *acting* in accordance with your profile gives you access to your extraordinary power so you can effortlessly manifest your life purpose and live it in every area of your life.

Knowledgeable Achiever/Rule Keeper
PERSONAL PROFILE SUMMARY

Profile	☐ This is my PRIMARY PROFILE ☐ This is my SECONDARY PROFILE ☐ This is my THIRD, FOURTH, or FIFTH PROFILE
My Core Soul Qualities (for this profile)	1 _____ 2 _____
My Defensive Profile Patterns	1 _____ 2 _____
My Vow Statements (How I self-sabotage)	1 _____ 2 _____ 3 _____
My Freedom Statements (Solutions to my Vow Statements)	I am open to _____ I am open to _____ I am open to _____
My Favorite Negative Pleasures (How I self-sabotage)	Something I do that I shouldn't do but get pleasure from: _____ Something I get pleasure from not doing that I know I should do: _____
Lower- and Higher-Self Traits (matched pairs)	Lower: Higher: 1 _____ / _____ 2 _____ / _____
Actions to take for living courageously from your profile	1 _____ 2 _____
Speaking Your Truth (ESSENTIAL WORDS you must say to others)	1 _____ 2 _____
Law of Attraction (People, situations, etc. that I am attracting)	In defense, I attract _____ In my core, I attract _____

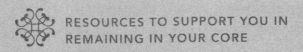

RESOURCES TO SUPPORT YOU IN REMAINING IN YOUR CORE

1. **Guided Meditation Audio Download.** *Your Subpersonalities.* Explore your higher- and lower-self traits through a guided meditation, available at www.discoveryourpurposebook.com/members.

2. **Bioenergetic Exercises for Knowledgeable Achievers,** available below and on the same website.

BIOENERGETIC EXERCISES FOR THE KNOWLEDGEABLE ACHIEVER

Movement is often the key to opening up feelings for the other profiles, but for the Knowledgeable Achiever, breathing and opening the heart before moving is more important. The following are some physical exercises that will help you do that.

EXERCISE #1: DEEP BREATHING. Your rib cage will be tight and rigid as a result of holding in your feelings and protecting your heart. Deep, full chest and belly breathing for thirty to forty-five minutes will let you feel your feelings.

EXERCISE #2: ROLLING AROUND. This exercise is especially good if you find yourself in the rut of always doing things the same way. Lie down on the floor or carpet and freely roll around. Try it for a few minutes with your eyes open; then close your eyes. Notice any parts of your body that don't press easily into the floor. Finish by lying on your back with your eyes open. Then get up and walk around slowly. Enjoy your body and notice how fast it wants to move without prompting from your brain.

EXERCISE #3: THE FORWARD FLOP. This exercise is a powerful way to learn to surrender to what is coming at you every day.

Start by bending your knees and letting your arms reach down to the ground. Relax your neck and face so they just hang in a forward flop. Keep your hands connected to the ground for the entire exercise if you can.

Now, let some tension and a slight burning build up in your legs by extending them as far as you feel comfortable. Full extension is not recommended. The heat that is building up in your legs will quickly want to go somewhere. Let it build up for a few seconds and then start pumping your legs up and down slowly, a few inches at a time.

Your legs may begin to vibrate, which is good. It will feel like exhaustion at first, but it is actually the release of tension. The objective is to get your legs to tremble lightly while you breathe deeply and release any tension in your legs and lower back. Be very careful if you have lower-back problems, or skip this exercise and go on to the next one.

EXERCISE #4: PRESSING THE EARTH. This exercise teaches you to hold your ground when you might normally want to run way.

From the Forward Flop, come up very slowly to a standing position, with your legs still pumping slightly, keeping a vibration going. Put your palms facedown and, as you press down into the earth with your legs, push down with your arms, imagining that they, too, touch the ground. Keep your head and neck loose, and feel the vibration moving up through your legs and into your body. Stay in this position for as long as you like, pumping until your legs and body tingle and vibrate. Learning to be this loose may take many attempts. Be patient.

EXERCISE #5: THE ARCH. This exercise teaches you that bending over backward in the service of others is essential for life but does not have to sap your energy. Quite the contrary, service to others is the path to empowerment.

From the last exercise, place your hands in the small of your back and bend backward slightly. Keep your head forward and loose and your knees bent. In this position, your vibration can move all the way up through your body. Do not be discouraged if your vibration is minimal at first. We all have body armor that has built up over years, and it may take some time to soften.

Once you feel strong in this position and are getting a good full-body vibration, let your arms hang and see if you can get them to vibrate out to your fingertips. Finally, relax your jaw and see if you can vibrate it. If you have back problems, be very careful with how far back you bend and always support your lower back with your hands.

Alternate back and forth between the Forward Flop, Pressing the Earth, and the Arch until you get a good involuntary vibration or trembling going through your entire body. Through this type of involuntary vibration, you begin to allow your body to break up some old holding patterns.

EXERCISE #6: SHAKING TENSION OUT OF YOUR ARMS. This exercise is especially good if you have a tendency to control certain situations or people and have a hard time letting go of that habit.

Extend your arms in front of you at shoulder height and let your hands go limp. Shake your hands at arm's length, as if you are shaking water off them. Shake them as hard as you feel comfortable. Do this for ten to fifteen seconds. Then let your arms drop. Feel how energized they are. Your arms may get so energized that they feel like floating up, so let them. All of your body can be energized like this; you just need to shake off the tension that holds it still.

PART IV

The Profiles and
Relationship Mastery

CHAPTER 12

Relationship Magnets: Soul Mates, Friends, and Co-workers

The Life Purpose Profile System can be a tool for relationship mastery, helping you to develop soul-based, conscious relationships that support your purpose-driven life.

The most powerful skill you can develop to enhance all of your relationships is to be able to see and draw forth the *core soul quality* of those people you are in a relationship with—whether it's your spouse or partner, friends, or co-workers. Seeing another person's greatness is not always easy to do, especially when you have vowed to reject certain defensive behaviors, but it is the path to real freedom and joy in all of your relationships.

In this chapter, you will learn how the profile system can help you to recognize your *relationship magnets*, those attractions to others you experience both in defense and in your core soul quality.

Relationship Magnets

Have you ever wondered why you continually attract the same kind of people into your life? People divorce only to remarry someone who may look different but has the same issues or fears as their previous spouse. You may quit one job because you are treated badly by a boss, only to take a new job with a similar type of abusive boss. Or you move to a new city or state and find you are attracting friends who, like your previous friends, quickly gossip about your difficult spouse or child.

These types of negative "relationship magnets" are the result of your living unconsciously in your defense—your projected mask and virtual reality. Your defense polarizes you to become magnetically attracted to the opposite defense for good reason—so your soul can bring that defense to your conscious awareness. Being able to recognize these unconscious negative attractions and reframe them with your core soul qualities can help you see that, behind the negativity of the defense, there are two souls who have much to teach each other.

The following is a list of those relationships that will teach you the most about yourself. The people you attract in these relationships have the highest likelihood of awakening you to your core profile qualities while also revealing your defenses in daily life.

- ❖ Spouse
- ❖ Parent-child relationships
- ❖ Employer-employee relationships
- ❖ Mentor/coach/teacher-student relationships
- ❖ Enemy/hate relationships
- ❖ Abusive relationships

At first, such relationships may seem dysfunctional. But keep in mind that no relationship comes into your life randomly. Every person who is in an important position in your life plays a part in helping you discover your life purpose.

When the core soul qualities of each person in a relationship are allowed to surface, they bring a richness and depth to that relationship, so it's like a match made in heaven. These core relationships may be long-term or short-term, but the goal is to see their potential and revel in the relationship magnets that are positive and awaken you daily to who you are.

Soul Mate Relationship Magnets

When people first meet, the deepest attraction they can feel is the pull of a subconscious awareness that the other person somehow makes them more complete. That sense, so often described in words such as *I don't know why I find you so attractive, but I am drawn to you*, comes from the soul reaching for balance.

The chart on the next page, Soul Mate Relationship Magnets, shows you the profile you are attracted to as a soul mate for finding balance and awakening to your life purpose. The explanations that follow the chart will help you understand the power both you and your partner have in the relationship for either releasing each other's defenses or keeping each other in defense.

Look for your profile on the chart and follow the arrow to find your soul mate's profile. Recognizing both your own and your partner's core soul profile qualities brings power and understanding to your relationship.

After you determine your primary soul mate combination, look at your secondary profile relationships in the section on soul mate combinations that follows. If you find that you are in a relationship coming from your secondary profile, you may want to bring more of your primary profile qualities into that relationship. When you do, you may see that your partner has the balancing factor for that profile as well. You'll also read about how to discover each other's defenses, and, finally, how to balance each other out and become supportive, growth-oriented soul mates.

SOUL MATE RELATIONSHIP MAGNETS

Creative Idealist/Thinker	↔	Their own ideas and genius
Knowledgeable Achiever/ Rule Keeper	↔	Emotional Intelligence Specialist/Poor Me
Charismatic Leader–Charmer/ Enforcer-Seducer	↔	Team Player/People Pleaser

As you look at the Soul Mate Relationship Magnets chart, notice that Creative Idealist/Thinkers find their soul mate through their own mind and genius. Often Thinkers will have a stronger relationship to their scientific studies, music, art, religion, or spirituality than with any other person. They may marry or have a family but usually only attract those who have their same profile, such as scientists, artists, computer programmers, and musicians. While these relationships can support the Creative Idealist's spiritual life purpose, they will not help Thinkers embrace their human life purpose on a practical level. For this reason, the Creative Idealists must find their soul mates through their secondary profile to help them focus on their earthbound activities.

In the remaining four profiles, there are two relationship combinations possible. While all five profiles can be combined and can learn from each other, there are only two basic soul mate combinations: Knowledgeable Achiever with the Emotional Intelligence Specialist and Charismatic Leader–Charmer with the Team Player.

Because the objective of all soul mate relationships is full balance and conscious awareness, your partner must hold whatever you don't have ready access to yourself. This includes both the good and the bad, and you must learn to love and appreciate the full range in them, and subsequently in yourself, in order to awaken from your unconscious defense and isolation.

Soul Mate Combinations in Defense

One of the most powerful forces in the universe is the desire for union between male and female. It is the core spiritual drive within us all, but if a person is living at a high level of unconscious defense, such attraction can be driven by an animalistic desire for pleasure, control, or safety.

A person living with a high level of conscious awareness will choose a mate whose qualities they love and desire but have never been able to express themselves. As opposite poles of a magnet attract, they quickly find common ground because they support each other in their differences. In their core, they create heaven on earth, the universal balance that can only be fully experienced in the union of the two.

However, when a person lives mostly in *unconscious defense,* he or she will be attracted to another person with the same level of unconscious defense. The ensuing battle between the two can create so much pain that the individuals begin to examine their own culpability in the struggle. But such self-inquiry is never guaranteed. For the deeply unconscious, these conflicts can drive them further into defense, dooming them to repeat it in many relationships throughout their lifetime.

Following I've described the two unconscious soul mate combinations: Rule Keeper/Poor Me and Enforcer-Seducer/People Pleaser. In their truth, people in these two combinations are drawn to each other to create spiritual balance, but in unconscious defense, they create a constant battleground.

In describing the following soul mate combinations, I use a male for the more aggressive traits and a female for the more receptive traits. In actual relationships, the roles may be reversed, or each person has one aggressive and one passive aspect in their primary and secondary defense/core soul quality combinations. These pairings hold true of same-sex relationships as well.

Keep in mind that the defenses described here are the most destructive relationship "killers" and are rarely all present at one time. However, if you see any of them in yourself or your partner, they should be addressed immediately. If your partner exhibits all of these unconscious defensive traits, you may want to reconsider your relationship.

Couple #1: Rule Keeper/Poor Me Soul Mates

The Rule Keeper is strong, energized, organized, and rigid in his approach to life; he is often successful, serious, disciplined, aloof, and critical. He may be a business owner or manager or a specialist in some field, and he likes to be the knight in shining armor, saving mankind through his ingenuity. He tends to be a know-it-all and a doer, and is usually dissociated from his heart and deeper feelings to show little emotion.

The Poor Me, whose energy often runs low and needs organization, wears her heart on her sleeve. She is overly sensitive and often feels the need to be saved from overwhelming situations. She may be in a mess financially or be a substance abuser to block her deeper emotions and wounds.

These two profile defenses find each other and try to fix each other. The Poor Me hopes that her knight will someday fall headlong in love with her and accept that her feelings are real even if they seem irrational. The Rule Keeper, believing he can fix anything, hopes that this sweet little Poor Me person can get her act together through his help so she learns to stand on her own.

Couple #2: Enforcer-Seducer/People Pleaser
Soul Mates

The Enforcer-Seducer can come into a relationship either as aggressive and powerful or needy and broken. Both positions keep him totally in charge of all decisions in the relationship. He can be narcissistic and conflict driven; he can also be a substance abuser and addict, never trusting anyone and often lying. He may be handsome and seductive, even addictive in his charm. He can be an overbearing workaholic boss or extremely lazy, working only when needed. He will overvalue his time or get others to do his work for him.

The People Pleaser is always working, usually by caring for family and others. She can be codependent and often feels like she doesn't know what she should be doing in her life, but she doesn't have the time to think about it and so stays stuck. She often has low self-esteem, will shift her opinions to fit the relationship, and is resentful of anyone she works for who does not appreciate her efforts.

These two profile defenses get together not to fix each other but to relate in ways that take them into even deeper suffering. The Enforcer-Seducer needs a servant to support him in his latest conquests. He often uses his considerable charm to entice a person into a marriage, then shifts to a task master who treats his spouse more like property than another human being. When she resists at all, he loses trust and puts her through more hell to prove her loyalty.

The only way a People Pleaser knows how to get love is to give her selfless devotion, so she is often drawn to a powerful person who needs support. Little does she know that his conquests come and go with the wind, and she is one of them. Over time, the People Pleaser takes up a passive-resistant stance in the battle of wills, always losing and so building up deep resentment, silently tolerating her partner's abuse.

Conscious Soul Mate Combinations

At their core, relationships teach you to let go of your defense. The beginning of a true soul mate relationship starts when you let down your virtual reality defense and freely express your core soul qualities within your relationship. This commitment to embody your core qualities can transform the defensive battles into the love and compassion of powerful adult souls. Through this ultimate sacrifice of old beliefs and behaviors, and this new commitment to another person, lifetime soul mates emerge.

Once you bring your own inner beauty and strength into your relationship, amazing things become possible, but the soul mate journey is not without challenges. The truth of who you are can be scary for your partner. For instance, when the People Pleaser begins to assert independence, the Enforcer-Seducer partner can feel betrayed. You are changing the agreement of your relationship from defense to core soul qualities, and it may take time for your partner to come around to the new terms. Once your partner encounters your soul, however, you leave the hell of a defensive life and begin to live in heaven.

Both of the following couple combinations are matches made in heaven. Even when the relationship begins in defense, which is common, the qualities each person brings forward in the other can be hugely liberating.

Couple #3: Knowledgeable Achiever/Emotional Intelligence Specialist Soul Mates

As the Rule Keeper defense meets the core soul quality of the Emotional Intelligence Specialist in his partner, he is able to see that she loves him for his heart and not for what he does in the world. She sees the heart of the Tin Man, forgives his criticism of her, and teaches him the ways of the heart. This shift allows him to let go of self-criticism and to know that love really exists. As someone who will always be a high achiever, he can begin to include his heart in his achievements, realizing that his ideas can create connections between others, not just a big paycheck.

The Poor Me defense who meets the core soul quality of the Knowledgeable Achiever in her partner is held in a wisdom that includes her deep feelings. He can help her understand the deeper context and spiritual calling that each emotion pulls her toward. Each person needs the other to reveal the secrets of the universe that neither could see on his or her own.

Couple #4: Charismatic Leader–Charmer/Team Player Soul Mates

As the Enforcer-Seducer defense meets the core soul quality of the Team Player in his partner, he encounters a compassion that lets him trust her and release his hypervigilant need to control people. She sees the insecurity that drives his aggression and reminds him that he is human and vulnerable—think Beauty and the Beast. Once he is able to let down his guard, he can feel his power and leadership, not as a weapon against the world but as a gift to empower others. He realizes that, without a loving support team he is alone in the world, and he comes to appreciate and adore his Team Player partner who supports him in trusting his instincts and fighting the good fight.

As the People Pleaser defense meets the core soul quality of the Charismatic Leader–Charmer in her partner, she finds that she no longer has to resist anything. Her partner now sees her greatest strengths and encourages her to express them freely in the relationship and in the world. He holds a love that is so big and deep that she feels seen and can know without a doubt that her life has purpose. She knows that caring for him and for others, and holding the relationship as her highest spiritual truth, is real power. He no longer assumes or demands but now asks for his needs to be met from a place of vulnerability, and she knows that it is safe to say yes or no and have complete dominion over her own choices in the relationship.

Social Relationship Magnets

We all need people around us who reflect our strengths or at least make us feel comfortable being ourselves. Whether we belong to country clubs, colleges, healing circles, yoga studios, military groups, or multinational corporations—these are all groups that magnetize you to others with similar tastes and interests.

Such relationships based on commonality can be good for your spiritual growth if you develop a sense of camaraderie and support from them. In healthy friendships, you find people walking a parallel path who can support you in the challenges in your life because they are going through the same thing. But if you use your like-minded friends to convince you how right you are and how wrong your primary mate is, your friendship can be detrimental to your primary relationship and your personal growth.

For instance, if you are a Rule Keeper, and your Rule Keeper friend agrees with you that your Poor Me husband is too weak to maintain a job and be a decent father, you learn nothing of the power of love. Or maybe your People Pleaser best friend who meets you in the line to pick up your children from school every day says you deserve much better than the Enforcer-Seducer "jerk" you are married to. If you listen to her, you stay angry or resentful toward your spouse or leave him, missing the opportunity to establish boundaries and power within a relationship.

When you live from your core soul qualities, not your defense, you get along with friends and co-workers, and navigate easily through relationships with all five profiles. But if you are having issues in those relationships, or you find that your friends are all the same, you may be relating to those people from your profile defense.

The Friend and Co-worker Defense Magnets chart below shows the profiles of people you are attracted to when you are in defense. You will see why you have chosen such friends, and how they both support and hold you back at the same time. Using this chart can help you become conscious of your defensive patterns so you can let them go and have healthier relationships.

You can attract friends through both your primary and secondary profile defenses. Look in the left column of the chart for your primary and secondary defensive profiles, and then go across to the right column to see which profiles you will tend to attract as friends. Those are the relationships that will tend to enable your defense rather than challenge it.

Often, friends and co-workers are attracted to you through your secondary defense, but you may not be aware of it. In that case, use the chart by looking first in the right column to find the profiles of your friends or co-workers, and then look back at the left column to see what defense you are likely using in relating to them.

FRIEND AND CO-WORKER DEFENSE MAGNETS

Thinker	→	Thinker
		Rule Keeper
		People Pleaser
Rule Keeper	→	Rule Keeper
		Thinker
		People Pleaser
Poor Me	→	Poor Me

People Pleaser	→	People Pleaser
		People Pleaser
		Poor Me
		Thinker
		Rule Keeper
		Enforcer-Seducer
Enforcer-Seducer	→	People Pleaser

You will notice from the Friend and Co-worker Defense Magnets chart that People Pleasers can get along with anyone because that is part of their defense. They think that if they are nice to people, they will be taken care of and loved. People Pleasers know how to support relationships, but in defense they tend to maintain some relationships that they ought to let go of.

On the other side, the Enforcer-Seducer cannot trust anyone who is not compliant or operating as he wants them to. In social relationships, the Enforcer-Seducer loves to take the lead. But as soon as the other person resists or demands space in the relationship, it is seen as a betrayal and the relationship is discarded. The Enforcer-Seducer gets along with very few people because he believes that anyone who gets too close to him will betray him. The Enforcer-Seducer eventually burns all his bridges in battles over who is right or who is in charge; he has few friends who put up with him, and most of these are People Pleasers. The Enforcer-Seducer may end up choosing club or social acquaintances over personal friends who might try to get to know him better.

There is one combination in the chart that is like oil and water: the

Rule Keeper and the Enforcer-Seducer. The Rule Keeper is competitive, and when faced with a challenge or conflict, he will not back down. He plays hard but "by the rules." The Enforcer-Seducer is competitive and uses any tactic to win. The Rule Keeper has tight boundaries, while the Enforcer-Seducer has none. The Enforcer-Seducer uses every opportunity to push him off balance emotionally and get the upper hand.

But as bad as it is when this combination is in defense, when Rule Keepers and Enforcer-Seducers find themselves expressing their core soul qualities, they can be a powerful team. Then the sage advice of the Knowledgeable Achiever complements the generous vision of the Charismatic Leader–Charmer. Every Charismatic Leader–Charmer CEO surrounds himself with Knowledgeable Achiever COOs, VPs, and managers to keep the business on track.

Let Your Soul Shine Through

By letting your core soul qualities shine, you are living your life purpose.

Your core soul qualities are your truth, and your defenses are a lie. Whatever you decide to express in the world is a magnet for others who are at that same level of consciousness. Your ability to attract a soul mate and good friends and co-workers lies in your ability to slowly expand your soul self in every relationship, especially the one you have with yourself.

As a human being, your deepest desire is to be seen by others for the perfection, love, and beauty that lie in the center of your soul. Your second deepest desire is to see and connect fully to the soul of those with whom you are in a relationship so together you can consciously support each other on your life purpose journeys. To let your soul have a place in your life, you must first take charge and be clear about who you are and who you definitely are not.

You will only be happy when you are *you*. The full-body experience of being who you really are will always give you a deep sense of inner peace, similar to the sense you had in your "secret place," as you may have discovered in the suggested meditation. If you build relationships that support you to be you, and that also remind you when you are in defense, then you will have the best chance of enjoying your life.

At first it may be difficult for you to see who your partners and friends really are beneath their defenses because you are accustomed to seeing them through the filter of your virtual reality and mask. But as you embody your own soul, and understand the profiles of others and yourself more and more deeply, you will begin to see through clearer eyes and not be afraid to see your partner or friend more clearly, too.

By doing the work in this book, you gain the skills to both express yourself fearlessly and be open to fully seeing the amazing gifts of everyone in your life. The best approach is to see their core soul qualities and respond to those qualities as often as possible. Respond to the genius of the Creative Idealist, the unconditional love of the Emotional Intelligence Specialist, the hero and leader of the Charismatic Leader–Charmer, the deep compassion and friendship of the Team Player, and the sage advice of the Knowledgeable Achiever.

You begin to appreciate and see beyond their defenses to the beautiful core soul qualities that have been kept hidden. And since you can only see in someone else what is already in you, then as you glimpse the power, beauty, and brilliance of others, you are awakening those qualities in yourself. This could be the most important work you do in your life, and what you gain from it will be well worth the inner work that you must do to own your greatness.

Acknowledgments

This book is made possible by all of you who have contributed to me and my work over the years. I could never have written it without the gifts each of you brought to me from your unique soul's perspective. My deepest gratitude goes out to you all.

In particular, I want to acknowledge:

My editors at Tarcher/Penguin for their support in working with me to bring this book into final existence.

My family for their support and patience while I spent long hours doing research in my study, and especially my sons Trevyr and Logan, who listened generously to my "crazy ideas."

My teachers, some of whom I've never met, who inspired me: Alexander Lowen, Eva Pierrakos, Dorothy Martin-Neville, Wayne Dyer, Deepak Chopra, Eckhart Tolle, and Martin Luther King Jr.

My team of editors and artists: Nancy Marriott at New Paradigm Writing and Editing Services and Rachel Dunham at Brand Therapy for their tireless efforts in helping me put my ideas into words and pictures to produce a book that could communicate my teachings.

My students, too numerous to mention but who have been part of my living laboratory as I developed my ideas into practices. Especially all those students who now work alongside me as teachers and administrators at the Rhys Thomas Institute to support others to find their life purpose and live an extraordinary life.

About the Author

RHYS THOMAS is a visionary author, speaker, and trainer in the energy medicine field. He is celebrated worldwide as a pioneer in energy medicine due to his synthesis and reinterpretation of energy medicine techniques for personal and professional transformation. He is the creator of the Rhys Method® transformational system taught exclusively at the Rhys Thomas Institute near Boston, Massachusetts, and as part of Rhys Thomas Coaching Programs.

When he was thirty-eight, Rhys had an awakening experience that stopped him from striving to be someone he wasn't and allowed him to embrace who he really was. He was introduced to what turned out to be the missing piece, a powerful form of energy medicine that profoundly changed his life. From his awakening, Rhys could see that he was not alone. He discovered that the source of people's pain was trying to be who they thought they were supposed to be and not truly knowing who they were. With this realization, Rhys developed an accessible system of self-understanding that moves far beyond any other current systems, now called the Rhys Method® Life Purpose Profile System. Today, Rhys has impacted people around the globe through his videos, speaking events, programs, and his institute.

Rhys is a graduate and former teacher at the Institute of Healing Arts and Sciences, and the founder of the Rhys Thomas Institute and Solstice Healing Arts Center. He has fifteen years of experience in energy medicine practice, which includes full-spectrum healing, crystal bowl sound healing, energy reading, and soul reading. He is a certified energy medicine practitioner, Reiki master, and second-degree black belt with twenty-five years of martial arts training. Before entering the healing arts, he had a successful twenty-seven-year career as a tennis professional and national speaker for the tennis industry.

Learn more and connect with Rhys at:

RhysThomasInstitute.com
support@rhysmethod.com
www.facebook.com/rhysthomasinstitute
twitter.com/rtiem
www.pinterest.com/rhysthomasinst/

If you enjoyed this book, visit

www.tarcherbooks.com

and sign up for Tarcher's e-newsletter to receive special offers, giveaway promotions, and information on hot upcoming releases.

TARCHER
PENGUIN

Great Lives Begin with Great Ideas

Connect with the Tarcher Community

• • •

Stay in touch with favorite authors!
Enter weekly contests!
Read exclusive excerpts!
Voice your opinions!

Follow us

 Tarcher Books

 @TarcherBooks

If you would like to place a bulk order of this book, call 1-800-847-5515.

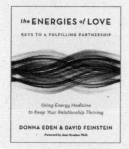

"Donna Eden and David Feinstein empower readers with knowledge and techniques from ancient energy healing and spiritual practices that will forever change the way you understand relationships. These are revolutionary ideas! I highly recommend *The Energies of Love.*"

—John Gray, Ph.D., author of *Men Are from Mars, Women Are from Venus*

978-0-39917-492-6 • $27.95

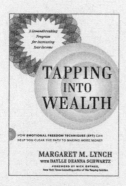

"There is no more powerful tool in the world to actualize change than Tapping. But there are times when the tool isn't enough, when you need the guidance, care, and nurturing of a powerful mentor who can pinpoint exactly where you need to go, what you need to explore, in order to get the fastest results possible. And this is where my friend Margaret Lynch and this amazing book come in."

—Nick Ortner, *New York Times*–bestselling author of *The Tapping Solution*

978-0-39916-882-6 • $15.95

An illuminating guide to one of the fastest-growing spiritual healing practices in the world and an essential tool for anyone ready to bring healing into his or her life

978-1-58542-649-2 • $16.95